The Challenge of
MATURITY

A Comprehensive Guide to Understand and Achieve Psychological and Social Self-Actualization As We Grow Older

William D. Eldridge, Ph.D.
The Ohio State University

UNIVERSITY
PRESS OF
AMERICA

Lanham • New York • London

Copyright © 1991 by

University Press of America®, Inc.

4720 Boston Way
Lanham, Maryland 20706

3 Henrietta Street
London WC2E 8LU England

Library of Congress Cataloging-in-Publication Data

Eldridge, William D., 1948-
The challenge of maturity : a comprehensive guide
to understand and achieve psychological and social
self-actualization as we grow older / William D. Eldridge.
p.   cm.
1. Self-actualization (Psychology) in old age.   II. Title.
BF724.85.S45E43   1991
155.67—dc20   90–25256 CIP

ISBN 0–8191–8177–3 (alk. paper)
ISBN 0–8191–8178–1 (pbk. : alk. paper)

The paper used in this publication meets the minimum requirements of
American National Standard for Information Sciences—Permanence
of Paper for Printed Library Materials, ANSI Z39.48–1984.

CONTENTS

Chapter 1

What About Our Past?

Chapter 2

Conflicts and Dilemmas of the Aging Process

Chapter 3

The Future

Chapter 1

What About Our Past?

History can reemerge at any time in our lives through conscious aware-ness, or as a more subtle background haze within our unconscious "sense" or composite definitional recollection of previous emotional or behavioral experiences. These acute and often poignant awarenesses, or their paralleled but abstruse panoramic backgrounds can assume identities as beautiful devel-opmental blossoms, metamorphosing positively within an enriched current environment; or conversely, they can savagely mutilate or cancerously devour our efforts to see ourselves as worthwhile dimensions of life's exciting drama, where their negative connotations also mitigate our hopes for tomorrow's rainbow.

Although attitudes, feelings and behaviors certainly have an indigenous character which places them within some valuational realm related to their good or bad purpose, outcome effectiveness relative to antecedent goals, or social "acceptability" as ameliorative human relations ligaments; these same mental or physical acts can also be "indexed" or functionally defined by their owners within a wide range of instrumental, experiential, psychological, philosophical, or spiritual interpretive domains which allow and demand that they be brought forward to here-and-now reality in an attractive, positive, inspirational, and growth-oriented existential package.

There is no question that everything we do, or did in the past, has some type of relevance and utility as it materializes within the living context of a holistic, animated scenario representing our stimulation, responsiveness, integration, extrication, or reciprocal domiciliation with various life forces or processes that make us, somehow, a part of our world's ecology. These causes or effects cannot, and should not, be erased from their meaningful position on the continuous highway of life's journey to and from its origin and ultimate resolution. They must stand, therefore, as symbolic reflections of cumulative cultural development, and as educative guidons to fashion a planful and enlightened future. They may also be transformed into usable energy sources and invigorating conduits to assist us in developing meaning-ful, happy, self-fulfilled, and socially responsible/useful agendas for our benefit and to help and care for those who share our planetary and spiritual "space."

In this context then, we should not defensively or delusionally attempt to escape from the bruises and painful emotional abrasions attached to our "mistakes" or "failures" or times gone by, especially since we were ingeniously and benevolently provided these wonderful opportunities to be truly "human" rather than artificially perfectionistic; and to potentially learn from the rich contradictions and spicy intellectual quagmires into which we plunged our struggling selves--but were given the effervescent anxiety and emotional disequilibrium as rungs on salvation's ladder to help us peer deep within our minds and hearts to understand one more elusive piece of life's Kaleidoscopic puzzle. We should, therefore, use this data along with those events we remember, as examples of human victory and resurrection, as necessary and very critical foundation cornerstones for a bio-psycho-socio-spiritual mobile temple which we can creatively use as a support structure, as well as a dynamic catapult to propel us more vigorously and resolutely into the final growth corridors of earthly life where some of the secrets and, heretofore, elusive formulas to our ultimate self-actualization, human fulfillment, and dignified relevance may enticingly await only those who insist on buying a ticket for the future.

In order to assist you, the reader and potential traveler, to consider some of the variably differentiated, yet interwoven paradigms which can be used to understand and constructively orchestrate the transcendence and resuscitation of past-to-present thoughts, feelings and behaviors; I will briefly outline some very basic but helpful strategies to deal with our past histories.

Skills Acquisition

Almost everyone who reaches a mature chronologic age has been blessed with life's generous apportionment of diversified exposure to physical, verbal, cognitive, sensory, and emotional capabilities; which we use to interface with, and adapt to a complex social environment. At a very fundamental level, these instrumental skills assist in gathering intelligence data from the world around us (touch, smell, hearing, taste), and convert "state of the environment" awarenesses into mental electrical impulses. These are sorted and implanted as concepts, symbols, or ideas for our decision-making, and finally "operate" externally as words or physical behaviors to manipulate portions of the material milieu to more fully meet our needs and align themselves causally or aesthetically in patterns which we have culturally and biologically learned are "essential" for our survival and well-being.

As the aging process chromatically moves along, many of us forget the detailed sophistication and lustered precision of the unique and individually meaningful skills we have mastered; and we also overlook many beautiful "trees," as time and cumulative amalgamation of interactive competencies focuses our attention on the more global "forest" of nature identity. This is not necessarily negative, however, unless the synergistic power of multi-skill reciprocation obscures the quality of the component parts which constitute the foundation layer of our identities.

An equally unfortunate, but external invalidation of skill relevancy, utilitarian quality, and personal sentimental attractiveness comes from a microscopic and delusionally self-centered, frightened, and production-hungry world which perfunctorily ejects older citizens from employment, family and community roles where dormant skills can be massaged into constructive use. New skills can sprout from the fertile soil of human interaction, challenges of system survival, and stimulative "productivity" quotients which incorporate a wide range of human talent, wisdom and creative energy. In these prevalent cases, or the similar/adjunctive situations where we each personally negate or veil our awareness of those skills and adaptive abilities (which made us unique and existentially "great" shareholders of the extraordinary flame of this life), we inadvertently sever the roots of our comprehensive selves, and thereby siphon one artery of sustaining psychic and physical energy which emanates from veneration of the learning which we fought so hard to obtain, remember, and use.

A central task, therefore, for every mature woman or man, is to recollect and re-examine as much previous experiential territory as possible, with the specific intention of defining and documenting each skill which punctuated important chapters in our ornamented historical growth. This is a very necessary and worthwhile task to commit to a written journal or "testimonial" biographic log because it proclaims the accumulation of qualitative assets, reminds us of the tenacious fortitude we summoned to overcome our own inertia and society's resistance in adding to our "bag of tricks." It also intimates that we examine the location and potency of our cognitive dissonant conflict in cases where we value a particular skill from the past, but notice we have failed to "un-mothball," polish, and tune-up this functional "friend" for activation in our present lives. As aging occurs, complacency, indolence, and self-derogation can insidiously cause the withdrawal of energy from interpersonal and self-enhancing skills which had been used previously to stay "tuned in" to various life processes, and to provide much needed personal satisfaction through the proud display of learned adaptive adroitness and the enjoyment of masterful outcomes which were created and caused by the active self. Although we might decide that some previously activated skills are outdated, they may have been subsumed within other skill clusters that no longer help us meet our changing needs. There are probably many others on the dusty shelves of our frightened, neglected, or socially ostracized egos which might provide very helpful initial thrusts for many of us to re-enroll in the mainstream of life and to begin a critical life-saving process of energy revitalization and self-nurturing stimulus-response-stimulus cycles which help us "leapfrog" toward vivified future goals and objectives.

As we list various skills which previously or currently form our essence and unique self-definition, some particular categorical examples might include:

1. <u>Listening</u> carefully to others to hear the secret, fearful, or special messages that occur "between the lines" or piggyback on other superficial word content;

2. <u>Tasting</u> with discriminative and benedective appreciation to fathom the richness of life's sensory pleasures, and to encourage others who explore the culinary arts and mysteries;

3. <u>Touching</u> children and other adults to share the provocative electricity and cradling support of human connection and to demonstrate "bridge-building" in a world of alienated ego and ethnocentrism;

4. <u>Speaking</u> with propagational sincerity and imaginative articulation to delight the ears and awaken the souls of recognition-hungry compatriots, and to encourage meaningful interpersonal dialogue as a vehicle for human learning, reconciliation of antagonistic differences, and appreciation of cultural and personal commonalities and symbolic linkages between worldwide "brothers and sisters";

5. <u>Analyzing</u> in a non-judgmental way, some of the complexities of life which younger minds have not resolved through repeated exposure, experimentation, and decision-making; and helping various segments of a sometimes misdirected and illusioned society understand the dynamics of our self-imposed psychosocial labyrinthine entrapments, while using a mature, self-assured and objective perspective to help illuminate the door to sensibility, peace, human love, spiritual awakening and non-alienation;

6. Creating beautiful symbolic representations in wood, ceramic, painted canvas, cloth, written words, food, plant life, etc., of the celestial grandeur of our incarnate perceptual and cognitive aesthetics, which can be used by others as referenced foci to excite or intoxicate their awareness and to invite new vistas of life's demeanor and relevance;

7. Waiting for the developmental unfolding of contingent actions or decisions, to demonstrate the masterful skill of disciplined patience, and to further illustrate the brilliance of hypothetical and correlational thinking which integrates strategic and tactical planning of our contributions, ideas, inputs, or confrontations to insure the greatest probability of successful social outcomes;

8. Withdrawing the ineffective, asthenic, or enfeebled maintenance of actions or other inputs from relationships, projects, or organizations to uphold higher principles of morality or ethics, and to planfully execute energy redirection as a reinforcement and educative tool to confront others with the relativity of their negative uses of power, and to produce learning through stimulation of conflict and support of negotiated resolution for maximum benefits to all.

Although only a few general areas of skills have been presented, they illustrate a vital perspective in viewing the deeper meanings of seemingly simple and innocuous thoughts or acts, and further suggest that the world in which mature or aging individuals reside may very dearly need and benefit from the rebirth and integrative inflamation of these skills within present day families, community organizations, and national cultures.

Relationship Development

The opportunity to have lived fifty or more years munificently provides a wealth of exposure, awareness, experience, appreciation, and facility with human interactions; which can result in life's latter seasons of growth, in the existence of phenomenally rich chasms of loving care with friends, spouses, or children; or can provide a woven fabric of interpersonal skills and associational adjustment frameworks as a vehicle for future satisfying liaisons. Although we must all admit to previously inaugural flounderings in learning to "connect," or must accept the confusing and sometimes painful endings of past relationships, much has, nevertheless, been learned and enjoyed which can be remuneratively salvaged in existing partnerships, or catalytically implemented to launch new ones for our future prosperity.

We often spend excessive time regressing to the safe and familiar "wombs" of the past with reluctance to inject transfigurative stimuli for worthwhile change, or frustratingly cling to illusory loyalties of earlier "commitments" while neglecting to pursue a plethora of exciting and fulfilling interactional bondings for the important journey ahead.

In cases where significant loved ones have died, many of life's veterans delusionally revisit childhood dependency entrapments, where guilt and fictitious perceptions of "loss of self" cancerously destroy the living being, along with the biologically deceased; and insane attachments to a new "victimized life script" are contracted which stipulates crescendoing emotional and spiritual suicide and the unconditional surrender of enjoyment of all living circumstances, plus social irresponsibility in this muted withdrawal from the mainstream of social life.

The key to constructive utilization of the existence, remembrance, or learned dynamic process of relationship building and maintenance, is for every senior individual to "internalize" and accept personal responsibility for "owning" the marvelous corporeality and basic essence of the actualized and qualitative "living self" in the context of human interrelationship. This means realizing that shared feeling, emotion, mental kinesis, spiritual reciprocal nurturing, and biologic interface constitute sovereign states of being which, because of the interconnections and combinations of human energy and emotional "electricity," can produce a fuller awareness and enjoyment of life's substantive refreshment and gratification and a direct result of the relationship <u>dynamics</u>.

A positive and permanent orientation to relationship quality also involves a "developmental" philosophy, wherein we all believe that the ultimate richness and enlightenment of life is somehow partly or fully enthroned at the end of a ribbon-like corridor which weaves the way throughout the complex linkages of people to one another; and may become illuminated when our investments and transfusions with others grow to the point that alienation, fear, self-centeredness, jealousy competition, and isolation are eliminated as we achieve some form of unified "oneness" with human physical and biological nature. This appreciation of the past, present, or future value of our experience and learning about associational growth and interactive vivication suggests a "functional" purpose of sharing which necessarily presumes that there is a hierarchy of qualitative relationship levels which can serve as a never-ending goal for the continual reincarnation of our affiliations, in search of a purer, deeper, more delicious, or more enlightened outcome of interactive "being."

In any case, whether the value of relationships involves the solidification of past warm memories which help sustain current "life forces," the quest and discovery of present pleasurable sensual or spiritual "feelings," or the goal-directed expedition toward futuristic personal or joint expansion and cultivation of the seeds of nature; the things that we have all learned and continue to fathom from our liaisons can be significant blueprints and anchoring mechanisms to guide the direction and undergird the value of our movements alone or together toward the sunrise of the future. Some of the most significant dynamics of past relationship experiences, therefore, will be briefly highlighted to stimulate thinking about the benefits of reaching out and maintaining connections which many people tend to forget as we sometimes allow or force relationship images to blur into the amorphous, cloudy mist of yesterday.

1. We learned to approach:

Any relationship from the past, whether reviewed positively or negatively, at least exemplified the courageous act of overcoming all or some portion of fear of rejection, and offered all or some portion of a trusting self; contained within the preliminary act of reaching out to someone else. This proactive expenditure of energy can be seen as a monumental thrust involving the explicit communication of love and caring, along with implicit articulation of the worth of another human being--in a complex confrontational package which simultaneously announces that acrimonious human distance and destructively fearful isolation must be forcibly destroyed if there is even to be any hope of constructing sunlit windows in the mental, emotional, and cultural walls which attenuate our full human nature and shared condition of existence.

These praiseworthy acts of invitation to join the human race may have been abandoned in wake of frustration and despair accompanying relationship disjunctions. We may continue to inversely "enjoy" the pain of martyred tribulation to manipulatively hope someone will approach and enjoy the sweet taste of "me," or at least suffer in the absence of what our questionably (but not-to-be-tested-again) qualitative selves could have given, but now safely retain in dry-dock where we don't win, but also avoid future losses which we feel will be lethal.

In either case, previous exposure and survival of the "initiating ritual" places all of us in a unique position of special power to know at least one secret concerning "convergence" of separate personal identities. It makes us extremely valuable, and possibly lifesaving, resources to younger, older, or contemporary lonely "souls" who, without the persistent cavalcade of our identity extensions, may never again breathe the resuscitative air of perceived self-esteem and dignity which evolves from conspirational interaction and unity.

2. <u>We learned to compromise:</u>

Historical or current relationships necessarily require compromise so that different needs, representing idiosyncratic parts of unique identities, can be met as a stimulative or adjunctive component of personal growth. In this regard, having learned to compromise means that we possess, somewhere in our conscious or unconscious reality, the ability to evaluatively prioritize and manifest various parts of a "flexible," as well as variegated personality storehouse, in a coordinated attempt to adapt to reality contingencies and take responsibility for creatively enhancing the probability of our happiness. This implies, of course, that we may benefit from the exhumation of the ability to view a wide range of personality parts or strengths which may be necessary to sustain emotional vibrancy, as role changes and life alterations require compromising ingenuity in defining needs for which there are available social rewards, defining new needs where we can exercise more control of self-rewards or nurturance, discovering virginal strengths which can be implemented to make previously unfulfilled needs incompatible with expeditionary accomplishments, altering the priority we assign to various needs so we can balance our ability to receive with the environment's ability to give and its need for us to give, or helping us learn to relate to new people or activities which may not correspond to our previous habits or preferences. Furthermore, this can provide exciting new avenues for self-fulfillment in the discovery of new types of associations and their commensurate undetected pleasures.

Compromise is ultimately necessary to sway, rather than break, in response to the varying winds of life's often unpredictable meteorologic emotional demeanor, and the lessons of previous relationship negotiations may help insure the flexibility and adaptiveness necessary for us to continually reorient the changing self in a complex correlational waltz with a world that is also changing.

3. We learned shared "reality":

Within the context of the lives we shared with others in our past, whether primary love relationships, significant friendships, or even brief encounters; we were privileged to occupy physical, emotional, mental, and spiritual territories which converged or interlocked to define, solidify, and valuatively italicize a part of "perceptual reality" known only to the two participants. This conceptual intersection not only permitted each individual to feel "validated" as a special aspect of their psyche or soul was known and appreciated externally, but the vortex, created and held in place by the collectively conjunctive perceptions, served as a magnetic focal point to help retain the boundaries and functional characteristics of the relationship. Furthermore, we directly or inadvertently struggled to "see" and appreciate the complexion and enriching depth of somebody else's "sunshine" which helped to expand our own awareness of the myriad qualities of life and its symbols, and provided an additional reference point to help us evaluate the import and meanings of our own former and potential future views of reality and our role in this drama.

This complicated and ethereal process which almost everyone, to some extent, encounters, enables us to transport an invitation for others in our current and future environment, to enrich themselves with a colorful array of new "visions" which we can share, and to expand the frequently narrow horizons of any of our psychic lenses, to learn new ways of self-fulfillment and to more distinctly reconnoiter available routes toward a more complete resolution of life's imprisoning conflicts and a loosening of the shackles, which we learned from childhood on, as an irrational and fearful way to avoid unknown encounters with ourselves and the world in which we live. The experience we bring as matured veterans of the "perceptual convergence phenomenon" can guide neophyte explorers toward a wealthier approach to self-esteem building, and can simultaneously open entire new mental and emotional galaxies to our possibly bored, jaded, saddened, or retroflective eyes which can entice the reinvestment and affirmative thrust of growth and developmental hunger the remainder of our lives and into any hereafter we can potentially "know" from the hard work of studying our realities of the present.

4. <u>We learned to feel secure:</u>

As the days and years of our lives move ahead, there is interaction between our posterior reflections of intrapsychic and personal losses in the hinterland of relationships which "appear" to be over, plus uncertain speculations of the future that are filtered through the diminutive lenses of childhood which dichotomize "safety" and "danger" relative to "known" and "unknown." As this seemingly negative phenomena attacks many of us, the feelings of security, trust and confidence in ourselves and our surroundings are forgotten as internal perceptions which any of us could bring to life presently through recognition of "having-been-loved-and-therefore-being-lovable-and-secure-in-this-permanent status"; and we also attack a circumscribed and discrete power to previous lovers/friends to the extent that security and warmth are frozen in past time and we assume cannot be recaptured in relationships of the future. This is obviously self-defeating and negates both our internal power to use memory and reconstructed reality "imprints" to activate helpful awareness and emotional sensations in technicolored present time, and frequently stifles our appreciation of the security we learned to seek and use in the past which we could likewise work to create again for ourselves in a radiant renaissance which is accented as a direct result of having experienced its meaning and nature previously. The internal depressive withdrawal and turtle-like creation of isolating emotional skills is an example of personal and social dereliction, in abandoning learned adaptivity through the creative use of historical chronicled recapitulation of satisfying emotional psychic "condition"; and through abstinence in forming new relationships to help others enjoy the fruits of interpersonal security. What a waste to perpetuate insecurity because we refuse to take control of our minds and bodies!

5. <u>We learned to receive:</u>

One of the most traumatic and personally offensive experiences reported by men particularly, but women also, during the traditionally perceived and operationalized aging process, is labeled "dependency"; and connotes for many the loss of autonomy, productivity, self-respect, freewill, and power--with the introduction of varying types and portions of public services, forms of personal aid or assistance, health care activities, financial support, advice and consultation, or even patronizing delivery of respect or emotional nurturance from younger members of families or communities. The insulting and derogatory connotations appended to these frequently necessary changes in formerly adjudged "independent existence" predestines the recipients to differential proportions of acute or chronic emotional misery as resistive minds counterpunch and flail at external intruders, while ignoring the enemy within. Moreover, the net result is usually retaliation of some sort from a rejected social network of "helpers," or withdrawal of necessary corollary ingredients of holistic living which leaves us more alone, angry, fearful, and unassisted with the attenuation of both physical and emotional energies from which a more willing "donee" could benefit.

The major point here, is that all of us, throughout diversified encounters with an "other" or "not of" environment have learned at various times to take, as an expression of caring for the self-actualization of the caring giver, and as one way to enrich and fortify particular parts of the "self" or "I" world, in order to progress subsequently toward additional growth with a newly aggrandize perception of "expanded self." Despite the fact that consuming and producing may have appeared as a balanced approach to healthy living, we all may have succumbed to an artificial separation of a unified reality of "being" through an unhealthy distinction between inner and outer self which signifies a constant preoccupation and struggle to empty and fill a psycho-emotional container through action and inaction--whereas (a) the container was or never can really be empty and (b) there is no differentiation between output and income because the same energy produces both with just a different object of directional bodily activity. If this existential explanation is, indeed, correct, than there can never be a loss involved in becoming "one" with the "giving nature" of the world around us because it is not really external to our natures anyway, and the main point of living is to always pursue building and expansion which is inclusive rather than exclusive of that which can be added to our resources.

Remembering how we received in the past, therefore, may help us to flow more harmoniously with the fluctuating themes and melodies of a changing life pattern, and exacerbate our abilities to achieve closeness with giving souls while simultaneously permitting, and therefore taking independent mental control of the warm swirling of nutritious energized psycho-cellular supplements throughout all components of our inter-dependent cognitive and biologic compositions.

Cultivation of Aesthetic Appreciation

As each of us wondered sometimes aimlessly, or other times purposefully, throughout the blithe mountaintops or woeful valleys of various proportions of antecedent years, our various sensory receptors were faithfully transferring valuable awarenesses and assessments interactively and reciprocally between the environment, our biologic cognitive acquisitional computers, and our cultural and personal self-reflective decision center where emotional valuation occurs and is coronated. Throughout this consciously poignant or unconsciously leavening process, the personality, using its encyclopedic mechanisms of movement toward progression/regression/balance/change/growth etc., tests and appraises competing states of "being," "self-esteem," "actualization," or "adequacy"; and ultimately decides on various acceptable and functional (not necessarily positive and healthy) psychic conditions which are stimulated and partly created by the natures of external stimuli and then in turn, are solidified and represented by retaining the external symbols as foci to remind us of who we "are." Because we undulate perpetually through various states of receptivity and attentiveness to learning and expanding the "self," various aesthetic symbols from the past have had differential impact on creating awareness and forming our identities because of the intricate and bewildering interaction between the intrinsic nature of the influential stimulus and the "absorbency quotient" of each person who is exposed to one of life's natural or person-made savory messages. Throughout the years, of course, some emblematic images or icons are retained and fortified as ritualistic and permanent retroflections of the internal feeling or identity we desire or represent goals for the future, while other recollections of meaningful artifacts, sounds, prismatic colors, fragrances, textures, etc. have either dropped out of utilitarian status altogether, are renting a room in our unconscious minds to await a functional "call to arms" at a later date, or have been fully integrated into a consonant and conflict-free unity with our mental images of the self and are therefore no longer separate, discrete phenomena. In any case, it is extremely important to transverse some of the aesthetic territory of the past to insure that important and growth-producing images and self-perceptions have not been lost to the clutches of plodding time or regressive and self-protective defenses, and to also insure that our receiving systems have not atrophied with the rust and decomposition that come with disuse, alienation, frustration, social disinterest and punishment, or natural slowing down but not elimination. To help revive our consideration of these relevant concerns which can be important and fundamental catalysts for future growth, I will briefly examine some of the more pronounced forms of aesthetic stimulation and symbolization which we all encounter to one degree or another.

1. Music and sound:

The path traveled by human ears is an extraordinary spectroscope to receive messages about all aspects of reality, as these dimensions are piggybacked and dynamically represented by the concomitant variations in tone, cadence, resonance, volume, inflection, modulation, notes, pitch, key, timbre, acoustics, phonics, reverberations, audibility, word selection, word combination, and sentence or paragraph connotation and meaning. The songs, noises, voices and, other sounds we have heard in the past have represented and symbolized defined aspects of our various "selves," have helped delineate the changing shapes of some present or desired components of the personality, have helped integrate these parts through their continual reemergence in social waves, (strengths, qualities, fears, perceptions, etc.) in a relationship pattern with other identity dimensions, and have provided a safe and secure imaged resting place so that our perceptions of self or inner views are kept safe from the bumps and bruises of external world affairs which are not designed specifically to validate or support the unique natures of any of us. The melodies, for example, of any one of our yesterdays have betokened who we were, what we believed, what we hoped to achieve, and what avenues or routes might be available to help us move into the intellectual, emotional, physical or spiritual future. In many cases, the sounds we heard in the past symbolically represented magnificent and glorious aspects of our human beauty and dignity. We may have lost sight of these essential parts of self as the old songs no longer appeared on the radio, their record albums were lost or broken, and new sounds replaced them, which constituted negative portraits of a prejudicially confining youth, and traditionally conceived productivity-oriented society, which generally excludes older members from the ranks of its contemporary and generationally replicated achievers. Also, we may have insidiously allowed our ears and learning skills to "close up shop," with the result that positive sounds of the past, which have been transported or retained in present time, or new auditory provocations which percolate in the air waves surrounding us presently, are either ignored by weary receptor channels, or fail to produce new learning because we are void of energizing anxiety. This occurs when an avid desire for new growth plunges our psycho-emotional-spiritual system into a state learning deprivation and crisis.

We can all benefit from the recollection of significant emotional events or salient intuitions or enlightenments about our personalities or relationships which are attached to particular musical compositions; environmental noises; animal, bird or weather sounds, or voice characteristic of people who influenced our lives etc.; as these stimuli and responses have been paired or correlated in our minds to the extent that either the event or the aesthetic/aversive symbol can help us conjure up the perception or awareness of "self," upon which it is predicated. The future, therefore, may be enhanced by resurrecting these memories or the sound symbols so that positive and self-fulfilling components of our values, goals, aspirations, or pleasure/pride in self can be used to sustain a healthy personality foundation, and also to inspire us to seek other desirable definitions of who we are, which parallel the dynamic images represented by the music or other auditory symbols.

2.   Painting, drawing, sculpture and natural graphic genre:

Although many people pursue full and growing lives without pervasive interest or consumer/producer expertise in visual or physical art forms, everyone has had at least peripheral conscious exposure to numerous creations representing message-laden announcements of colors and textured composition, sketches and graphic shapes, architectural construction and physical form and silhouette, or fabricated shaping and molding of various free forms or relief designs. As these purposeful or incidental exposures to the world's creative tableaus occurred, their discrete, blended or juxtaposed natures most probably had some influence in our unconscious worlds, to provide prototypical or orthodox "data" as a structural normative configuration against which to compare and contrast the form and meaning of reflected personality frameworks which organize and direct emotional content and behavioral purpose. In some cases we might have felt secure in comparing our inner worlds to the "strong" characteristic of a building or rock formation, while specific murals with their unique colors and associated spacial displays may have intrigued our searching spirits and inspired emotional expansion or ventilating conceptual emancipation. In other situations, "encounters" and mental/emotional interactions with a sunset, a sculpted figurine, a piece of textured cloth or a cartooned drawing may have echoed our inner tranquility, relaxed acceptance of refueled nurturing energy, or sense of humor relative to inner paradoxical contrasts which were mirrored externally for clarity of awareness.

The important point to keep in mind is the relevance and learning potential of our active as well as passive <u>interaction</u> with the substantive and material natures of graphically displayed symbols, whether through our creative authorship of their temporary or ultimate form, or through receptive inhaling and imprinting of their informative and guiding auras and tutelaged ministrations.   As a result of the process as well as outcome of interactive "communication" with these alternate configurations of life anatomy, we may gain some insight into the "truth" about our own participation in the holistic symphony of autonomous or choreographed existence; we may diagrammatically understand part of the formula for the type, direction, and potency of future actions to adapt or continue growth; we may clearly appreciate the causal or associational linkages between various parts of "systems" so that our own relationship performance takes on new "functional" meaning, or we may notice parallel aspects of our human form which unify and "secure" our identities with the powers and characteristics of natural or spiritual phenomena, and we may actively attempt to model the relational dimensions of an external object or artistic creation as a way of self-actualizing our own integration of formerly perceived disparate personality parts or ideational values.

For the future, we can benefit from a fuller participation in the actual creation of artistic designs and graphic projects which can serve as tributes to our own unique views of the world, and as communicational bridges to initiate and sustain consciousness-raising dialogue with other younger or older "feeling" individuals. Many years can be happily spent in training for improved artistic competencies, while at the same time the expanding experiences of color and configurational and diagrammatic appreciation can bring our surrounding natural and constructional environments into clearer crystallization as representations of values, human spirit, cultural goals, or spiritual dimensions of our life-energies which, through greater awareness, can provide depth and richer profundity to our thinking and feeling processes.

3. <u>Horticulture and zoology</u>:

The abysmal pervasiveness of social notions linking human "aging" with the "death" process is a mandatory challenging reveille for all of us to sharpen our retro-focus, to identify previous relationships and their attendant energy transfusions, where we have interacted with other forms of biologic or agricultural life. Nature teaches a series of valuable lessons about the ecology and continuous progression of energy and active dynamic vitality throughout the internal and external systems of living things, which most of us have been exposed to in some active or passive format through past nurturing of house or garden plants, walks in the woods, or relaxing moments on the lawn, the care and loving affection provided to favorite pets, exposure to the "earth" sciences through formalized forming roles, or observations of animal life and reproduction through visits to the zoo or observations of "nature" documentaries on television or in books.

In all these cases, we probably accumulated an array of values and principled ideas about the beauty and inherent significance of these complex, yet simple, excursions of germination, vegetation, evolution, maturation, and decomposition. These guided us toward an involved and interactively responsible human role to participate in, facilitate, and enjoy the living animation around us, and maybe provided an explanatory and analytic paradigm to help explain some of the ups and downs we encountered in our own lives.

This former learning can be extremely valuable to help us remember and continue to use our nutritive propensities to advocate and support all life processes, and particularly, to reflectively study the movement of energies and effervescent potencies within and between our human organisms and spirits, so that we always maximize our appreciation of the life forces within which we have significant parts to play. Also, we can consciously manipulate, expand, conserve, efficiently employ, induct, or emanate the power of our potentially invigorating selves to help others share with us in the wondrous phenomenon of existence.

The possible reinvolvement of our skills and interests in direct care of plants or animals can produce "dividends on invested energy" as the reactive and generative "life" grows and achieves various states of "blossomed" verity and actualization as a result of our own giving and as a returned gift of beauty, animal, friendship, and sustained maturation. It is important, futhermore, for all of us to remember how to receive the various gratuities of nature, which we can enjoy in a pure form from nonhuman entities which may remain unincumbered by reciprocal demands for nurturance, or other cognitive/emotional baggage which can turn authentic giving and receiving into manipulative dramas of delusional and illusional childhood proportions.

4. Writing and drama:

Although most women and men never become professionally or even substantially involved in writing (other than routine letters), or perform in dramatic plays or productions, almost everyone has observed the contrived and schematic presentation of emotionally resonant role enactments in the theater or on television, and we have likewise been exposed to numerous styles of recreating or representing the "world" through imaginative alternation of word selection and positioning in numerous forms of poetic or prose manuscript. Many, obviously, have also demonstrated "who we are" through the actual writing of letters, diary entries, school projects, employment reports, and a host of miscellaneous notes, memos, etc. The important point to remember about the dramatic or compositional experience we have encountered, is that our past probably contains a multiplicity of piquant and provocative examples, where otherwise mundane or seemingly inconsequential "reality" was elevated to an emotionally passionate, glowing, thrilling, tantalizing, demonstrative, enthusiastic, etc. demeanor which may have increased its learning value, experiential significance, or stimulus value for additional action or energy investment on our parts. This implies that each of us who experiences any decline in the enraptured or stimulative nature or conduct of our lives may be able to understand the process by which drama or writing can invigorate fertile participation in life, and that we can possibly take more responsibility for housing personal neurological, emotional, or spiritual activity to help ourselves or those around us to attain the fullest level of scope, connotation, augmentation, or impact in our lives and interactions.

Some of the specific techniques or approaches that might be used are briefly listed as follows:

a. Use of hyperbole to exaggerate some aspects of our conversation, writing or even thinking in order to accent various significant values, and also to draw others into more energized or even confrontational dialogue to ultimately enrich the investment of emotion and the quality of any outcomes which evolve.

b. Use of simile to compare otherwise diverse or unlike ideas or objects so that our speech or actions become flavorfully interesting and innovative, and also to expand our creative awarenesses beyond "known relationship" between ideas so that new routes toward ok—

understanding, interpersonal connection, or unorthodox plans and activities can enter our lives to replace and actually improve upon the narrowness of role definitions and activities which have been forfeited or relinquished because "society" has lacked the foresight and originality to connect its "aging" or mature members to new and heretofore disconsonant functions.

c.   Use of metaphor in attitudes or words to associate accepted descriptions or definitions of our commonly known environment, with other known or unknown phenomena so that the richness of the second concept or idea can be enriched by the implicit comparison that occurs with this transference of ideas. Although this process has direct application to writing and dramatic symbolism, those of us who are not experts can also accept the challenging and inspirational task of communicating flexibility, openness, profundity of understanding, expansive awarenesses, and imaginative description and analysis of interconnected parts of the world. This process can help everyone escape the monopolistic incarcerations of our provincial ideas and beliefs, and help build bridges to braid personalities into new meaningful alliances that illustrate both uniqueness and holistic unity among all people. The use of metaphor is at least one way to improvisationally connect ideas and people through the special characteristic of descriptive nouns and verbs which functions as a conveyance to transfer one set of ideas or perceptions to another without losing the quality of either one.

d.   Using personification to illustrate to ourselves and others that nonhuman ideas or objects can be "brought to life" by attaching personal names, pronouns, or status/action attributes; which ultimately can result in seeing the otherwise neutral, frigid, supine neighborhood of our lives from a more absorbing and attentive viewpoint and can also be reversed to note the ways in which we have allowed the repetitiveness and circumstantiality of our "activities" to convert our "persons" into lifeless and inert objects representing anti, pseudo, or non-human entities. Any approaches we can remember from the dramas or writings we have previously experienced which remind us how and why we can breathe life into any ostensibly defunct or exanimate components of our lives (ex. Tin Man in Wizard of Oz) can enrich our existential relationships with all parts of the world, and constantly remind us that we are still alive and have an important responsibility to fulfill as completely and qualitatively as possible the requirements of this "condition of being" which we have earned or been given as part of a "cosmic function" with which we share proprietorship and may not be able to avoid--even with biological cessation of one component of this systemic phenomenon.

e. Using the notions of <u>irony</u>, <u>farce</u>, <u>paradox</u>, <u>allegory</u>, <u>catachresis</u>, <u>allusion</u>, etc. to illustrate for our own learning, as well as the edification of others, that many values, concepts, rules, or inter-pretations of, and by, "social" culture are possibly extremely subjective, pragmatically dysfunctional, inverse, or opposite relative to their real or intended origin or destination, and rationally ludicrous when honestly considering the interpersonal distance, human alienation, personal ostracism, practical complication, or miniscule and irrelevant interpretation which result from the thoughtless implementation of social controls, orientation methods, and reward/punishment mechanisms which were developed by women and men (maybe mostly men!) but which now have become Frankenstein monsters that control and inhibit our lives. Members of older generations must be particularly tenacious and vigilant in the attention-getting activities of behavior, thought, speech, and feeling so that younger generations who are just learning many of our social "insanities," and cohort groups who have become subservi-ent over the years to incorrect and inane definitions of what "was," what "is," and what "should" or "might" be can be gently but force-fully confronted, through grammatical and dramatic means, with the unwise and cancerous perpetuation of attitudes, values, or beliefs which negate, prohibit, and actually destroy the quality of extended life which should be a sweet smelling flower for all to enjoy, forever.

f. Using <u>comedy</u>, <u>whimsey</u>, or <u>buffoonery</u> in the selection of stimulative reading material or audio-visual entertainment, to lubricate the tiresome and sometimes painful path of life, and particularly to remember the humorous aspects of past events or obstacles which, by using retrospective comedic wit, and facetious interpretation allowed us to emerge from otherwise negative situations with a positive view of self, and probably the courage and optimism to either reattack a difficult challenge, or move on in life to better opportunities in the future. Remembering the jokes, funny stories, puns, gags, witticisms and the general role of humor or comedy in our lives can help us evaluate the extent to which we still endeavor to see the "light" side of circumstances. It could possibly propel our sometimes lazy or despondent minds to work harder to unearth the cheerful, buoyant views of events or people, and to discover or rediscover the amazing effect of permissive exemption and independent latitude in rejecting traditional explanations and accepted perspectives about the world and its inhabitants, in favor of the deviant, unexpected, reversed, exaggerated, minimized, or otherwise altered versions which comedy and humor deliciously allow.

g.   Finally, using behavioral techniques, manners and general style to periodically capture the various dramatic orientations of melodrama, spectacle, mimicry, denotation, gesticulation, charade, mystery, motion, or other demonstrative or subtle symbolic communications to not only sharpen and intensify the meaning of daily communications about our needs, disappointments, demands, and expectations from an often uncaring society, etc., but to likewise stimulate the gusto and enchantment of routine interrelationships and to signal the clear intention of living and enjoying life to the fullest extent with the investment of energy and animated activity to exalt our biologic, emotional, and spiritual organisms to their highest state of activity, energy production, and prolific generativity of the living process.

5. Photography:

The 50, 60, 70, or 80 plus years that many individuals have lived certainly provided considerable opportunity and undoubtedly much direct experience in taking pictures of family and friends, scenery, animals, homes, and various blurry fingers accidentally protruding in front of the camera lens. Although photo-historical theory and traditional album accumulation is typically retrospective to transport us to previous times of pleasure and emotional satisfaction, and thereby enhance the quality of heartfelt sentience in the present. Our serious examination of all aspects of antecedent photographic skills and experiences can teach us all a lot about ourselves, and suggests important opportunities to "develop" the quality of present and future activities and emotions. The union and integration of the photographs and her or his "representational machine" reminds us of the value of "oneness" and indivisibility in some life areas, which facilitates the smooth and efficient accomplishment of distinguished outcomes where we modify some parts of self-definition and deportment to blend and mold ourselves around the intrinsic and functional characteristics of an otherwise "foreign" and incongruous object. The relation between camera and operator requires appreciation of the delicate intricacies of exposure profiles, shutter light requirements, angle demands, distance requirements and subject/object "receptivity," along with equally challenging "human operator idiosyncracies" of interest and subject reduction capability, tension control, physical balance, environmental awareness, emotional patience--all of which illustrate that life is a complex symphony of ostensibly contradictory but potentially interwoven factors which, when "negotiated" with tenderness, patience and attention to detail, can produce a "summative product" that in some ways may be greater than could be accomplished by any singular component alone.

Cameras and photographic protocol also usually provide a carte blanche opportunity and open, or at least tacit, invitation to interact with other people or the environment which can demonstrate interest and relevant penetration into the "energy field" of corporal permutation and sustenance, and often translates into an affirmative occasion for the circumspected subject to be highlighted and honorably referenced in historical record as a significant participant in some portion of the world's apocalyptic manifestation. These somewhat artificial and secondary, yet effective liaisons can be utilized in each of our futures to communicate to our "models" the value of their existence, and to also serve as an introductory statement of our intent to engage, "touch," and enjoy the mysterious yet comforting pleasures of human contact--even if initially vectored through a camera lens.

Photographic outcomes, additionally can make a value statement to reflect and hallow the "artists" special comprehension of the "facts of life," and the variable quality of finished products can attest to the goal directed and challenging pursuit of excellence with each new change or enhancement of the pictorial declarations which evolve and mature. History, therefore, can be partly created or influenced by the innovative photographer who designs and selects different prospects for re-creative documentation, and those who pose in various contexts and configurational scenarios can learn more about themselves and appreciate a wider range of sensory and aesthetic images with which they do and can project their "selves" to others.

6. Culinary arts:

In this category, there is no question that every person reading this book has had considerable experience, and those of us with bulging waistlines may have even had "experience overload"; although we may all have forgotten or failed to appreciate the emotional and spiritual significance of prideful preparation of interesting and satisfying foods, the delectation in consuming quality cuisine, or the interpersonal brother and sisterhood created or enhanced through the special meal's unifying conciliation. In all of these cases, we have been provided with a wonderful model to help us experience substantial depth of pleasurable appreciation, and to sharpen our sensory and divine levels of discriminative gratification and raptured fascination with life's gift of biologic nurturance, as it also functions to access various inner chambers of our aesthetic need for exquisite refinement and comprehensive satisfaction. The decision to invest more time and effort in the preparation and savoring of various food or beverage substances, or to use dining opportunities more purposefully and attractively to enhance relationships, does not depend necessarily on financial wherewithal, but necessitates searching for heightened awareness of taste and pleasure sensations, and the pursuit of creative variations in simple or complex recipes or mealtime atmospheres, so that formerly boring and ordinary food-related experiences are embellished cosmetically, compositionally, and environmentally to carry our minds and emotions great and exciting distances away from the seemingly less adventuresome trappings of the dietary and caloric substances. These explanations of taste, cooling, preparation, display and design variations can be developed into personal objectives for increasing knowledge, experience, and self-esteem, and can also provide enlivened discussion and excursion formats for friends to pursue different experiences in each other's residences and also in dining out experiences.

Philosophical Values

Throughout the varied courses of our lives, we have, for both specific purposes and general orientations, espoused and practiced traditional as well as unique modes of functional explanation, logical reasoning, causal analysis, dissertational argument, hypothetical decision-making, conflict synthesis, information deduction and induction, identity-confirming rationalization, and destiny validation, etc. These thinking and feeling processes have evolved from, and also shaped various definitive views of ourselves and the world which have provided security boundaries to replace parental protection and control experienced in childhood. They have also served as calling cards and communicational semaphores to help us initiate and establish congruent relationships, and our life-context visions have also projected goals and consequent evaluative criteria to guide the selection of actions in the present which we hope will produce positive self-image reinforcements in the future as a result of replicating the positive past, or correcting for its undesirable or dissenting previous outcomes. In all of these cases, our philosophies have symbolized in our minds the value and meaning of our actions aimed at developmentally becoming a person who can be defined by our inner ego authority as "good" or "satisfactory," or defined by our self-selected or pre-determined external authorities (God, Buddha, Life Energy, Spiritual Entities, etc.) as "pleasing" or "conforming"; and/or in simply being in a state of existential identity, awareness, peace or unity with self and the world wherein we attach the spiritual and emotional labels of "self-actualization," "enlightenment," "security," or "fulfillment."

The changes in life which accompany aging or chronologic maturation quite often gradually or suddenly impact accustomed states of physical health, conditions of dependence or independence in autonomous self-care and personal management, accustomed financial states and adequacy of living standards, residential alterations or relationship modifications, and substantive additions/deletions, etc. All can seemingly force us to ignore or even discredit the ideologic mental constructs which may have successfully made everything "fit" cohesively together in a balanced "whole" at other times in life when changes were either not occurring or were planned and anticipated; or can distract our abilities to use these contemplative guidelines to either synthesize current changes (including suffering or loss) and redefine their negative connotations, or to creatively use past "insights" or "principles" as foundation starting points from which to comparatively develop new philosophical postulates or personal axioms which are more appropriately suited to reflect the "new" individuals we have become in our current state of biological, psychological, social, and spiritual existence.

Some of us may uncomfortably discover that new life "data" does not "compute" with previously trusted explanatory "anchors," and we may consequently realize question marked areas of ignorance about the full latitude or domain of our beliefs, which we can respond to with possibly unhealthy redefinitions of current events or circumstances to achieve artificial consistency with the narrowly known beliefs. Conversely, we can also allow ourselves to be challenged to "revisit" or "tried and true" notions about reality. Through reading, consultation and personal meditative reflection and examination, we can pursue the unfocused or darkened recesses of our philosophical territory to maybe learn that these are theorems, syllogisms and theses which provide very adequate and even triumphant chariots to transport us confidently into brightly horizoned futures through some form of affirming and perfumed recognition and appreciation of the present. The systematic and disciplined investigation of our philosophical past cannot only open new therapeutic, consultative, or friendship associations, but can also provide hours, weeks, months or years of exciting learning and discovery which we can subsequently use to boost our self-worth as more educated individuals, but can also provide an impetus to help us teach and care for others who might also benefit from the process of becoming knowledgeable, and may become personally enriched and "saved" from negative or self-defeating delusions with awareness of new and exacting truths in their lives.

We may also discover that we had "intellectual" information and aware-ness of particular philosophical beliefs, but had never taken the opportunity, or really learned how to emotionally "experience" and deeply "feel" the consummate abundance of the transformed cognitive ideas within our souls, hearts or innermost spirits--which may imply that the specific concepts of the theory, creed or personal doctrine can be replaced as we grow with more comprehensive or enriched explanatory notions of greater width, depth or inclusiveness; or that enhanced emotional serenity comes with increasing absence of competing or conflictual concepts about ourselves and life, as a greater acceptance of peaceful coexistence of a variety of philosophical canons with which we feel a greater sense of acceptance and unity through a maturing appreciation and acceptance of the arbitrary, subjective, or uncontrollable nature of life so we actually relinquish mental ideas as we accept and appreciate the vulnerable and imperfect "self" which we may possess.

Regardless of the particular philosophical ideas and guidelines we embrace, or have entertained or stringently utilized in the past, there are several specific directions which our re-examination of "self-in-the-world" can take to help us learn and grow within the latter 50, 40, 30, 20, 10, or even one percent of our seemingly known biological, psychological and social lives.

1. Resolution of past conflicts:

Everyone who lives has, to some extent, experienced conflict which seems to inevitably accompany childhood struggles to grow within paradoxical controlling and powerful ego-deflating parental roles, which interact with equally contradictory needs for dependent security as well as emerging autonomy for the child. The complexity and obvious potential for confusion, misinterpretation, differential interpretation, and unresolved questions of desirable outcome can be seen in at least one diagram which depicts the problem of simply "matching up" the "amounts" of parenting activity with somehow associated child activity:

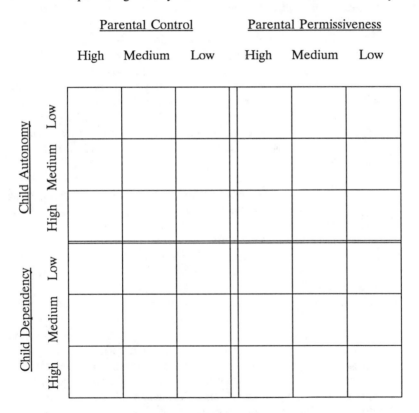

Because of the difficulty of separating our unique and independent selves from the psychological and social identities of our parents and "families of origin," as well as the accompanying task of seeking and utilizing the protection and nurturant "authority" of parental rules, values and reward/punishment systems; each child must make many cognitive and emotional decisions throughout various critical developmental crises prior to "official" adulthood. In the process of defining ourselves, our parents, other people, and the universe at times when we are too immature to even perceive (let alone understand) these arduous notions, we are prone to "locking in" erroneous, deceptive, self-defeating, narrow, or time-limited "truths" which help us survive specific trials of fearful and perplexing development, as children. But we do not realize that these temporary "foundations" probably will become obsolete, or at least require contemporary modification as our needs and circumstances change in adult life. In many cases, we register very negative, delusional and prohibitively incarcerating definitions of ourselves relative to incorrect positive or negative views of parents with whom we are angry or resentfully needy, whereby these concrete ideas perpetually take up residence in our unconscious minds, and serve as an antiquated formula or "map" for life which limits our abilities to think, act, or feel in fully self-actualized or fulfilled ways. Because we often do not learn new "realities" or fail to trust or test new philosophies which come along in life, we may persist in using ancient guidelines to assist our travels in a modern world--and sometimes suffer with the frustrations of these limitations forever.

One exciting way to examine and understand the meaning and decision-making/behavioral impacts of childhood mental formulas on our current lives and future attitudinal opportunities, is to compare each aspect of our images of "us and the world interacting" with various types of old or new philosophies. This is helpful so that we can decide whether or not we look differently, have altered options, possess a wider range of meaningful identities, or can have ownership of greater degrees of self-esteem or gratification when our behaviors, ideas, and outcomes are reflected or compared to one philosophy as opposed to another. Each separate conglomeration of life analyses indigenously possesses an interpretive "blueprint" or framework which assigns values to existing behaviors or ideas, but also authorizes (through our allegiance to that philosophy) new values, feelings, ideas or behaviors which can help "unhook" us from many limitations which our existing philosophies impose on our various outcomes in life. For example, we may have believed for 60 or 70 years that leaving home during adolescence was "bad" or "wrong" because "honoring" parents, according to one philosophy, might mean "doing exactly what they want for our lives" regardless of our own needs or interests. An alternate philosophy may free us from lifelong guilt if we explain "honoring" parents in terms of independently fulfilling the self as a tribute to the quality of parenting which helps us appreciate each unique person as a free agent in life.

Also, the very process of examining various philosophies may help us realize that selection of life agendas and logic to validate decisions is a very subjective phenomenon singularly fashioned to fit individual personalities. In this regard, universal proclamations of the real "truth" in life, especially as they were articulated by parents, may be viewed with a larger "grain of salt" and as much less "carved in stone" than the children we once were that had been socialized and conditioned to believe.

2. Personal security:

One of the most essential ingredients for developing and maintaining a stalwart fortification of personal boundaries and identity-confirming self-images, is the presence of a network of pragmatic and visionary creeds for existing and functioning. A set of consistent, harmonious, and trusted directives helps us pilot the general nature of behaviors, and evaluate the degree of conformity of more specific acts which support our beliefs about the type of person we want to be, so that we establish foundations of congruent approaches to life which facilitates predictability and confidence in facing an uncertain future, based on customary uniformity of past conduct. Principles of living which are contained within the postulates, laws, axioms and corollaries of encompassing philosophies also help build symmetry and balance in our lives because they typically represent the positive dimensions of honorable living, which we use to help counteract the guilt experienced when our thoughts or actions are displeasing to the dictates of parental authority which we all retain to some degree in our memories. Philosophical indoctrination also prescribes attitudes and behaviors relative to societal customs which we have conditioned ourselves to depend upon to navigate our course through the pushes and pulls of cultural standards of conformity and deviance.

Whether or not the philosophies of our younger days represent a pure and crystallized "truth" which has become ineradicable as our directional compass, or whether we prefer the "cafeteria" approach in picking and choosing the most appealing parts of several maxims or in continually experimenting with a continual parade of new proverbial truisms; the very fact that we have some idealistic cornerstones in our lives can provide immeasurable personal security and stimulating optimism to continue interacting and struggling to achieve the highest standards of thoughts, feelings and behaviors which our personalized mottos and gospels specify as ideal.

3. Problem solving:

Each new stage of living seems both inadvertently and deliberately equipped with various major and minor adaptation challenges, which represent mental puzzles to be solved for greater understanding, skills to be learned to enhance our enjoyment of new interests or to improve environmental comfort, adaptation of novel or renovated perspectives or attitudes to help us accept unchangeable life circumstances or to reverse their definition and breed a positive strain of awarenesses. Finally, there are transition life passages to be negotiated so that ulterior movement can continue with minimal fear and irresolution lingering from our occupation of less sublime or horizontally different levels of development.

The fact that problems or stumbling blocks exist at all suggests that at some level we posses a limitation or deficit which prevents advanced warning of impending dissonance in our balanced approach to living. We are unaware of the stimulative ripples we initiate which causes a "surprising" evolutionary backlash that we narrowly fail to recognize and therefore plan ahead to integrate the external influences of contingent needs and expectations of our social environments. We create problems unconsciously to enact pseudo resolutions of childhood dramas to achieve self-worth. We are isolated from communication networks where information is exchanged to direct opportunistic use of surrounding resources, or we are not actively seeking our own fulfillment by placing strong bricks of achievement and fulfillment on the foundation of our personality domiciles so that we can withstand the stormy tempest which almost always comes to herald society's resentment of our individuality and our own childhood fears of independence.

The examination of past, present, or future philosophical viewpoints can help us discover or renew awareness of the "nouns" and "verbs" available to us to label different aspects of our perceptual or activity "field" as within the scope of awareness and anticipatory predictability (e.g., realizing we cannot get changes in Iranian oil prices and, therefore, plan a shorter automobile vacation six months in the future). Also, to discover new "action words" which create a wider range of adaptive options for ourselves in terms of the cognitive, emotional or behavioral repertoire of steps we can take to include, exclude, assimilate, integrate, approach, avoid, wait, stimulate, respond, facilitate, amalgamate, reduce, increase, modify, combine, or separate various parts of personal or relationship dynamics which help us to avoid entrapment, delay or failure in handling the obstacles which come up in life requiring our analysis, action and some form of resolution.

One way to understand something about our problem-solving ability and its relationship to philosophical orientations is to simply peruse a standard dictionary and, after noting a variety of nouns or verbs with which we may not be familiar, decide whether or not we could use this particular concept or idea as part of our normal daily activity to enhance or sustain our ability to deal with various problems that arise. If we conclude that we are unable to put any of these symbolic ideas or actions into practice, we can then think about basic life philosophies which may not agree that particular options are good, functional, or conforming to principles by which the world is believed to operate. Futhermore, ask ourselves why certain privileges, rights, choices, discretions, etc. are not available to us, and whether our lives would be easier, more sane, more enjoyable or have greater success if we changed or modified philosophical visions to incorporate other explanations of cause, effect and operational procedures of life to moreover allow exacerbated capabilities for us to influence sub-outcomes, react positively to externally-generated obtrusions, nullify our perceptions of the power and control of certain forces in our minds as social networks, take other forms of affirmative action to move ourselves to higher or lower planes of relevant influence and responsible "being" or to produce self-serving frameworks of feeling or behaving which are incompatible with the simultaneous negative influences of outside forces (e.g., I won't feel guilty when someone else blames me).

Although the reliance on philosophy can also be used as a clever psychological escape from pressures of responsible action or confrontation of life's fears, it cannot be counted on as a panacea to "solve" all problems. We can certainly benefit a great deal from retroflection on our beliefs and principles to make sure they allow us the widest possible capacity and facility to confront and resolve the enigmas and obstacles which confront us, while at the same time providing a set of ideologies and reveries to help us see past the "thorny" problems to the "roses" of life.

4. Understanding origins:

Each and every one of us at different times in our lives has struggled, conjectured, debated, feared, joked, or been awed relative to the question of our inception and specific or general purpose as life forms on this earth. This is typically an evolutionary, theological, mystical, astrophysical, cosmic, biogenetic, etc. issue which has been studied by the scholarly and inquisitive minds of every culture in every historical era with varying degrees of discovery, insight, scientific or spiritual "proof," dismay, confusion, future investigatory inspiration or abandonment. Yet the masses have yet to agree on a common empirical or supernatural explanation of cause, purpose and eventual destiny which is universally accepted. We are left, therefore, with the individual responsibility and creative challenge to grapple with this ultimate investigation, and to hopefully arrive at either satisfactory temporary or tentative hypotheses, or a definitive conclusion which can assist us in our latter years to appreciate and celebrate the struggles which we have previously endured; to possibly explain and give beneficial meaning to the personal and material losses and associated suffering; to provide a mental and emotional place of peace and happiness in our present life status to calm the disturbing pains of anxiety, guilt and fear; and to help usher our future plans and activities so we can complete any developmental cycles to which we aspire or are destined or produce rewarding and non-destructive interactions with ourselves or others which we and they can define as honorable, good, helpful, revelational, supportive, stimulative, etc.

In the pursuit of this demanding and perhaps never-ending task, many of us clearly sense the mental and physical disciplined rigor and tenacious fortitude which are required to "know" the seemingly "unknow-able," and decide either to withdraw from the contest altogether, to passively (but usually resentfully) accept someone else's hard-earned dogma in life, or to arrive at accustomed or simplistic deductions which may provide an artificial or "subcutaneous" mantle of security, yet fail to deeply explore and understand the intricacies and wondrous mysteries of life.   Thus, we accumulate the personal compromises which usually accompany mediocre or impotent efforts to attain competence and profi-ciency. Another alternative, however, which can provide a long-term stimulus and test of courage, and a plentiful supply of goals for study and analytic learning, is for each of us to make a commitment to read, attend lectures, enter discussion groups, meditate, pray, visit shrines of prophets or mythical sages, to think profusely and resolutely in an effort to expand our knowledge and wisdom about the inception of our planet and its living and nonliving inhabitants, and to bolster our value and utility as friends, children, parents, grandparents, citizens, etc. to help others who struggle with despondency and skeptical defeatist pessimism to possibly discover a ray of sunshine or hope in an otherwise cloudy and depressing existence. Our discoveries may certainly cause confusion or even more questions, yet the "process" of searching can be an exhilarating reward in itself, and can have real and lasting benefits as various puzzle pieces fall into place, and we can test our newly discerned philosophical propositions within the behavioral framework of interpersonal relationships which we can enjoy and improve with new learning which occurs.

In areas of life which represent past as present smudges or scars on our identities or ego-chronicles of the attempted accomplishments, embellished and augmented benedictive acclamation of the virtue and function of our existence can help to retroactively transform quagmires into adaptive enunciations which can become energy-filled springboards for even greater forms of fulfillment and personal success in the future.

5. Relationship development:

It is always amazing to listen to people who live in a world that is becoming rapidly overpopulated as they discuss their fears or current relationship condition of being "alone." Although it is always time consuming and often delicately toilsome to construct rewarding personal affiliations, most would attest to their value, although we might remain perplexed about why specific "sparks" or stimulating "couplings" emerge or retain their permanency. In many cases, the instrumental necessities of managing daily life dictate social and functional role differentiations whereby we team up with complementary "skill-bearers" to accomplish short or even lifelong tasks. In other situations, which might also include sharing of pragmatic chores, relationships may serve to emotionally nurture and support areas of self-concept which are less stalwart, or to pair with other passionate streams of rewarding sensation or self-enhancement to give their spiritual apparition and experiential manifestation in daily activities, and increased energy and sanctioned imprimatur to attain greater richness of feeling. As these emotional relationships move toward a more pure, lofty, and deeper spiritual or "cosmic" connection, many of the instrumental or even affective/ sentimental components may pale as they reach such heightened levels of intensity as to require a "celestial" berth in the unitary minds of the relationship actors, so that the comparatively elementary emotional components of worldly "personhood" do not self-disintegrate, but can perch themselves at a higher pinnacle of shared magnificence and develop unincumbered by the narrower constructs of dependency-related feelings to predominantly maintain childlike perceptions of protective security.

In any of these various relationship scenarios (instrumental, emotional, or spiritual), the feeling and sensation aspects may sometimes or even frequently interact with each other to the point that their undefined catalytic influences result in confusing or frightening unknown "disconnections" (which actually represents a connection union of which we are ignorant or inexperienced, or have previously selectively and subjectively identified as "negative") which causes the relationship to dissolve gradually or volcanically, or never even get off the ground in the beginning. At other times, the emotional interdigitations of two sets of ideas, values, awarenesses or feeling "concepts" may seem to merge successfully on an obstructionless avenue of unification, yet become pelted by particles of daily life maintenance notions which are obtrusively seeking to be integrated where there is no relevant or ornamenting capability in the elevated emotional/spiritual spectrum (metaphysical-beyond, transcending or above the physical or instrumental). Also, the demanding tasks of physical survival frustratingly get in the way of more pleasurable mental connections with others, or are unable to be paralleled and acted out as representatives of supernatural symbols because we have not learned to "index" our perfunctory duties as vibrant reflections of a life, feeling, meaning or world beyond.

When we experience these types of discordant conditions of relating various emotions to one another, both with individual psyches and between people as well as connecting the worlds of mind/heart and matter, the philosophical values and beliefs can function as invaluable "synthesizing," interpreting, summarizing, or diversifying mechanisms and platform planks to open doors toward unification of otherwise seemingly divergent "units" of reality (feelings, behaviors, ideals, etc.) which would return to inactive states of inertia and fearful seclusion with an overarching philosophical idea or value within whose protective womb the singular emotions and behaviors can join bonds and receive nurturance in their associational configuration.

An exploration of the basic concepts of old or new theories of life can result in a list of "principles of life" which might help us decide more clearly what we need in relationships with others, and provide a stronger linkage tether to view the combinations of feelings and emotions which may alone, be very distinct and different for each person in a dyad. But when seen from a more abstract and profound perceptual lens, it may represent a combination of feeling events which accomplishes a great deal for our "special life journey" and allows us to move beyond definitions of differences at the present level of feeling--behavior tangency, toward a developmentally more mature experience later on. We may also use philosophical goals and objectives to place relationship needs and outcomes into a ranked hierarchy of differential function and priority so we do not feel cheated when any particular relationship does not meet all of our needs; but can enjoy the associations we have with others in their fullest dimensions because each has a unique philosophical or ideological purpose and level which can achieve 100% quality as a complete and non-comparable entity.

Our life values, when articulated in the words and grammatical phrases of a "philosophy," may take on the nature of "operational" objectives so that our concentrated perusal of potential new relationships can be fueled with a purposeful dynamic energy which might help us use corroborative feelings to "act out and get on with" our intents to "be" or "become" a special person and to be clearer in sharing with others the types of emotions we desire from them or can help them develop which will ultimately be a benefit for our own growth. In these and the other cases mentioned, relationships can become true and permanent partnerships as philosophical ideals take on the role of categorical "books" in which two people can jointly gaze and "believe" the same things about their small collectivity, and can also be retained as welcomed beacons in the stormy seas to direct us toward safe harbors when misconceptions and childhood fears interfere with the separation and unification of feelings and emotions as part of a ballistic system of security and interpersonal harmonious sharing.

6. Evaluation and change criteria:

   Almost every philosopher who discusses life as a growing process of personal development stresses the value and necessity of internally and externally induced change for several important reasons. First, change in the ways we perceive ourselves and view our own meaning and behavior relative to the ongoing forces and energies of life may become stagnant and concretized "still" pictures of what "used to be" when we felt secure or became developmentally "plateaued"; or may represent mental and emotional "oases" to which we cling to avoid the pain of past or future traumas to our self-esteem. In these cases, life may have moved ahead without us on board, and change of some portions of our ensnaring opinions, beliefs, values, discernments, etc. may help adjust our reciprocal energy exchanging positions to a more paralleled and congruous status relative to life's partnership and ability to enrich our lives.

   A second arena for change might occur when we are sufficiently "tuned in" to the "voices" of life which "talk" to us at one level of our behavior or identity, but have reduced capability to solve immediate problems or to enjoy unknown benefits which are available in additional realms of existence (physical, emotional, spiritual) which we do not have the skills or enlightenment to access for a more complete interplay of various and different parts of our personality (e.g., heightened sensual and sexual pleasure by developing physical stimulus and response capabilities, when we have predominantly interacted with life from a successful and adoptive, but comprehensively limited cognitive framework). In these cases, we are not necessarily regressing or "fixating" ourselves in the past from a horizontal time-line perspective as in the first example, but we are digging more deeply into the vast vertical regions of one or more dimensions of the "self" to use the inherent "equipment" that is indigenous to that province of our personality.

   A third condition wherein change occurs is often precipitated by the physiologic changes and modifications of our "selves" which naturally accompany the aging process, or emerge as secondary influences of disease entities which interact as expected or unanticipated contaminants of the evolving system composed of our mental and biologic functions. In either case, the psycho-emotional charge required may not necessarily represent a greater "quality" or a superior capability of emotional or spiritual awareness which "transcends" a more elementary level of self-actualization, but may represent a need to either slow down or speed up what we are already feeling or thinking in order to accommodate the time delays or limitations which our external world and physiologic "soul-encasing" apparatus dictates. Expectations for goal attainments may require some retardation of the mental and emotional preparatory scaffold-building, or decreased life-span predictions may conversely mean that we must open the throttle to arrive at a desirable or satisfying psychodynamic or spiritual station in life before our physical self passes this point of departure from the world in its presently "known" context. Of course, change may also result in a qualitative shift or acquisition of broader perspectives to understand or accept life's "limiting" contingencies as a way of achieving a spiritual superordinate victory for the holistic and metaphysical self--although this does not necessarily have to be the case in order for "linear" rather than lateral vertical change azimuths to introduce themselves.

Finally, change may be necessary or desirable in our lives as a way of simply providing diversity or enhanced "electrical" recharging of emotional spirits which dissipate themselves through the arduous task of scaling life's hurdles and/or working out the solutions to existing or experimental formulas for our independent, dependent, and inter-dependent personalities which were written in bold script during childhood but are rewritten or at least challenged in numerous healthy or pathological ways by us and others throughout life. Change for its own sake may "re-enthuse" our tired minds for the challenges of living, and remind us of the joys and excitements which we have ignored or "swept under the carpet," and captivate the idealistic and enthusiastic "child" in us to "smell the roses" which are still conceptualized in our minds as positive stimuli, but which we have ignored through our occupation of somnolent attitudes and neglectfully clogged and unused nasal passages, which can be pressed into service by "pricking" our resting selves through changes in ritualistic patterns, traditions, role activities, or states of conscious or unconscious awareness. Diversity may spawn revitalization of atrophied or dormant parts of the self which are fully adequate for exquisite growth and fulfillment but have fallen inadvertently into various states of disuse.

In considering each of these major types of changes which we all probably encounter at different times, there is an important role for philosophy and our personal life-defining value doctrines in helping us evaluate the stimuli for change; the status we occupy before the change is proposed or induced; the process we experience in going through various alterations in thoughts, feelings or behaviors; and the adequacy of the outcome once we believe the metamorphosis has materialized. Philosophical views, therefore can help us in the following ways:

a.   Breadth of change: As change occurs, we are sometimes pressured by self or others to gobble up large portions of new and unfamiliar portions of behavioral or conscious reality, which can easily confuse our efforts to determine the degree of deviation of any action, thought or feeling from an acceptable range of options which consistently represent the basic identity we feel is right for our lives. Focusing on the "fit" between our ideals and new actions can assist in sorting out which changes must be relinquished because they compromise our "self-integrity," and which innovations that we have previously avoided can now enhance our lives and concomitantly give us feedback that we are still "us," although we can flexibly try new things as a stimulating reflection of our identity.

b.   Value comparison: Our propensity to maintain buttressed personality security often results in ownership of monolithic and petrified dogmatic "truths," which interfere with appreciation of the human qualities of other "truth-merchants" and ends in isolation and alienation where none of us really cares to know or love ourselves or others. A disciplined and vigorous comparison and contrast of every philosophical concept or ideal we can unearth can help us evaluate and "factor out" the varying dimensions and content of different life theories so that we can place ourselves within the hypothetical confines of various simulated approaches to learning, and decide how our feelings of happiness, success, fulfillment, peace, and relevance, etc. would be different in our self-generated injections of alternate "definitions of feeling self." Beginning with a study of relationships between philosophical ideas in terms of analytic categories (e.g., depth of explanation, richness of concepts, comprehensiveness of options, importance of relationships, applicability of external outcomes, autonomy of the self, value of unity with nature and cosmos, role of pain and suffering, importance of dependency on others, rewards of material accomplishment and acquisition, immediacy of rewarding payoffs, value of deferred gratification, integration of mind and body, degree of need for external manifestation of principles, etc.); we cannot only decide what "oases" seem best, but also develop some "hooks" upon which to hang various conforming or deviant behaviors to help us reward the positives of inner values, and convert the negatives, to avoid further destructiveness of ourselves or others with continuation of anti-philosophical feelings or acts.

c. External control: Sometimes changes occur in our thoughts, feelings or behaviors with which we are in serious disagreement, and experience considerable guilt, personal shame, compromise of honor and integrity and confusion about why we are different and what has caused our nose-dive from previous levels of satisfying performance or self-esteem. Very often we decide that the demon represents an internal destructive seed which we had heretofore kept hidden, but have become so weakened by life's stresses or selfish for pernicious pleasure or gratification that our evil selves have wrestled control from our tentative grasp for all time to come. In many of these cases, certainly, we may be the culprit as our cognitive defenses for various reasons allow fears and childhood impulses to take over; although often times, the change we experience is mandated and indefensible relative to the massive power bombarded by external social forces against which we are helpless victims and must "rationally" acquiesce to survive socially and keep the personality from experiencing psychotic or neurotic disorganization and regression.

The application of philosophical theories and propositions here can help place the self-relative-to-society in perspective so that "rugged individualism" as one extreme, and "passive marionette" at the other, do not emerge as the only honorable explanations of our ability to sustain ourselves in a world composed of both inner and outer stimuli rewards, and punishments. A philosophical position might suggest, for example, that some degree of vulnerability to external pressure is both normal and efficacious, and that total existential self-sufficiency and isolation, at all costs, is pathological rather than honorable. We might decide, in this regard, that our "weakness" to external power is extremely normal given the needs we have and certain social and environmental contingencies, and that true self-actualization comes from acceptance rather than resistance, or from delayed and planned resistance rather than petulant, abstinent, and rigid protestation and renunciation initially at all costs.

Other philosophies, conversely, may guide us in the direction of accepting total responsibility for every action, which gives us confident support in confronting social forces to control us, and provides victorious options when society "seems" to win through its controls and judicially enforced norms for conformity and punishment for deviance.

d.   Transitional "waiting": Change among human beings is a frequently discussed, but typically infrequently or slowly occurring phenomenon, even in cases where apparently massive or dramatic behavioral alterations manifest themselves, followed by a ripening maturational stage where the changing "inner self" more slowly catches up to the often exploratory, "behavioral self." In thinking about the principle of "change" itself, we might consider that the personality generally seeks to establish a ratifiable state of equilibrium or balance "within" the "world-defining" confines of philosophical ideals or values, and may view itself (certainly through socially "learned" and not necessarily naturalistically true reasoning processes) in various states of inadequacy, crisis, imbalance, "wrongness," etc. when it is "between" more definitive positions or beliefs about life itself as any topic of interest or necessity.

Although philosophies can help us know, to many extents, where we are in conceptual space and time, and provide "retroflective" rewards for "being there" (having a dependable and consistent belief or view), we often use the concepts of these laws of life as stable and immovable palisades to control anxiety about the unknown, and fail to discover or utilize equally functional philosophies from our past or present to validate the "process" of locomotion as a growth stage or status in and of itself, which can have various degrees of purpose, longevity, depth, and outcome meaning for ourselves and our significant relationships.

From an evaluative standpoint, the definition of each of us as qualitative and growing individuals is at least partly, and maybe largely dependent on the ways in which we acquire, hold, and relinquish various views of self and others (including behaviors which accent these opinions and values), and the growth which actually occurs as a direct by-product of struggling, fighting, suffering, working, etc. to learn and change, which may be more beneficial as a dynamic exercise in thinking and feeling in the face of fear and anxiety and psychosocial conservatism, rather than the outcome of that growth which, in some respects, may mean that we plateau, rest or stop the energy flow which was necessary to help us "arrive" at various states of "being." Philosophies can guide us to understand more about how and why we attempt and complete life changes, and can provide various types of satisfying rewards which are not necessarily dependent on outcome resolutions of "who we are," which may be less within our control and constructed by varying degrees of social expectation, pressure, and available role positions which might confirm identities or values that are uncomfortable, outdated, premature, or incorrect for any one individual. The "between the lines" philosophical perspectives may also shed light on the platforms at both ends of the acrobatic tightrope and help us to redefine the ends based on a different perspective about the transitional middle and the relationship of all parts holistically.

e.   Depth of inner change: Although everyone's personality style, intentions, values, goals, fears and general human qualities are frequently observed and evaluated relative to public physical actions and words, we, of course, realize the italicized prominence of each of our deeper inner selves; and entertain various gradations of belief about the existential degree, to which the "world lives" and life actually occurs and is ratified within the psyche or innermost chambers of the individual mind, rather than collective consciousness which may exist through social group interactions. There may never be resolution, clarity, or even minimal understanding of the ways in which separate identity essences, energies, dynamic awarenesses, feeling states or spiritual conditions of enlightenment actually exist, function or interrelate between people, so the only way of truly "knowing" or "perceiving" anything in life may reside exclusively within the "idio-psychic" cognitive and emotional machinery of each separate knowing-self; which may paradoxically never be able to know-itself-knowing, and may only perceive and reflect upon that which is outside itself. So we only have "self"-awareness from the variously interpreted reactions and feedback from other people in our lives who are observing-us-observing-them.

In the case of either the unitary, existential and solitary view of reality where everything only has substance and value because we choose to produce various concepts and symbolic images in our minds and to somehow reward ourselves for their manufacture; or the convolutional interpretation of life's meaning relative to the qualitative process and outcome of interpersonal ecumenism, whose profundity is determined by the richness of shared perceptions of the "we" and "our" components of social and cultural outcomes--we can employ philosophical notions of value, and definition and identity domains to give greater meaning to mental images of "I am," "I do," "we are" or "we do" which evolve as we grow to become wiser and more knowledgeable of the life phenomenon.

Changing the frequency, intensity, nature, duration, illumination, focus, complexion, luminescence, vibrancy etc., of our innermost thoughts about ourselves or others in the act of either behaving or simply "being," may have little or no meaning without the valuative accompaniment of broader concepts which describe the ultimate benefits of life, toward which our various internal changes are proceeding, or which at least testify to the importance of altering our thought contents as styles of thinking and perceiving as necessary preludes to the achievement of enlightened sensation and consequent wisdom or understanding through the disciplined use of the single mind or relationship of mental energy to break down or at least weaken the fortifications of ignorance, fear and inertia which insidiously assume command authority in all of us.

Various philosophies or ideals about the way life "should" be in its numerous aspects can become important rungs on a ladder which we can use to explore the farthest inner sanctions of our minds to attain (in action and/or belief) those very conditions of ethereal adequacy which confirm the intrinsic and achieved virtues of living; and some philosophical canons will serve as direct motivators to attach the ultimate value of life to the steepled or descendent search itself, by which we struggle and endure the pain of pushing sensation and cognitive apprehension to the limits of endurance. This may produce spiritual edification unilaterally, or may represent the necessary explosive assault strategy to conquer our fears and excuses, and subsequently arrive at some or all of the "truth" as a result of decision-making during the calm after the battle has ensued.

In any of these cases, the efforts we make to examine and understand the very private and deep parts of our selves (alone or in relationships) can be phenomenally enhanced and validated by use of philosophies and value tenets which might have been dormant parts of our past lives when we were not interested or able to change, or these ideals may exist as future aspirations toward which our inner struggles and conflicts can be purposefully directed.

Survival and Continuity

At the age of 50, 60, 70 or above, it is probably safe to publicly declare that we have "been around," may have been born at night, but not "last night," have "forgotten more than many people will ever learn," and may even be a "classic." The important message submerged in proclamations of historical chronometry and experiential "weathering" is related directly to the process of "aging," and reminds us of the fundamental significance of physical, emotional, mental and spiritual exercise, utilization, disciplined and tenacious engagement, toil and strain of calisthenic perseverance, struggle and exertion, and absorption of the pain and corrosion which becomes an integral and defining component of each mature "self." The parallels between our fascination with old, seasoned, and even "deteriorating" buildings, cultural artifacts, monuments, civilizations, parts of the landscape, etc.; and the aging phenomena within ourselves may be an important connection to observe, study and understand as a distinct and separate life occurrence, irrespective of the external outcomes or accomplishments which have been the results, rewards or grid coordinates for accomplishments of various life tasks or goals. The contoured lines and wrinkles in one's face, the seemingly wearied recesses of eyes which have looked at the world long and "hard," the vivid and sometimes mysterious aphrodisiac of gnawing or intense pain of veteran joints and muscles, the labored gait of ambulatory movement which seems deliberate and courageous, and the paradoxical beauty of formerly traumatic scars and "corduroyed" roughhewn abrasions; all can speak loudly of the glory of persistent survival and of the difficult yet conquerable interface between person and environment which represents an intimate oneness with nature, even to the extent of having been changed by its power, yet illustrating our capacity to maintain continuity with the unique essence of the self which was strong enough to emerge from an indeed worthy and powerful force which visibly and spiritually impacts the self-in-need-of validation.

The telltale signs of conflicted existence, within an arena of birth and death, newness and oldness, thesis and antithesis, confirms we were really here and a participating part of a difficult and challenging journey, drama, or role play which demanded the flexibility of body and spirit to sway with the energies and will of the "architect" of life who plays the game with serious and impactful sincerity. Yet our "injuries" and "erosions" herald that the involvement was not mediocre, but characterized by enthusiastic and spirited participation from both principal players (life and us). Whereas each may have been "stained" or "colored" by the caring interdictions of the other, with the result that each half are more closely united as the "dance" continues as a result of the bumping, friction, and energized altercation of vivacious forces trying desperately to fulfill the ultimate destiny of working alone and interactively to be fulfilled.

Recollections of the uphill climbs, plateaus, backsliding, and victories of our unique histories may help us appreciate the monumental and divine "production" of exciting and meaningful themes which have interacted powerfully within and through the telekinetic communicational transformer which is our mind/body configuration, and the wear and tear which is observable and perceptible relative to our "machinery" attests, in its own right, to the involvement and qualitative ordination and baptism of each of us to the "miracle" of life, and confirms the value and strength of the human spirit or "grace-vessel" to emerge, grow, learn, and piously accept responsibility for contributing somehow to the overall scenario and life adventure.

This awareness of the instinct, intent, demand, thirst, drive, disposition, proclivity, or incontrovertible necessity to survive can become an optimistic invitation to plunge headlong into an animated and active future "till death us do part," and can confidently reassure us of the mission or assignment many of us have received to keep taking steps along the difficult but navigable path of life. This is important since we have, for some almost preposterous reason, managed to survive a difficult but nonfatal holocaust which has left us battle-weary and frayed, but nonetheless alive and capable of some function for which we have been indentured and trained through former rigors of invalued communion with the almighty competency and torque of life.

Productivity and Accomplishment

One of the most important aspects of our past to recollect, study and make positive decisions about are the examples of personal and social success or achievement which we can use to inoculate ourselves against negative or depressing dimensions of our present lives, and also transform into useful and rousing self-reliance and resolve about future goals. As we get older, the sharpness of antecedent images may blur to varying extents with the camouflage of linear time or the hazy amalgamation of events which we lazily lump into general categories and fail to punctuate with accolades cross-referenced with spiritual or philosophical pennants of adequacy or personal success. In some cases, also, we may perpetuate or resurrect distinctly negative memories of assumed "failures" which we never gave ourselves "permission" to really learn from in the beginning, and which have not been converted over time to assume new representative symbolism of the "best we could have done at the time," a "brilliant resolution" of pressing problems in conflict with internal/external limitations on our perceptions or actual skills in adaptation, or "the only way things could have occurred" due to external contingencies or by personal resistive blindness and stubborn narrow-mindedness which had to be harshly confronted in order to change.

Also, the demands and pressures of survival in the here and now world may entice us to divest energy from remembering the "good" from yesterday, and in fact, the pains we choose to attend to and perceive in our daily lives may even contribute to a contaminative and cynical retroactive process, whereby the past is redefined relative to its "contribution" to an unpleasant present, and causal linkage to the unhappiness many of us have refused to relinquish in order to move happily onward in our lives.

In any and all of these cases, we can potentially benefit a great deal by reviewing both major and minor events which previously occurred in our adult lives, in an attempt to learn about their positive contributions to learning and growing at the time of occurrence, and to possibly work through various procedures to assign them value and proactive meaning for present as well as future time. Some suggested impacts and affirmative contributions of successes or accomplishments are these:

1. Validation of energy: The act of goal attainment almost always involves overcoming the inertia of personal fears of failure and lack of optimistic discipline in our lives, which combines an ability to defer one form of physical gratification (personal pleasure, rest, etc.) in favor of a higher order of spiritual and emotional reward which comes with hard work and personal creativity to build anything in life (including ideas, feelings, or relationships) which did not exist previously. We often ignore or incorrectly believe we have lost or depleted our energy reserves when, in fact, we have probably only transformed or diverted their direction to less productive or dormant states to either satisfy the demands of unconscious

psychological conflicts or to take time to rest and recuperate from external demands which require engagement by our psychologic machinery. Remembrance of previous energy investments and the outcomes can affirm the causal relationship between "work" and some form of "success," and suggest that attributes possessed in the past may not be as far removed from our intentional control and revitalization as we might erroneously assume.

2. <u>Importance of behaviors</u>: Quite often, as we labor to connect ideas in our minds about "who we are" and "what is good or positive" in life, there appears to be an enormous chasm or hiatus between these two potentially converging points of idealistic identity confirmation, which can usually be shortened by the infusion of specific observable behaviors in between which we can use as islands in the stream to represent either something about life which culture, history, the community, or someone else in our lives defines as desirable; or to signify a component of who we are or want to be which we hope will also be needed and rewarded by social forces outside of ourselves--but which we are at least tentatively willing to accept as O.K. in our own minds.

As we mentally peruse the past, we can identify specific behaviors which helped us to feel good about ourselves, and can possibly become more motivated to "get moving" toward some tangible action-outcome, rather than sit around indefinitely to wait for an illusive and maybe permanently vacationing "good feeling" to emerge which will precipitate a consequent "good deed." Therapeutic experience about human motivation and change tells us that we can, at various times and circumstances, begin making positive life changes by <u>either</u> initiating the right behavior even if we don't feel positive, <u>or</u> starting out with a positive feeling of self-esteem and then allowing consistent behaviors to flow from our perceptions.

3. <u>Continuity of personality</u>: The reminiscence of <u>series</u> of successes or accomplishments which are connected to stages of life, continuous projects, themes of goals, etc.; or even the identification of separate and otherwise disconnected results or actions which are associated only by time occurrences or proximity to one another--can help each of us to see an overall and more global "pattern" of successes (some big, medium or small) which leads to a logical deductive conclusion that we posses an internal and parallel "success agenda" or "achievement inclination" or "positive personality style" which is consistent, reliable, firm, effective, and

dependably ingrained as part of our personality make-up, which also presupposes a healthy layer of self-esteem and confidence as the underlying foundation. We can easily forget that, as whole persons, we are wonderful, adequate, adaptive and successful because of our internal qualities that are permanent, especially as external forces or temporary crises can weaken faith in ourselves and our ability to think through and solve both minor and major challenges of living. Looking at past sequences or collections of accomplishments can remind us how competent, in the long run, we really are.

4. Opportunities to learn: In some cases (hopefully not too numerous) we will remember unsuccessful behaviors or negative results of efforts or our failures to take any action, but we can use this information in a very productive way by realizing that the best growth and development in life may come from our mistakes rather than triumphs, and we can reflect on the fact that life, God, nature, etc. cares a great deal about us by providing examples of improvement needs, and that the world actually "talks" to us continually until we open our eyes, ears, hearts and minds to start listening to the "truth" about how competent we are already, and how competent we can become in the future.

Thinking about the reasons for "non-success" or "success not yet achieved," (rather than defining failure) can help us learn other approaches or tactics for the future which will provide a greater yield on invested energy," and we can grow even more by appreciating our opportunity to learn and by conducting incremental "experiments" in the future to improve on the strategies and goal attainment efforts which we previously utilized with unsatisfactory (or "not yet satisfactory") results.

It is always hard to turn off the faucet of hurt, shame, disappointment, embarrassment, depression or disillusionment from past "paradises lost," but the discipline and concerted effort to courageously accept and honestly face the insufficiencies of yesterday can boost us to unimaginably lofty heights of personal victory and can reaffirm that the most perfect life is the one that humbly accepts the beauty of imperfection as the very essence of humanity.

Chapter 2

Conflicts and Dilemmas of the Aging Process

Introduction

Those of us who have experienced, or soon anticipate the numerous aspects of developing, adapting, "surviving," and otherwise "working through" the later years of life know first hand, or have certainly read or heard about, the challenges as well as the difficulties of handling the many physical, psychological, spiritual, economic, cultural, and social changes and problems which "aging" seems to usher into our lives.

In many cases, the alterations and metamorphoses are engendered by uncontrollable physiologic, economic, and sociocultural stimuli to which we must respond in the most adaptive fashion possible. In other instances, however, the "changes" we expect or experience relate causally to our subjective interpretations of the "self" within an advanced developmental "crisis" or "obstacle course," which we correctly or incorrectly learned about in earlier adult years. In this light, our perceptions of who we "were," what we have "gained or lost," what "options" await in the future, and what "strengths" or "weaknesses" we possess to continue life's journey may largely determine either the wonderful adaptive horizon we anticipate, or the horrible conflictual obstacle which we create as the mental image of our senior years.

The following pages, therefore, will begin to unfold various issues and truths/illusions which we will all, to one degree or another, face successfully or through struggling as life continues on its trek into tomorrow.

The Process of Change Itself

1. Physical Alterations with Aging

As the human body (and mind) continues to interact within its own associated cellular, chemical, and organ systems, and as these respiratory, cardiovascular, musculo-skeletal and neurological functions "relate" as stimulators to bodily activity and responders to the external environment, various changes occur. These have significant impacts on overall physical behavior, and our consequent interpretations of our bodies and the psychosocial "self" which our mind "believes" is somewhere encased within this receptacle composed of skin, bone, muscle tissue, water, and blood.

Although some parts of organ systems continually undergo cell rejuvenation and are always "getting younger," many parts of our minds and bodies progressively and at different rates experience (a) cumulative decreases in important enzymes and other body fluids which serve as stimulators or helpers to activate other functions of cells and organs, (b) a slowing down of some cognitive and behavioral capabilities (response speed, flexibility, duration of performance, etc.) due to the accumulative effects of cell loss and degeneration of internal as well as interchange mechanisms through a "wearing out" process, (c) the habituation and consequent "failure to thrive" of various systems where energy becomes bound, and therefore lost, as a result of personal habits and physical patterns which alter our abilities over time and finally, (d) the "weathering" effects of the pathogenic, toxic, corrosive, or contaminative substances which we consume or otherwise introduce as artificial stimuli to our internal organ systems, or the effects of sun, weather, environmental pollutants, and other atmospheric conditions which continually bombard our extremeties as well as inner bodies with various noxious influences.

As physical changes inevitably occur as a result of the combined influences of the above factors, the alterations in our responsiveness to the needs and demands of living are perceived mentally as a comparative ratio between previous capabilities to behave in certain ways, and expectations of current or future behavior, wherein the correspondence or differentiation of these two "performance outcomes" is assigned a psychological and social value weighting which we typically decide is a valid and relevant index of self-esteem or personal adequacy/well-being.

Physical change, of course, in and of itself is neither good nor bad unless we refuse to alter the degree of pressure and "work" we expect from our bodies to the point that our physiology can no longer naturally incorporate and balance the amount of stimulation or "trauma" which usually results in some form of physical discomfort or pain.

Otherwise, any conflicts or displeasure we experience with the physical aging process (irrespective of specific illnesses which will be discussed separately later on) are probably the result of one of the following perspectives in our minds, which represents essentially incompatible and disjointed outcomes for the necessary harmonious relationship between our minds and bodies.

a. Real Slowing Bodies--Artificially Speeding Minds: In this fairly common scenario, many of us may recognize correctly that particular or general bodily operations are pursuing some path of declination or limitation of former capability, and react fearfully to our social definition of "loss" by trying to increase our mental "productivity" as a form of compensation. Although some forms of compensatory "undoing" or "equalization" are normal in all domains of life, this reaction in many ways may impose excessive demands of a mind-body system which actually hastens or exaggerates its inability to handle stimuli or adjust to stress in ways that younger years allowed. Although most of us will never overcome our "capitalistic" and "industrialized" orientation toward "building," "accomplishing," "winning," etc., sometimes we may feel better about change by increasing efforts to produce on a graduated and realistic decreasing scale where a little slippage is expected from the beginning, but simultaneously changing the mentally perceived social goals and objectives we use to measure outcomes so that we have a greater chance to "produce" or "win the race" which is more appropriately attuned to our adult interests, talents and capabilities.

The other dimension of increasing mental "attacks" upon a world that we might feel is "devouring" our former essence, is that our neurologic and cognitive capacities are also changing (although not necessarily in the same direction or at the same rate as physical change) so speeding up mental "work" may prove to be fruitless if we concentrate on "rapidity" of activity or processing, "amounts" of new ideas learned, or "correctness" of recollection from the past--when, in fact, our minds may actually be able to cover more ground in areas of "depth" of awareness, "connectedness" or expansion, already learned ideas, or "reduction" of amount of information to more simplistic principles or truths of living.

It is always easy to play mental games to fool ourselves into believing that we can actually "overcome" physical changes in later years when, in reality, we may have never truly controlled physical or biological process in any substantive ways which actually altered the course of developmental history. As a matter of fact, the accomplishments and completed tasks of younger "triumphs" may have been even bigger delusions of control and superficial applica-tion of sociocultural values because artificial, imposed, and external demands on a natural bio-neurologic system may have even caused or heightened some of the deteriorative processes and problems experienced as pain, discomfort or limitations as we get older. One blatant example of this is the unnatural and inappropriate stress and damage of some sports (e.g., tackle football) whereas injuries and stress damage of early participation are directly linked to major orthopedic, nervous system, musculo-skeletal and other internal and external problems of living healthy lives in later years.

b.   Real Slowing Bodies--Artificially Slowing Minds: Another "solution" to basic physiologic itinerary which some of us will choose, is to assume that any diminutions of physical activity necessarily dictates that our cognitive processes must also slow down to balance our "self"-systems. Deciding, therefore, that we are "getting old," or "heading for the last roundup," etc., may usher in conscious or partly unconscious controls on cognitive sparks, mental alertness, recollection ability, etc. These may reflect a type of depressive reaction to punish ourselves for decreased "productivity," a balancing act to bring our minds into harmony with our bodies so we feel a whole and unified sense of self-image, or a secret effort to gain some power and control by reducing others to defer to our "limitations" and by avoiding presumed failures we believe will ensure as our "declining minds" match our "declining bodies." We may even exaggerate the constraints, shackles, or "disabilities" we perceive within our physically changing selves as a type of resigned "fait accompli" which may reflect our alienation from a physio-productive social "youth" culture, or disappointment at incorrectly presumed losses of previous or future "conquests" which primarily functions psychodynamically as a form of self-pity which is really a backwards way of loving a "self" we feel is unlovable. In this case, it's measured by a complicated matrix of unresolved childhood wishes and subjective societal expectations which we internalize as "parental substitutes" to handle our dependencies. As a secondary danger, the slowing of our mental energies probably interacts with physical enzymes, neuro-sensory processes and other organ-maintenance functions to further retard physical reception of mental stimulation and physical output overall, so the picture finally may emerge as a race between mind and body where both are running backward, and the winner is the one who goes the slowest.

The important point to remember in helping to avoid this conflict and eventual loss to the whole integrated body-mind "self," is that our mental capability should mostly be measured against its own internal need for stimulation and inherent hunger for growth, which should not be artificially correlated with physical body changes, but should reach a "natural" harmony and parallel with its own neuro-chemical changes and developmental path. Its inevitable limitations in functional capacity and adaptive responsiveness will dictate its own natural levels of reception, retention and output which we should not engineer relative to the "ups or downs" of body activity.

c. Real Slowing Minds--Artificially Slowing Bodies: There are natu-rally occurring changes in neuro-synaptic and cognitive-electrical energies in our brain cells and tissues which create different amounts of regressive slowing of various capabilities, including retrieval of information, responsivity to internal and external stimuli, abstract reasoning, conceptual flexibility, and other forms of information generation and processing. These mental changes, of course, are integral components of our central nervous system and our holistic organ complex, so our bodies, in some indirect or direct ways, may also "slow down" to either naturally accommodate our neuro-functional capacities, or react as a secondary diminishing of physical endowment as losses "upstairs" also eventually filter "downstairs" as well. There is little we can do, given the current relative infancy of neuroanatomical research and theory, to alter this normal development, except when extraneous correctable disease processes can be eliminated or retarded to help diminish their negative impacts on "fueling the fires" of inevitable changes.

An important "piggybacking" problem for many of us, however, is that we may prematurely and exaggeratedly jump to the conclusion that alterations of some cognitive and perceptual functions, signals a more massive decomposition of all parts of mental performance, and also that physical decline will parallel this negative regressive "failure." Although some chemical, dendrite, alpha brain wave or electrical activity, etc., does experience alteration, our cognitions in particular ways may compensate for these "losses" and the "deficits" we experience in earlier stages of aging may, in fact, be partially the result of removal of obstacles or energized impediments to a more balanced, harmonious, relaxed, and unpressured functioning of mental process which was potentially more seriously altered in younger years with value-laden pressures to perform, anxious mental fears of failure, or simply habit-forming patterns of processing information and using mental tools which artificially altered the normal activities--which may, to some extents, return as aging reaches particular stages of its development.

We may, furthermore, "decide" to slow down our other physical activities, life-elasticizing energies, or brain-stimulating cardiovasculo-chemical output to the extent that further cognitive slowing occurs in response to lessened stimulation from other parts of our body-systems which, when active and vibrant, help us think and plan and mentally create in more productive and rewarding fashion. In this light, most of us would "rationally" agree that we don't want to "throw bricks on an already overburdened life-boat," but some socially learned and culturally reinforced mental gymnastics may take over, whereby we (a) become angry with mental changes which may or may not really matter relative to our current state of life/achievement/status/need for performance, etc., and we consequently punish our bodies even more for this "sin" or "wrong-doing"; (b) we "pace" ourselves so as not to hasten the impending "doom" of mental and physical collapse and approaching death which, in reality, probably drives a nail in the coffin of our spirit to live and thrive and really speeds along the neurophysiologic retrogradation; (c) we feel decreases in social and psychological power as previous dimensions, potencies and frequencies of thinking aptitude undergo physical change, so we unnaturally become physically less powerful to reduce and manipulate others to take care of and defer to our infirmities--which we ultimately reason and gives us greater degrees of control over others when we believe we are losing control of the self; and finally (d) we try to avoid dissonance in our images of a whole and congruent self, by arranging our physiology to more closely "fit" our neurology, which, unconsciously, we often believe results in more benefit to a system which is "balanced." Although the seemingly symmetrical apportionments are often achieved by lowering capacities of both the body and mind, these often may not be synchronized at all because exogenous or external decisions on our part probably do not control, (or further disorganize) the natural relationship between our bodies and minds which exists on an internal or endogenous basis.

d. Real Slowing Minds--Artificially Speeding Bodies: The condition of cognitive, mental or neurologic "adjustment" to reductions in chemical or enzyme supplies to the brain, wearing out of frequently used parts, brain wave decreases in potency or regulating patterning, etc. has been discussed; although an additional reaction from our ego or personality control center may involve the desire and practice of accelerating bodily activity to (a) force our minds to "get in high gear" which may overtax their already struggling capacities with pressurized stimulus overload, or exhaust us physically which necessitates mental response to help compensate for the loss of balanced internal equalizing forces in the system; (b) produce observable, social data to attract the attention of our minds and help affirm the competence and viability of both physical and brain acceptability in our social-valuation frameworks; (c) to further exhaust the mind and produce greater slowing to justify any real or imagined declines on the basis of our autonomous self-control and choice of a "tiring regimen" rather than more honestly accept the forces in life or nature over which we have limited or no control at all, and to further confront our neurotic fear of the unknown which is only frightening because we learned this as children--not because there are "necessarily" any real dangers in what we have not yet experienced or cannot know in life.

As suggested previously, we are uncertain of the exact correlation between many mind-body actions and are even less sure of which causes the other to change first, so we may actually become or believe we become more active and stimulated mentally when, in fact, the "increments" we experience are actually indicators of energy related to mental regression or loss, or only temporary energy surges which do not last or actually cause more lasting, longitudinal damage in the future. More, faster, harder, deeper, etc. are not always or necessarily better, although the "productivity" capitalistic econo-culture in which we live strongly leads us to believe that these "truths" are valid and reliable guidons for social and psychological living.

e.   Real Speeding Minds and Bodies--Artificially Slowing or Speeding Minds or Bodies: Although most scientific studies certainly have "proven" or strongly suggest that the physical "development" of aging tends more toward decline in functional neurologic and biologic capacity, we should all keep in mind several factors which may alter, modify or even reverse the conclusions which are reached about this nature, direction, rate, and purpose of bodily movement toward some known or perhaps unknown outcome.

(1) Limited Knowledge of Mental and Physical Domains: Although most theories of gero-physiology or gero-neurology and their consequent measurement techniques and instruments are oriented toward the process of physical and mental decline, regression, patho-deterioration, etc., some or all parts of our anatomical systems may, in fact, be growing, progressing, or regenerating in ways we simply do not understand or cannot yet measure with current levels of technology. Although the "ultimate" phenomenon of "death" seems to blatantly contradict this viewpoint, we also know that many individuals die because of the apparent combined effects of natural process and specific disease, and science has not yet been fully and comprehensively able to separate the two conditions to unequivocally understand the separate and unique natures of either one. Elimination of the disease contingency at its primary origin (which may be in childhood, or much earlier in adulthood than we suspect) may reveal a much different "growth" lineage in later chronological years than anyone has ever imagined.

A correlate of this possibility, of course, is that "natural demise" without apparent disease complicity may really reflect the insidious presence of some form of pathology which we do not understand or cannot measure, as has been illustrated with the discovery of cancer which now accounts for one "terminal" cause which was undefined and assumed to be "normal aging" in earlier historical time periods.

There is also some medical authority consternation in explaining why some cellular and organ systems continue to actually grow when other parts of our systems seem to be "in reverse," and the relationships between the "active energies," "passive energies," and "regressive energies" pose many question marks in medical science, to the extent that we may not be definitively positive as to which life force is actually destined to survive, although the "negative dimension" seems to be winning, although could potentially be neutralized or reversed earlier in life with yet unknown alterations and corrections of negative diet, activity patterns, thought processes, health treatment, hygiene regimens, environmental patho-infectious influences, breeding practices, etc.

(2) Mental Decisions About Loss: In numerous cases in my own experience with clients, family and acquaintances, individuals who experienced despair or hopelessness with the pains of their own aging, or the losses of significant others through death, nursing home confinement, "irreversible" coma, etc., actually willed themselves to stop living and typically "passed away" six months to a year after they "decided" to give up. In these personally known cases, and I am sure numerous other medically documented ones, there was no specifically diagnosed cause of death related to continuing or new disease entities in the person's organism, so the explanation was explained "naturally" by medical authority, and defined as "loneliness" or "tiredness" by friends, family, and sometimes mental or spiritual health professions.

The "decision" and "choice," in these cases, to alter and control our bodies to the point of eventually, but quickly, halting organ functions can also be considered in reverse perspective to suggest that our mental powers may enable us to alternately choose to continue living at times when we "allow" our bodies and minds to slow down. Although ultimate "wearing out" or functional atrophy of our physical systems may be inevitable, the integrated role of mental value decisions, redirected positive thought energy, associated changes in neurological electricity and cellular revitalization which relate to our physical, chemical and organ systems, may certainly slow down the "aging process" and, in fact, actually boost the living and growing developmental continuum to some levels beyond those attained in earlier life periods.

(3) Cultural Views of "Fast" and "Slow": Another consideration of the overall life process is that its negative, deteriorative, regressive, and "pathological" components actually come at the beginning rather than the end, as we commonly believe, as a result of our learned and culturally determined mental and physical "inputs" or "stimuli" to a system which may not necessarily be in need of the regimen to which it is exposed. The various forms of physical exertion to play and win at competitive games or sports; the frequently exaggerated importance and traumatic results of overeating and undereating to meet psychosocial rather than nutritional needs; the mental strain of performance pressure, guilt, and excessive worrisome responsibility; the artificial and negative side effects of drugs, alcohol and a multitude of medicines which bombard our systems; the effects of environmental pollutants and other toxic influences, and the excessive or diminished influences of other natural and cosmic phenomena, (plants, dirt, sun rays, animals, lunar gravitational forces, etc.) which we may modulate incorrectly due to social custom rather than natural "oneness" with our world (e.g., may be allowing excessive influences of sunlight for "social tanning," but diminished influence of soil energy through social compulsive cleaning of homes). All of these may actually deteriorate and age our bodies and minds from childhood through middle adult years, at which point many of us feel we have achieved success, grow tired of "working" at life, or experience major mid-life changes which may scream out at us the need to stop aging and start living, although excessive physio-neurologic damage may have already started an irreversible chain of events to occur which refuses to allow us to return to our pre-traumatic developmental path which might, if allowed to run its natural course, change the entire outlook of every chronologic age or focal point. The goal then, may be to remove obstacles to living at an early age, rather than try to enhance either processes of deterioration or remove the results of nonliving

as we get older. A single matrix will help explain at least four outcomes based on differing views of life:

	Sociocultural Activity as External Potent Stimulus	Sociocultural Balance and Harmony with Nature
Life as a Continual Growth Progression	Artificially Induced Aging in Youth or Boost to Life	Possibly No Aging or Decline with Advanced Chronology
	RESULTS	
Life as a Continual Declining Regression	Artificially Postponing Death with Some Life Benefits in the Middle	Appreciation of the Meaning of Dying or Need to Change Culture to Postpone the Unnatural

In the above cultural perspective, what we think is a "slowing" down in later years may actually be a more qualitative aspect of progressive living which (a) we don't realize exists, (b) early blockages have ruined or (c) intervening disease has sidetracked; so that the mental and physical capacities we experience may really enable us, without the negative influences resulting from the reversed perspective earlier, to correctly participate in a life of greater depth, appropriate pace, more simple and unified conceptual reasoning, a fewer number of irrelevant recollected facts, and physical relaxation which are all considered to be cultural signs of decline rather than advancement, or something in the middle which is more neutral and neither "pro" nor "con."

(4) Life Existing in a Metaphysical Realm: The last perspective I want to discuss here suggests that life itself, or "developmental" progression cannot be conceived relative to our presently known ideas about the physical changes we believe we can see and measure, and that other forms of life may exist or begin to emerge for our minds and bodies as "perceived deterioration" or "death" evolve. As in the case of a rapidly spinning spoked wheel, as the wheel reaches a certain peak of excessive forward speed, our eyes begin to see it slowly rotating in the opposite direction or apparently

moving backward. The slowing at the "presumed" end of life may actually be a higher, deeper, more profound level of progressive forward movement which our cultural views will not permit us to believe, and the bodily and neurological changes which seem to contradict previous growth patterns, are really a more advanced, conserving, efficient, pure, and less encumbered transitional process to move us to a new realm of existence. Just as the approach of sleep prepares our bodies and minds to slow down, so that our tired organ and cellular systems can actually regenerate and speed up (including the massive, highly active unconscious world of dreams, fantasies, images, memories and even color/sound coded symbols which burst into excitingly animated life); the "dying phenomenon" may be an even more heightened form of regeneration and superior activation which our narrow and undeveloped perceptual skills and social value beliefs will not let us understand until we evolve to a higher state of awareness and wisdom.

Of course, traditional religious beliefs as well as psychic and spiritual sciences and philosophies suggest there are numerous types of "hereafter" lives, conditions of "being," places of "residence of the soul," etc. which may simply be examples of rationalizing the feared unknown, handling guilt about past irretrievable disappointments, or dreaming about a paradise we desperately want. Although they may correctly know that aging is a preparation for a transitional new life, these cannot emerge until we have fully dismissed our past mental processes and physical "homes" so that we can be born again, but differently, into a new and possibly better form of life.

For each of you reading these words, which may seem strange, "way out in left field," or radical given your present belief system, you might remember that most of us actually fight, resist, oppose and try to overcome disease, stress, "deterioration" or even death processes to the extent that our mental and physical "defenses" prevent our learning to "flow" or "integrate our wills" with the intentions and directions of nature. In this regard, then, we may never be able to "see" the other point of view and most likely will not try to become more unified with physical and mental changes, accept and enjoy the apparent "slowing," and redirect our powerful personal and collective energies to "tune in" to a newly emerging form of life which we may only understand when we relinquish our insistence on alternate and opposing views. In fact, there may be many exciting and phenomenally enjoyable aspects of life which we all miss from childhood on, because we conform to culture's norms and prescribed beliefs and behaviors which tell us who we are, what we should do to succeed in life, and how we should explain everything we see and experience in ourselves and the world around us. Unfortunately, in some respects, society has also credentialed particular "knowledgeable experts" who are the professionals we seek to "explain" those phenomena we do not understand--but maybe physicians, ministers, counselors, economists, or politicians do not really understand either.

In considering all of the aforementioned mind/body variations related to physical and neurologic changes, there are several summary points which I believe may help us all begin to adapt and learn about these, as well as other aspects of our growth and development:

Point #1: Physical change is not necessarily a uniform and all encompassing process of decline or deterioration of all organ systems simultaneously, so we can "vitalize" many aspects of thinking and believing by not allowing ourselves to become depressed or alienated from our changing selves.

Point #2: The ways we learned to handle change, illness, and physical alterations as younger individuals may not only contradict the natural order of life, but may not help us to adapt in mature years. We may need to learn new ways of thinking or behaving--or not thinking or behaving to be "productive"--to flow more smoothly with the new person we become each day.

Point #3: Our minds and bodies often work to compensate for the deficiencies in either one, which is good to a point unique to each person's values and living styles, etc., but we can also use physical or mental energy in destructive and stressful ways by artificially minimizing or exaggerating our attempts to compensate in traditional, materialistic, or concrete ways.

Point #4: What often seems like loss, decline, or regression may, in some ways, be a return to a more natural or normal condition of our physical and mental being, which becomes possible or even necessary as we grow older or younger later in life and have either (a) removed the unnatural psychophysical stresses which led us to believe we were "normal" previously in life or (b) we put our minds and bodies through such trauma throughout life that "breakdown" is the only way to say "enough is enough." In this case, we may need to change the ways we live life from the outset, and also consider accepting our return to a more desirable condition in later years, rather than resisting with maybe incorrect illusions of a previously "better" time.

Point #5: Physical disease, in some cases, seems to go hand-in-hand with particular aspects of physical and neurological aging, and can certainly be complicated or exacerbated by the "weakened" conditions of some bodily systems--although for many of us it may be most helpful to conceive of aging and disease as separate, since the disease pathology is increasingly responsive to medical technology, and because our efforts to strengthen the non-diseased parts of our minds and bodies may help avert or ward off the disease viral or bacteriologic pathogens which may not as easily approach a healthier host environment (body or mind).

Point #6: The measures we use in our own lives to test out our adaptiveness, just as the research tests and instruments in medicine and science, may "expect" certain negative performance outcomes for us, and therefore we may convince ourselves through "logical data" that we possess certain types or degrees of incapability. In fact, what we may discover, as some scientists have learned, is that changes in what we observe or how we approach a measure of "competence" may allow us to become aware of even more capability, performance efficiency, or adaptiveness than we experienced at even vastly younger chronological but culturally influenced years.

Point #7: The culture within which we live plays a major role in defining, actually from the earliest years of childhood, what "old age" will be like, and what desires/needs/activities etc., we should or should not pursue, and even how likely we are to accomplish particular goals for ourselves, which are often contrasted or compared by cultural "spectacles" with our past lives and the current "youth" oriented society. We must remember, therefore, that culture seems very powerful, but is created by each of us individually and can change in some ways to more correctly correspond to our correct and idiosyncratic desires, rather than continuing to postulate stereotypes about "maturing" which are incorrect, narrow-minded, or destructive.

Point #8: There is possibly a very sophisticated and complex correlation or reciprocal association between our minds and bodies, which each of us should be very careful in interpreting relative to our plans to use one or the other unilaterally, and which may be so powerfully connected that major outcomes (e.g., fatigue, physical or mental illness) in one area can be greatly determined by inputs from the alternate half of us. Also, in this light, we should remember that a natural "team work" may exist which needs relatively little external or planned manipulation, so in some cases we may need to "leave ourselves alone" to evolve naturally, rather than "making," either or both parts "perform on cue."

2.   Social and Culture-Related Changes

In addition to the physical and neurological transformations which constantly and sometimes vigorously push us to adapt, accommodate, reconceptualize, integrate or separate, or otherwise establish balance between our "ideal" and "real" selves, society is also progressing (although often I think we are regressively moving backwards) and changing itself, while simultaneously viewing and "making decisions" about its maturing members. There are a host of political, economic, demographic, religious, hygienic, geological, astrological, phenomenal, cosmic, etc., etc., forces which history has connected through developmental evolution or catastrophic trauma to the process of social change.

These changes have, within various time-spans, locations, circumstances or degrees of potency, influenced values, our social symbols, health and mental well-being, community organization and living styles, language and communicational media, dress and interactive customs, government, business and production energies, and every type of social position and way of behaving within these various "functional" cogs of the social wheel.

As every variety of metamorphic alteration impacts the world we live in, we have either changed our views of "us," "them," and the world to the extent that people have passively or actively revolted to cause the change, or we have experienced powerful influences by small groups of "leaders" in power, or by nature "having its own way," whereby we have had to change our behaviors and beliefs (either to adapt or to defend ourselves) after the change-stimulus has already occurred. For each cohort or age-similar group of people who stimulate or respond to the cultural mirror we have constructed of brick, asphalt, steel, wood, cloth, chemicals or food to represent our "selves," and for the multi-age groupings who live during and after the social metagenesis, there are often significant expectations of change in the individual and group roles which are occupied as the changed culture assumes a collective conscious "eye" and "mind" which sensitively or cruelly tries to "fit people" into the newly formed "mold" of society. The criteria for goodness or appropriateness of "congruent fit" are usually related to the following considerations (which may be rational or falsely incorrect):

(1) new skills, strength or energy are "considered" necessary for productivity to provide economic security;

(2) specific mental capacities are "valued" for creativity, rapidity or information processing, or other forms of leadership;

(3) linkages with past values, "successes" or behavioral styles are feared as stimuli to control energy to move ahead;

(4) "differentness" represents "criticism" of the new status quo, where sameness is assumed to contribute to lessened conflict in goal attainment;

(5)   possession of physical attributes, money, or political power are treasured as <u>foundation security</u> girders and <u>connective bridges</u> to help insure success of projects and to alleviate fears of loss;

(6)   removal from the mainstream to obscure moral dilemmas of social responsibility, control guilt, and lessen the potentially excessive demands of human need and dissatisfaction on precarious new social systems;

(7)   insurance of "failure," degeneration, or chronic weak vulnerability to provide consuming markets for some primary but mostly secondary systems of production which are needed as support functions for primary economic and political interests;

(8)   support and isolation of competition for scarce or uncertain "production" roles, or time out to prepare for advanced or future roles to guard against decline or deterioration related to projected expectations or unknown impacts;

(9)   removal from productivity to provide validated opportunities and recognized "expertise" in recreational, spiritual, emotional or other reconstitution functions for "resting producers" to return them quickly and effectively to the demanding workplace after brief rest periods.

As each of us ages, therefore, society will change and assign values to others and ourselves--and to the various things we do, think, or feel--to the extent that more or less will be expected of us as we become central or peripheral to different systems, and commensurate with the ways our needs and "payback" resources are defined by those in control; and various social and cultural opportunities will be opened or closed for our potential utilization and benefit.

One of the most significant and central changes, therefore, which we and society may experience simultaneously or at different times, relates to profession (we will discuss "homemaker" in a separate section), work or employment activities.

a.   Employment Roles

The economically buttressed and production-enticed society within which our parents taught us the proper "work-ethic" values of achievement, efficiency, punctuality, perfection, diligence, etc.; is also the same conglomerate of jobs and performance occupations which measures utility, worth and effectiveness on a scale punctuated with chronological or linear age as a major criteria of role retention. Because of some real (but often exaggerated) declines in physical strength and efficiency with aging, and even more distorted beliefs about mental deterioration, coupled with a "youth-ethic" and general economic need to hire younger and cheaper employees, most maturing men and women are removed from their work excessively prematurely through retirement policies, unacceptable job reassignments, salary reductions, or social pressure and discrimination.

At this slightly variable point in time for each of us, serious psychological trauma and acute or even chronic disorientation can ensue because of several extremely important factors in our culture-related socialization and learning from childhood through adulthood which place us "adaptively" in often precarious, highly vulnerable, and "trapped" positions in a world which often clearly says "We don't want your ideas, energies, service, or presence any more, for any reason--so good-bye." Some of our psychosocially learned handicaps are these:

(1) We often view ourselves so narrowly that we neglect to develop a wider range of job skills, interests, hobbies, philosophical ideas, relationship outlets, or levels of personal being (layers of spiritual growth, for example); so "job" becomes the predominant focus of our significance and value.

(2) We sometimes neglect a comprehensive view of the "work" world where we might begin early, and progressively maneuver ourselves (within one business/company, or between organizations) into positions which insure greater job security, or more closely match and accent the changing physical and mental natures of the "new" person we continually become as we age.

(3) We frequently define the "value of life" relative to the goals of our careers, or the material commodities we acquire secondary to the salary "payoff" of work, so we retire with a permanently blocked, or at least vastly diminished capability to possess the "good, true and beautiful" as we have forced their essence into "production" or economic "ownership" concepts. This usually means that success is translated into "concrete" accomplishments or quality/amount of possessions, which are often unavailable in retirement, and detract our energies from other goals in personal relationships, learning and educating ourselves, pursuing broader goals of community improvement or change, or enhancing other qualities of our "self" which are independent of occupational or professional roles.

(4) We are likely, also, in avoiding fears of aging or displeasures with years of rigorous or boring work, to glorify retirement as a perceptual playground in the sun and perfect relaxation nirvana. This may not materialize, and eventually appear very depressing as we are unable to make drastic adjustments in our work/play ethic, or as habituation makes this presumed paradise becoming boring as it lacks balance and diversification.

(5) In our youth, most of us spent monetary "fortunes" renting doctors or medicines to produce physical pleasure (not always absence of pain), or we consumed considerable time and effort "youth-inizing" ourselves to avoid accepting or integrating physical discomfort as a normal part of life, or learning to control and pacify our stressful minds to the point that many illnesses would probably not have developed. In retirement, therefore, the pain of illness and aging may become a "horrifying bedfellow" with whom we have not reached satisfactory qualities of unification, acceptance or understanding to allow greater flexibility and congruence in dealing with some inevitable displeasures of maturational change.

(6) We also "stereotype" ourselves in gender, ethnic culture, family, or other constricted role expectations, which not only reduces the number and quality of "personal and social

attributes" we believe we have, but locks us into the loss of these capabilities to maintain self-esteem once we have retired and society reduces its interest in many traditional roles (employee, mother, leader of the clan, etc.). At the same time we are ignorant, fearful, or otherwise unprepared to experiment with, or adapt other role characteristics (e.g., emotional nurturance among men) to expand and enrich our opportunities and sensations in life.

In light of the above, and I'm sure many other ways we "trap" ourselves in not preparing for the deplorable, yet existing discrimination and elimination of older citizens from culturally "pedestaled" work or employment roles, there are some tips we can all use as we approach the traumatic "exorcism" of our "selves" from the "production" components of society, or as we handle the psychological and social losses we experience when we realize this option appears to have been permanently removed from our lives.

(1) Psychological Preparation or Adaptation

    a.   Many people view work roles as one-dimensional, and see only the most immediate or obvious function of accomplishing a task or completing a project, etc. Although the symbolism of doing a job well, or using our special talents is very necessary in maintaining self-esteem, we frequently do not push ourselves to clearly identify the two, three, or more dimensionality of our present or former employment activities, to appreciate the symbolic functions which our actions also serve. This form of mental "depth perception" applies a blueprint overlay to every job, and gives it greater meaning with "texture, shading, motion, brightness," etc. to expand its purpose in terms of richer meanings of creativity, artistic coordination, rhythmic timing, thematic interrelationships, precisioned delicacy, or ultra-sensitive elegance/gusto/seasoning, etc. An example of this is the auto mechanic who feels she is conducting a symphony orchestra when "tuning" an engine, or the carpenter who "hears beauty" when sawing a piece of wood or planing a smooth cabinet surface, etc.

The main reason, of course, for this "expansion of perception" is to provide a road map to other occupations, hobbies, or mental awareness we experience in private so that job loss does not remove the deeper aspects of our "souls," but simply takes away the superficial accouterments which we decide are not the "meat and potatoes" of our existence. Detachment from the "externalities" of work, and attachment to the more internal, qualitative aspects dramatically expands the options we have to continue the symbolic functions of our "meaning" in life, long after our specific jobs or formal careers are prematurely or appropriately ended by society or ourselves.

b.   Most of us have learned, as young children, to view the decline, removal or externally forced modification of "things" in our lives as loss, because our fragile egos learn to believe that everyone must care for us through giving us symbols of their love, and that ownership or possession of anything in life is a necessary component of "filling our empty selves." When job loss or change occurs, therefore, in this "deficit" model of defining the self, many of us perceive an actual injury to the "feeling" part of our identity, and actually believe that some part of us has been removed. Although specific behaviors in a particular work setting are certainly "lost," we are much wiser to remind ourselves that a "chunk of ourselves" has not been removed, and that a whole series of new opportunities are now available to our enterprising and creative personalities whereby we can even more fully learn and grow to feel "full" inside, without the "crutch" which we have been, maybe-not-so-generously, provided by life.

This internal psychological process is called reframing by many counselors, and simply means viewing ourselves as full rather than "empty," and turning our socialized concepts of loss into conception of opportunity for gain (making lemonade out of sour lemons).

c. Another approach which some people have used effectively is based partly on the medical disease-prevention model of "innoculating" us against certain illnesses (polio, smallpox, etc.), whereby we are given small doses of the actual diseased pathogens or micro-organisms to build up tolerance so our body cells can more effectively combat bacterial or fungal invasions at other times. In career or employment situations therefore, it may be helpful to "envision" the discomfort and confusion of eventual work disruptions by actually changing jobs, or careers, or at least work sites several times during our lives. This causes us to become less attached to the dependency-related "nest" provided by a lengthy secure "position," and force ourselves to adapt to change or disruption in small increments at times when we can adapt more easily, learn from mistakes, and "map out" a strategy to help us when we are surprised by sudden disinterest of employers, or traumatic discrimination which will precipitate emotional crisis if we lack experience or plans to handle change.

Changing other aspects of our lives may also help engender this "flexibility" or responsive latitude so we do not become rigidly trapped in unreal illusions of "stability" or concrete predictability of the world around us. Therefore, we can learn to view ourselves as constantly moving and, like water, capable of "dancing in coordination" with the cracks, bumps, curvatures or obstacles of the terrain. Changing wardrobe, place of residence, some less desirable friends, rigid habits, etc. can help us train for the bigger or more fearful modifications of lifestyle which await us in the later years of employment activities.

d. Another approach which is somewhat opposite of the first idea of experiencing symbolic depth in our careers, is to actually minimize, in some respects, the socially learned predominance of "career" as a significant "definer" and "reflector" of the adequate, successful or achieving "self" in the world, which obviously is a difficult, but not impossible, task if we begin late in chronologic life. In looking back upon years of accomplishment and hard work which are slowly or abruptly ending, we need to remember the interpersonal relationships, religious or church activities, our hobbies or personal projects, home improvements, and even new ideas we acquired--all of which may have been "lumped" together in our memories with work recollections, but which must now be "heterogenized" or diversified to bring some aspects of the background into clearer focus, and to mentally redefine work in a permanent or temporary position of lesser importance. Realizing the "we" are not our "job" or "place" of employment can facilitate the psychological process of "centering" our values and views on us as a whole "pie," within which work or career is only one slice. The removal of this portion late in life leaves numerous other "aspects" of our "whole being" (thoughts, feelings, non-work behaviors) to enjoy and savor for all eternity and beyond. This technique involves the cognitive skill of "transferring meaning" from one object or area of focus to another, which requires us to realize and use the full extent of "mind control" we possess. But remember, from an existential philosophical perspective, that everything we perceive or believe may be totally subjective, and, therefore, fully under our control to transfer value, eliminate outdated ideas, or add totally new concepts to our mental pictures of ourselves and the world.

e.   One additional way to prepare ourselves psychologically for the somewhat distant, immediately impending or already culminated loss of work roles, is to adopt an affirmative, advocacy, somewhat indignant, and adversarial view against the world (not the helplessly ignorant or frightened prejudicial people in it). This will or already has treated us unfairly and uncaringly in removing a work "option," which this same world has also taught is (especially men, but increasingly women as well) an "essential cornerstone" of our social "adequacy" and psychological esteem. Although I am not suggesting that we delusionally refuse to accept and accommodate to reality, or that we become angry and disgruntled "victims" of a "sadistic" culture, some of us can fortify our psyches with emotional goal-directed resolve, and diminish the negative effects of loss with tenacious energy and philosophical "righteousness" in the refusal to willingly accept external decisions which affect our opportunities to live and thrive in a role-oriented society. The resistance we launch, in these cases, may not result in the sustenance of our previous jobs or work roles, although some businesses or organizations may be pressured (through guilt, affirmative action or age discrimination, litigation, social protest/boycott, or union-type collective bargaining) to find other acceptable (maybe not ideal) work roles for older employees, or develop advisory or consultative positions to continue to benefit from the wisdom and expertise of senior staff who "know," but maybe can no longer actually "do" the job because of physical limitations, coordination contingencies, or other factors where specific age-diminished reactions truly jeopardize the safety of the employee or the quality of the end product or service. Also, the development of a mental covenant to actively and insistently pursue some form of work role wherever we can discover or <u>create</u> one, by ourselves or with family/friends/investment partners, etc., can provide considerable opportunity to use imagination and purposeful vitality to challenge ourselves to meet our needs. This can also give us additional "reasons" for "attacking life" and trying to enjoy the benefits it sometimes reluctantly hides, until the seekers and fighters among us insist on "playing the game" and receiving some reward for participating or at least making an effort.

(2) <u>Social and Behavioral Preparation and Adaptation</u>

    a.   As all of us age, there is no doubt that some physical and neurological declines in muscle strength, visual and perceptual acuity, movement flexibility, stamina, reaction speeds, etc. occur (with and without the added burden of specific illness) which become particularly problematic in certain work activities where accomplishment hinges closely on the physical capabilities of the worker. Jobs, therefore, which are "physio-specific" or "neuro-precise" may place aging workers at progressively increasing disadvantages in efficiently, effectively and safely complying with production demands; which means that changes in job specifications, output expectations, work procedures, or equipment/tool/machine capability (e.g., computers and electronically operated machines) is the only way some workers will be able to survive in certain jobs. In cases, however, where the organization has not boosted its "high-tech" capability, or insists on the philosophy of employee "expendability," we may be required to continually "migrate" within the system of varying work roles, into positions of management, supervision, decreased physical demand, etc. so that we move to jobs more suited to our changing natures rather than expecting the job to change to "fit our altering contours." Increased education, skill cross-training, management preparation, voluntary acceptance of modified (but usually lower paying) positions, or improved "literacy" on computers and high technology equipment can be one approach to help insure increased "survivability" within employment situations. This would otherwise eliminate us if we refuse to prepare, plan, explore and flexibly seek different situations which make us less "visible" as "defective or inadequate performers" and reduce demands and stress in vulnerable areas of our bodily systems. This approach, of course, takes time and sometimes delicate preparation, and particularly necessitates changes in beliefs and attitudes about our self-images ("I was born a lumberjack and will always be one"), especially if we have already been "excised" from the work force and need to carefully re-enter at a more appropriate role which is correlated with the new physical person we are today, rather than the one we were yesterday, or idealistically always dreamed about--which may never come true (Cinderella's mice and pumpkin do not always turn into white horses and a beautiful carriage).

b. Another "social" skill or strategy which is helpful in pre-
venting, delaying, offsetting or compensating for job loss
is the comprehensive and sometimes meticulous building
of social and employment "networks."   These are
comprised of key associates, consultants, employers, or
friends within a variety of work sites, who can assist us
at critical points in our personal change process, or in
their organization's "transition" points to learn about and
possibly secure new job placements which accomplish the
psycho/neuro "graduation" and job "suitability" goals we
have for reducing probability of excessive stress
demands, performance failure, or obsolescence in
keeping pace with age-correlated criteria of job
retention.

Networks also provide psychological support and
informal learning about better attitudes and skills to
handle job transitions, plus they create reciprocal
"helping" systems where we can also facilitate and
contribute to the well-being of other maturing workers
who find themselves in similar dilemmas or "challenges"
of their own.

c. In some cases, the loss of particular jobs is stimulated
prematurely by observable declines in efficiency,
production speed, physical or emotional stamina, or
independence in completing one's work without seeking
the assistance of other employees, or allowing the struggles to "keep up the pace" to become manifest to
management through our complaining, anger at the
"system" which is making our job harder, or more
concealed protestations of absenteeism, lateness for
work, or other passive-aggressive ways of communicating
stress and disappointment.

The problem here, is not aging per se, but an
interactive effect of the initiation/response/recovery times
in performing the instrumental tasks of our jobs--paired
with the nature of the work which requires particular
dexterity, visual, auditory, or mental recollection/
manipulation skills which, in fact, do become modified

with increasing age. Since most employers are not acutely sensitized, or particularly innovative in modifying job activities to more closely match changes in employee capability to interact with equipment, devices, or other implements, the growing "mismatch" between people and things widens, and diminished outcome eventually "points a critical finger of blame" at the worker.

We can help ourselves to a considerable extent in many work roles; however, by assuming more responsibility early on, for examining every technical aspect of our jobs to originate and construct modifications which will correspond to our individually changing physical needs, while at the same time not drastically altering the final result of our work in either completion time or quality of the product we build or facilitate. This approach can be handled, in many cases, fairly "quietly" so the boss is not alerted to aging as a "big deal" relative to his or her productivity concerns, and in some instances may even temporarily or permanently cause increases in worker output, and can be used to further enhance our status as job innovators, initiators, and responsible employees who help the company improve.

Some simple examples of changes include: larger lettering on documents, electronic devices to heighten sound amplitude on telephones, simplified paperwork "check lists" to eliminate tedious work with manuscripts, mechanical modifications on tools or equipment to facilitate operation in cases of arthritic movement restrictions, relocation of files to decrease "travel" distance, organization of production schedules to eliminate time/energy consuming unnecessary or laborious steps, or implementation of any other "shortcuts" or manual assistance procedures to lighten, speed up, or simplify any components of our jobs which will "naturally" reflect ineffectiveness as our bodies and minds change with age.

d.   As some of us strain to adapt to the energy losses and stress demands we experience as older adults within various work roles, we may tend to "hurt our own causes" by psychologically giving up the "fight"; and thereby decreasing our activity boundaries and levels in an effort to "save" energy, or to symbolically express anger at ourselves, fulfill a deterministic "destiny of decline," or to purposefully control our own failures rather than have this "degrading" experience foisted on us from outside "management" authorities or powerful environmental circumstances.

In contradistinction to this inverse "self-salvation philosophy" of controlled decline, however, some research suggests that older adults are actually "stressed out" in some ways from "under" rather than "over" arousal, and suggest, concomitantly, that we thoughtfully force ourselves to increase numbers of different activities, or energy invested in any one activity, to (1) remove self-imposed mental inhibitions to heightened productivity, (2) to stimulate the electrical, cardio-vascular, muscular, hormonal, and other bioenergetic forces in our body/mind system to become more active, (3) to create more "attractive stimuli" (event potentials) in our worlds to which we may choose, or be environmentally forced to respond, in order to resolve problems and actively plan adaptational adjustments, (4) to generate anxiety in our systems to "shake up" the sometimes "slug-like" and dormant compulsive habits which maintain behavior and attitude at minimal levels of mediocrity, (5) to call forth the "flexibility" some of us have learned through life experiences, to overcome and compensate, to some extent, for the individual deficits which trap us frequently within one type of behavior pattern (which may not occur for younger workers), but allows us a fuller range of adaptive responses in other behaviors where younger "competi-tors" have not yet "learned" a performance repertoire, and finally (6) to combat the slowing and almost addictive effects of "stimulus persistence" which means that some aging adults have varying degrees of retardation in disengaging or recovering from the impact of recurrent influences and demands on our systems to accommodate--although altering the "stimulation experiences" to which we are exposed may "dislodge" us from the seemingly mesmerizing and dominating effects of a behaviorally conditioned, but declining response compulsion on our parts.

We may test out this "activity hypothesis" by "psyching ourselves up" for our boring work routines, involving ourselves in non-required aspects of our jobs, interacting more vigorously with others in our work setting, or just making daily efforts to speed up or energize our regular activities and reward ourselves psychologically for "trying harder" or exhibiting greater effort.

e. The final suggestion for this admittedly abridged list of social and behavioral approaches to deal with past or future job loss, is for some of us to think seriously about the benefits of owning our own businesses, pursuing limited partnerships with friends or colleagues, or investing capital in economic or money market ventures which will pay dividends based on the hard work we have previously done to earn the money, rather than future "labor" which is dependent on physical capability as opposed to the mental work which some of us may find easier as it relates to the "investment" or "owner-ship" concepts of earned income.

Obviously, many people will lack the financial capability to achieve an investment base, since we must have some money to make more money. Although consultation with qualified investment or small business counselors can highlight many opportunities of which we are ignorant, and good consultants can often guide us through the complex labyrinth of bureaucratic red tape to help us discover workable combinations of loans, down payments, limited partner stock options, govern-ment incentive programs, and marketable ideas for business or investment which can actually result in successful and lucrative options to the traditional employment role.

We must realistically remember that there are significant demands in this type of "work" also, but we may determine that the flexibility of maneuvering work hours, the delegation of responsibility, the selection of less physical production and product options, and the use of mind rather than body predominantly may extend our meaningful "work life" far beyond the impaired or "apparently" natural limits which may be associated to more dependent roles in the work force.

b.   Family Roles and Structure

As the aging process pursues its course in our lives and those of our adult children, it seems that some very important decision dilemmas evolve relative to the structures, functions, symbolic rituals, and ideologies that surround the important and complex phenomenon of "family" living. The historical recurrence of some of these change or decision junctures incorrectly suggests that there is a natural, normal, or inevitable reorganization that occurs within and between generational subgroups of extended families. While, in fact, some changes may be precipitated because we are initially afraid they will occur, or as a result of other age-related percep- tions of ourselves or other family members which represent conflicts about our positive vs. negative self-images which we have not resolved internally, but choose to "work out" within the context of the operations and ideations of the family system which we "learned" as children was both a "cause and effect" of the quality of our individual being.

In other cases, however, some changes may be required to adjust to the demands of the new "selves" we happily or unhappily become as we get older, so that optimal levels of our well-being and that of our children or other relatives can be achieved through the modification, addition or elimination of various support, caretaking, facilitative, or receptive-beneficiary roles which previously had limited or controlled our abilities to achieve the fullest state of personal comfort or psychological happiness. Although these changes may occur with little or no frustration or psychic distress, they often are accompanied by varying degrees of confusion, fear, anger, disappointment or irresolution because they represent disruptions in homeostatic or balanced life systems which we use as external anchored focal points to reflect our internal stability and emotional security.

In either case, changes which we "manufacture" in our minds as necessary, or changes which must occur as practical and necessary means to "survive," I will discuss several important domains of family life and organization which generally become intricately involved as stimulus or response factors related to aging.

(1) Leadership, Control and Power Changes

As each of us grows older, the family "nest" continues to empty as young adult children pursue jobs, college, or their own independent family existence, and changes in our own careers means that the household may no longer be predominantly organized around a routine work, school, and social activity calendar that greatly influenced its "purpose for existence" for many formative years during our younger adulthood. As the functions of parenting, supply and maintenance for employment, recreation to recuperate and prepare for work/school, and general household preservation decline or become less necessary or important, the leadership opportunities previously exercised by men or women increasingly fade away from former role requirements, and we each may experience the loss of power, personal significance, self-affirming authority, and security-producing control which were invested in, and a "payoff" from, family leadership structures. Men may cease to be "instrumental" leaders of activities, productivity philosophies, ideologic values, or "physical" caretaking and home maintenance tasks; while women may experience shrinking pedestals of "affective" support, "homemaking" nuturance and interrelationship engineering, and psycho-emotional inspiration and foundation-building for the developing personalities within the family. Modern changes, in these "traditional" gender roles, of course, may substitute different leadership responsibilities for men and women, and some research even suggests that some couples almost totally reverse leadership roles as they get older and feel the need to balance life with exposure to the activities, responsibilities, and rewards formerly experienced by the spouse of the alternate gender-role orientation.

In handling the gradual or sometimes sudden awareness that children no longer require as much direction and emotional bolstering, and that spouses no longer need our unique skills and talents to help hold their family-related functional roles in place, the family, together, is no longer headed in a specific and unified direction which needs our guidance, planning and validation as a worthwhile journey or "cause." There are several important "power-restoration" steps we can take to help prepare for, or handle the change and perceived psychosocial loss we may "cause ourselves" to experience.

Step #1: We need to transfer some energy for self-esteem from areas of "responsibility" for others and for activities within families to the leadership we can exercise in guiding our own continued development, and realize that the "control" which emanates from the dependency of others is simply the absence of control within our own lives.

Step #2: We may benefit from reorganizing our views of family life to diminish the importance of household "things" or behavioral activities which become less necessary or less accessible as we age and families separate, and substitute the positive control of emotions, ideas, symbols of relationships, etc. which we need to maintain in our hearts and souls as more powerful connective linkages to significant others as the frequency of actual physical association diminishes, and as the accessories which formerly surrounded these activities no longer require purchase, maintenance, packaging/unpackaging, transportation, storage, and planful discussion of "what" rather than the "who" of family life.

Step #3: We may need to relinquish narrow definitions of our "leadership expertise" in family-related functions to allow a fuller range of contributions we can make within marital or friendship structures, community activities, or individual growth agendas, so we do not necessarily surrender the need for healthy power to be important to ourselves and others, but simply expand the audience who can potentially benefit from the influences and guidance we provide.

Step #4: We may handle the eventual loss of family "system-generated" power by beginning as soon as possible in our lives to assume more equal, interdependent, and parallel cooperative roles with those we formerly controlled or led, so that bridges of friendship and shared independence will reduce the likelihood of children having to drastically separate emotionally or physically to "reject" our control. This will contribute to closer relations built on mutuality as we experience less painful and resentful loss when families change, and at the same time have created other non-power dependent associational structures to carry over into new relationships when the nest becomes physically altered, but not emotionally deprived or sterilized.

(2) Added Caretaking Responsibilities

The trend for many older individuals to live much longer lives due to medical health-care advances, better nutrition, etc., on the one hand means that some of us will be responsible for providing financial, emotional convalescent, or invalidism care for our adult children; and on the other hand, those who remain healthy will also experience varying types and degrees of increased emotional and physical "dependency" from spouses (especially longer living women caring for men), brothers and sisters, or friends.

The financial, physical, and emotional demands of these "caretaking" roles in families or friendship groups can represent a major adaptational obstacle for many of us who have not previously learned the responsibility and techniques of emotional as well as physical giving, and the time and effort we expend meeting the needs of others can also plunge us into psychological conflict and frustration in pursuing our own goals and needs in life. Also, some of us may destructively convert feelings of loss, compassion, or sadness for "helpless" loved ones into guilt or anger we use to blame ourselves, or even abusive behavior or feelings toward those we are caring for because they represent our own fears of dependency, weakness, or "irrelevancy" and we angrily want them to improve or "be O.K." so they stop representing a "mirror" of our own selfishness or fearfulness.

One of the best ways to prepare for the emotional struggles and burdens which may accompany potential nursing, feeding, medicating, bathing, physical therapy/maneuvering, decision-making, and psychotherapeutically supportive roles, is to learn to view our individual personalities as more completely "whole" or "worthwhile" depending on the degree of skill and creative ingenuity with which we can "help others to help themselves" to any degree. It is certainly hard to reward the self for unselfish things, because this contradicts the natural instincts we all experienced and learned to control as children; although we can, in many respects, mentally train ourselves to view the "payoffs" in life as directly connected to the emotional and physical love we give to others--which we can also conceptualize as making compounded deposits to our own "banks" of self-esteem and relevance to ourselves. In conjunction with this approach, we should also gain experience and appreciation of being vulnerable and dependent on others for love and support, so we learn to avoid "denying" this human quality--not deficit--in ourselves, and realize that caring and being cared for can actually be viewed as gains or self-enrichment opportunities for both giver and receiver, rather than as losses for one or both parties.

We can also help ourselves by remembering that there is (a) a philosophical limit on how much we should do for others without robbing them of their independent ability to help themselves or accept their helplessness, (b) a pragmatic limit on our own emotional and physical energies required to keep us emotionally and biologically alive, and (c) a natural limit on how much we can really accomplish in reversing, delaying, obscuring, or otherwise comforting others in experiencing the feelings and psychophysical sensations which life gives in a unique way to each of us.

Caretakers can, therefore, circumvent considerable guilt by planning ample time away from "serving" others in order to healthily and ethically/morally "feed our own souls." While, at the same time, helping those in dependency roles to also take responsibility for themselves in providing some doses of their own emotional support, and also becoming stronger by accepting the limitations of their condition through patience, transcendence of aversion to pain thresholds, and development of other fiscal and mental resources to "survive."

Caretakers can also ask for help from community or church organizations or groups who can provide professional or volunteer assistance with the burdens of home care, and we can also accept our own limitations and remember the value of our love when we have to arrange temporary or permanent "custodial" nursing home services so that we and our loved ones can both complete our natural lives with a higher quality of comfort, satisfaction, and whatever "life energies" we can develop to reach our fullest individual potential.

(3)   Increase in Dependency Roles

In addition to the responsibilities which age-related changes usher into various caretaking roles, all of us eventually experience some degree of dependency, contingent reliance, protective indemnity, or external guidance/control from others, our own physical and mental states of being, various forces of the fiscal and physical environment, or even supernatural or cosmic destinies and "authorities" which may govern our entire lives or portions thereof from start to finish.

Although dependent existence is a phenomenon everyone undergoes in early childhood, our maturing biologic and psychologic systems, indorsed by family and cultural rituals, cause most of us to progressively seek "independent" adult living and to either (a) learn to fear dependency as a recollected state of parental control of helpless child-victims, (b) lose sight of the positive benefits and strengths which accompany trustful acceptance of support from others (this is especially true for men in Western societies), (c) feel O.K. about dependency "conditions" but forget the "skills" needed to participate effectively in this necessary but also nuturing process, while simultaneously avoiding inappropriate or exaggerated forms of control by others, or (d) continue to be involved in dependency relationships with people, places or things, but label each of these circumstances as independent and free options which we have chosen.

As illness, slowing or altered capability for sound decision-making, financial insufficiency, emotional isolation and loneliness, or natural physical incapacity forces us, or necessitates our choice of limited or extensive degrees of extrinsic-reliance on family, friends, public services, medical care, drugs, prosthetic devices, nursing services, legal guardianship, etc., we can personally contribute a great deal to a smoother transition of this highly inevitable life change, and to its eventual "successful" outcome representing minimal psychological resentment and conflictual resistance on our parts.

-- a: We can avoid a great deal of guilt about imposing on others by remembering that giving love, attention, care, and support may be the most direct route for others to experience self-esteem and fulfillment. Many self-centered and "materialistic" behaviors we performed or experienced earlier in life may represent defenses, avoidances, and hindrances in accepting and enjoying our true interpersonal giving and receiving opportunities.

-- b: We can prevent considerable anger at our dependency-assumed "weakness," "vulnerability," "failure," etc. by considering perspectives which contradict "achievement" and "activity" oriented cultural ideologies. This can allow us, conversely, to view self-control and personal power as more predominantly attainable through "acceptance" of limitations and autonomous (i.e., nonresistant) choices to allow other people or functions to provide the caring attention and help to which the deservably lovable parts of us are entitled.

-- c: Each of us can also pointedly remember that dependence or provisional connectedness to external sources of energy, nurturance, structure, or guidance usually does not encompass all aspects of our personal or biological domains of behaving, thinking or living. We, therefore, continue to exercise control over many avenues to freedom, individuality, creativity or self-direction, and can build esteem and confidence despite the fact that some parts of us may seem to be in various conditions of "bondage."

-- d: In the context of relationships, we can also more actively participate in negotiating reciprocal roles of inter-dependency, whereby we can actively recruit oppor-tunities to help and care for others, while offering them the "opportunity" and "advantage" of helping us meet our own needs related to the aging process. This ratio of helper to helpee roles contributes to a balanced social system where everyone, in turn, can employ their "strengths" to not only take care of others who are temporarily or permanently dependent in some life-areas, but each of us can be "independent" in creating unique and effective "agreements" whereby others can help us meet our own needs as well. This, of course, requires awareness of self (i.e., needs), honesty in defining areas where we are deficient, and qualitative communication to engage, monitor and support the efforts that we have enabled others to make on our behalf.

-- e: We can all benefit a great deal by viewing the connection which many of us form between "dependency" plus "vulnerability" with a third idea of "human adequacy." This means that the conversion of a psychosocially negative concept into a positive one can free us from the defenses we all employ to control or avoid the anxiety we experience as we anticipate or actually encounter this "state of being" at any time in our lives. If we all learn to openly express our fears of losing control, letting others see our weaknesses, or handling the obligations of responsible adequacy after we have received from others, we may progressively learn that dependency is actually, in and of itself, a freeing experience and one among many opportunities for a more fully qualitative human experience.

(4) Decline in Activities

As we all have certainly witnessed in others, and can
anticipate for ourselves, the physical changes in our body's
capacity to collect, store, and metabolize energy as affected
by reduced vascular capacity, cell loss and organ structural
deterioration causes some degree of "slowing down" in every
aging human being. This obviously results in reduction,
modification or substitution of behaviors which occur within
interpersonal or family structures, and may have several
important reciprocal effects on others who partly define their
"selves" relative to the deeds and actions of persons who
actually experience the activity changes or declines. As family
"systems" theory explicates, when any individual changes
perceptibly within a "balanced" set of interdependent role
expectations and contractual formal or informal agreements,
others may experience "disequilibrium" or anxiety as they must
"redefine" the changing person and possibly forfeit some of
the benefits of emotional "need gratification" which were
provided by them, which may now require "satisfaction" from
within each other individual who makes up the marital or
family unit. Some of the most typical and problematic activity
declines, and ways to compensate or adapt to them, which are
experienced by maturing members of marital dyads or more
extended families, are as follows:

Activity Decline #1: Reduced participation in family meal-
times, outings, work responsibilities, babysitting, shopping,
sports and recreation, and other physical activities;

Problems: Other's guilt in leaving you behind, inconvenient
schedule rearrangement to accommodate your activity
threshold, additional work responsibilities for younger family
members, changes in some of the family's preferred activities;

Resolutions: (1) Affirmative acceptance and communication
of your needs to remove responsibility from others, (2) family
meetings to jointly define new roles for others so that equity
is maintained, including relevant less-active responsibilities for
ourselves, (3) honest discussion of "negative" feelings, and the

"losses" we all fear when change occurs, (4) family assertion of its basic activity priorities, and their consultative guidance to help you find and accept something else to do when you cannot participate, (5) affirmation of the important contributions of all family members, or marital partners, irrespective of particular natures or degrees of physical behavioral activity, (6) family analysis of "activity" relevance to insure that some less active "actualizations" of the "selves" involved (which would more closely match your activity declines) might be beneficial to all involved (e.g., more reading, quiet reflection, etc.), and (7) confrontational challenges from family to insure you are not "making excuses" for yourself, seeking sympathy, manipulating, etc.

Activity Decline #2: Progressive withdrawal from family or couple discussions, debates, arguments, decision-making or planning functions, leadership services (discussed previously), and other forms of verbal interchange;

Problems: Family disappointment at loss of your contributions, increases in conflict which your "buffering" role prevented, fears of responsibility/failure as others are "on the air" more frequently, pleasure (laced with guilt) that your negative inputs are reduced, inertia and family "floundering" as they must proceed on their own steam without your guidance;

Resolutions: (1) Family planning to continue the spirit and nature of your input through selective solicitation of your "benefaction," or assignment of this contributory "function" to another member who becomes your "proxy," (2) family analysis of your "inhibiting" role in their conflicts, followed by joint efforts to help everyone grow from the learned awareness, (3) your feedback to the family about the frustrations or "failures" of your communications, which may have precipitated or hastened your fearful or rejected withdrawal from action where you or "they" might adjust, (4) family planning to assign you a less active, but significantly "potent" role in consulting about some family decisions, or offering certain types of feedback at key points (but not recurrently) within discussion scenarios.

Activity Decline #3: Alteration or removal of your emotional and spiritual energy, attention, feeling, awareness, hope or other form of nonverbal and essentially nonphysical (although probably metaphysical) additions to the collective energy of the family;

Problems: Sadness of some members by not having your specific attention, general "sense" of energy loss without clear answers as to "why" or "where," fears of inability of some members to find their own source of "ego-power," irresolution of some positive behavioral outcomes without the fully collective spiritual or energy/psychic "imprimatur" at the start, middle or finish;

Resolutions: (1) More careful planning of critical times when your emotional input can be powerfully used, although on a limited basis, (2) family discussions of their "spirit" and ways to boost its energy and power to not only help you to re-energize, but to capitalize on the increased strength of everyone, (3) family consultation requests to seek your wisdom and inner light to help the younger members carry on your image, function, and psychic "specialness."

(5) Communication Changes

The physical changes in our auditory, visual, speech, olfactory, and sensory capacities for touch and physical sensation due to cellular loss, structural deterioration of various body parts, and neurological/central nervous system alterations of function causes each of us to continually emerge as a new and variably altered apparatus to receive communicational stimulation from the environment, and to process it cognitively with a consequent response back to the outside world. As our sensory and neurological "receivers" become progressively modified, we may (a) fail to perceive various "cues" which are sent or available to us from the physical world or significant people near us, (b) mix up signals which exist simultaneously, and either cancel some out or confuse our minds in the "data processing" stage, (c) receive the communicational light, sound, sensation or verbal messages too late to provide a relevant response to meet our own needs, or those of the sender who expects a response, (d) use our memories and "experience-rich" mental processes to "make up" for the communications we fear we have missed, or to simply process the information through our own filters which may delay the response, or neglect consideration of its differential meaning to the sender who does not have our mental "code book" or agenda criteria, (e) perceive stimuli which do not exist because our electro-chemical mental "machines" are experiencing internal malfunctions in formulating correct images to represent physical reality, which sometimes we replace with ideas and awarenesses from our unconscious past, (f) respond predominantly to stimuli which are familiar, so we can feel comfortable with a more predictable and habitual response which has been successful for us previously, (g) receive the noise or extraneous cues in the environment, or only certain parts of complete messages which are sent, because changes in our physiology have produced inability to receive certain tones, sound waves, light shades, or bodily sensations; or have caused heightened "sensitivity" to particular forms, intensities, times, organizational contexts or cycles of "sensations" which might be available for our awareness and consequent personal decision-making, (h) perceive some stimuli to be more intense, significant, powerful or intrusive than they actually might be perceived by a younger person, and therefore "recruit" communications which are more acceptable or stimulating, or decide not to respond to the more salient messages, (i) adapt or become habituated to typically presented communications to the point that their poignancy is reduced and responses are categorically de-emphasized, routinized, or eliminated, or (j) receive the stimulus adequately, but delay the response due to extra age-related processing time, or natural slowing of biological and physical behaviors which serve as the visually noticed response to the sender.

In all of the above cases, the possible breakdown, misinterpretation, or abnegation of communications in relationships may be predominantly a function of changes in our bodies, although numerous steps will shortly be discussed which will help us and others in marriages, friendships or families to accommodate and compensate in many ways for the obstacles which changes in the communicative "apparatuses" engender. In other cases, however, those around us make significant assumptions about us as aging individuals totally, or they formulate opinions about our communicational capabilities or interests which, correct or not, can alter the nature, style and effectiveness of interpersonal exchanges of stimuli and responses which have varying degrees of importance to the emotional lives of the communicants. Some of the typical behaviors in others are as follows: (a) they assume we will not attend to certain message "content" or to stimulative "process" so exclude us as legitimate intended recipients of information, (b) they fail to realize the receptive capability which we do possess, and therefore communicate "around" us with messages intended for others which are about us, or may be inappropriate or hurtful when we cannot help but to intercept the message, (c) they direct intended messages to us, but do not adjust the tempo, amplitude, pitch, style or method of stimulation to increase the probability of our timely and accurate reception, (d) they become impatient with our acute or chronic slower response times, and deliver too many "chained" stimuli for our processing "systems," or fail to wait for the delayed response which we formulate and deliver at our own pace, (e) they decide that we are unable to cognitively understand or logically handle complex, abstract, intellectual or sophisticated information, so moderate or eliminate the contributions we might make to significant issues or important family interactions. Finally, they attempt to be sensitive to "special conditions" of our communicative receiving or sending capabilities, but exaggerate their "adjustments" of stimuli or responses to the point that we are insulted or patronized, or the communication pattern is too drastically altered to allow comfortable and normal interaction sequences and behaviors.

Regardless of ourselves or others as the primary instigators of communication problems which are directly or secondarily connected to correct or assumed aging phenomena, the following guidelines will help all of us adapt and continue to communicate with relative maximal effectiveness:

Guideline 1:   Family or marital units must continually identify and support everyone's <u>communicative strengths</u>, so we can all work to improve our deficits based on positive incentive model, and to help counteract stimulus or response mental "cautiousness" for fear of failing in communicative interchanges.

Guideline 2:   Each member should identify specific areas of their <u>reduced</u> communicative sensitivity, awareness, intake capacity, processing accuracy, feedback potential, or response inadequacy so that everyone can adjust their behaviors accordingly, and also discuss their emotional feelings about any "losses" or system changes which may become burdensome or neglectful of any person's needs.

Guideline 3:   Everyone must learn <u>patience</u> as communication patterns are slowed, speeded, or otherwise modified artificially so that a "new environment" actually comes into being before some stimulus-response sequences are completed; but remember that speed and accuracy do not necessarily vary together, so a slower response may actually be a more qualitative one for the system's benefit, particularly as one member "works over" the response within their own conceptual framework to produce a result which may have a more potent or comprehensive meaning.

Guideline 4:   Members of caring relationships should also keep in mind that "aging" does <u>not</u> mean that everyone in the same age bracket is <u>identical</u> in the type, degree or specific occurrence time of various communicational assets or deficits, so that each person should be "profited" based on <u>their</u> continuing behavioral trends relative to past behaviors, and then compared in terms of communicational "functionality" with the "potentials for flexible accommodations" of those in the primary social group with whom the maturing person interacts both regularly and infrequently.

Guideline 5:   Some research data suggests that a wide variety of "decremental slopes," including those related to perceptions and sensory-motor communicational stimuli and responses, can be delayed with concomitant demonstration of various successful and adaptive behaviors, and with increased physical health and fitness on the part of the aging person. This awareness and practice of body/mind maintenance, of course, should be encouraged among all members of family units.

Guideline 6:   Stimuli which are presented within the interactive "net" should be introduced with the widest array of multiple inputs (verbal plus visual plus tactile stimulation, etc.) to increase the likelihood of reception by each unique (younger or older) information processor, and messages should contain as much clarity, simplicity (not compromising the quality of the content), delineation and magnitude as possible to insure that they are received in the original form intended by the sender.

Guideline 7:   In cases of doubt, everyone should seek and specifically elicit direct feedback from message recipients to insure that valid meanings persist through the processing stage, and to correct any distortions or even negations which materialize at the point of when the message "transfers" from the environmental air and light waves into the sensory and then cognitive/neurological receptors of the intended receiver.

Guideline 8:   Those with problems in communicational sending or receiving should be assisted by family members in "practicing" their skills in awareness of stimuli, accurate perceptions of meaning, non-distortional processing of implications of the input relative to their response, and delivery of clear, "receivable," and timely responses which help meet the needs of the original message sender. Sometimes, in this context, family members may be required to discuss their emotional or cognitive "agendas" so that each family participant can become a better communicator relative to the symbolic meanings which underlie specific message contents. Older adults or mature children, sometimes therefore, must be confronted if they persist in developing their own "self-reflective" meanings to communications, rather than being sensitive to the needs of others.

Guideline 9:   The entire family must work together to study the home or living environment to identify detrimental aspects of furniture placement, acoustic capability, quality of light, prominence and salience of visual images, feasibility for touch and personal communicational contact, and distracting noises or interruptions. These should all be modified and then tested to determine any changes in the quality or quantity of communicational interactions which materialize.

Guideline 10:   The family or marital unit, jointly, should do a "content" and "process" analysis of the typical types of messages sent and the styles of associated stimulus, response or processing techniques, to determine which aspects of the patterned interchanges have become regimented, routine, ignored, boring, misunderstood, innocuous or typically offensive so that creative changes and exploratory modifications can be implemented to produce higher quality techniques, more noticeable inputs, greater continuity and accuracy of responses, and generally more interesting and rewarding interchanges of a caring and complementary nature.

(6)   Recreation-Leisure Changes

The topic of leisure-time activity is an interesting one because, in some cases, retirement or maturing years brings an increase in valued hobbies, sports, relaxation, etc., which had been prevented in a fuller participatory context due to the earlier time/energy/attention constraints of employment, child-rearing, other social "obligations," and life achievement interests and demands. In other life histories, however, the aging process, along with its illness or disease components, actually reduces the amount and philosophically/emotionally-valued quality of many recreational activities which have to be curtailed or eliminated from our lives. In trying to understand some of the changes in life as recreation waxes or wanes, we will consider the interaction of several dynamic or dimensional variables which apply to recreation (as well as many other activities) as noted in the following matrix:

	Active Recreation	Passive Recreation
High Symbolic Meaning	a. Increase b. Decrease	c. Increase d. Decrease
Low Symbolic Meaning	e. Increase f. Decrease	g. Increase h. Decrease

a. Increase--High Symbolic--Active Recreation: In this particular scenario, the availability of time, money, role flexibility, freedom from stress, etc. means that the aging woman or man had probably put an important part of personal identity and self-fulfillment "on hold" during younger years, with possibly mounting frustration at the lengthy inability to "play seriously" as much as would be necessary to be self-actualized through the "payoffs" that are symbolized with the high energy recreational attitudes or behaviors. The initial excitation and developmental rewards from a more active recreational lifestyle or singular interest will be extremely stimulating. Physical changes over time may eventually reduce the intrinsic rewards of this pattern, and necessitate either a transformation of the symbolic meanings of this self-actualization to more "passive" pursuits, or necessitate major changes in the symbolism itself which we may discover is unnecessary in our lives or has already been met previously or is not related to any particular "activity," is a defensive escape from fears or previous disappointments, or must be met in some other way in the future.

In this form of active use of time and psychic/physical energy, we may also have to adjust our thinking about the importance of outcomes of an active sport or hobby, since "successes" will diminish if we maintain the same "scoring" formula or standards of actual performance, so we may find it advisable to incrementally emphasize "input effort," spirit or enthusiasm, since "absolute skill" may increase temporarily with practice, but will most probably diminish with advancing physiologic restrictions of age.

Within the context of relationships, other people may develop a set of expectations about the type and level of activity, relative to their needs as well, and also have to "adjust" as this "baseline" profile changes over time. In some cases, we may become so excited about this "opportunity" that disappointment relative to subsequent declines and the "losses" of the interpersonal sharing which revolved around the activities may be difficult to tolerate. We, therefore, should work out "contingency plans" with significant others so that the relationship bonds can remain firm through the substitution of alternate "bridging mechanisms" between "hearts" and "souls" which do not relate to type or amount of activity. In this light, there is also a major dilemma if someone in a close relationship has severe activity limitations (either because of preference or physical deficit), because increases in activity on the part of one individual may cause temporary or even permanent emotional separation and the associated problems of resentment, alienation, loneliness, and reaching out to others for love and nurturance. These possibilities should be considered as activity divergencies are noted, so that the emotional connections are not weakened due to the activity disconnections, although these differences can certainly be used for learning about the self as well as about the relationships which exist in our lives.

b.   Decrease--High Symbolic--Active Recreation: The problems related to life changes with this personality picture usually involve varying degrees of reconciliation with the past, where we have been active with a great deal of meaning relative to the "core" of our identity, and experience heightened frustration when time becomes more available in past retirement years, yet age-related changes force modifications or reductions of previous patterns. It is essential that we work hard to not allow ourselves to equate decrease in activity with decrease in worth, and we must do a good deal of mental "work" and logical thinking to realize that the internal "images" of self-realization, adequacy, fulfillment, etc. are in no way directly or even rationally "connected" to our physical bodies or activities--except as we have chosen subjectively to form the symbolic, idiosyncratic linkages. As we remind ourselves of the power we have to "arrange" some parts of "reality" to our "likeness," we must also remember that others in our family may experience the "loss" as well, which means we must help them understand the transformation process in our heads by which we establish our priorities irrespective of "activity quotients," and help them realize that they must also meet their own identity needs without too much "vicarious" reliance on our activities as interpersonal symbols and referents of their image states of being.

In some cases, alternatively, we may discover that formerly high activity levels or energy "cathexes" (investments) were more defensive in nature than adaptive, and actually served as poor substitutes for the "peace of mind and body" which might enhance our states of "being" rather than more actively "becoming." We may decrease activity by choice or natural limitation and realize that the compulsive and ritualized recurrence of activity made us "believe" it had been symbolic content, although it may have only protected us from fearful unconscious "phenomena" which we now know do not, or never did exist; and we may be able to diminish the behaviors and more fully accept our "selves" with the same type or frequency of behavioral criteria. Others in the family, however, may be surprised to discover who we "are" without certain defensive facades, which may or may not be an easy adjustment for them. We also may be saddened to learn that we do not really know ourselves once certain character-defining activities are extinguished or adjusted, and we may experience mild, moderate, or even severe mature "identity crises" as we seek to learn more about us when the external trappings of high energy fun are no longer functional as self-reflective mirrors.

c. Increase--High Symbolic--Passive Recreation: This form of change or adaptation may be necessary as a way of maintaining the value and demonstrated presence of self-esteem or identity images, while harmonizing our inability to physically continue more active recreational endeavors. Our social "learning," however, has emphasized broad concepts of active lifestyles as "healthy" and "good," which is echoed frequently by the younger generations to handle their own fears and power differentials with their "seniors"; so our minds must grapple with conversion formulae to transform equivalent "units" of active behavior to units of passive behavior without losing the meaning of either as past, present or future indices of our historical significance.

Passivity, however, may reflect heightened speed of processing complex data in our minds without the delays of associated slower physical "corroborative mirroring," so we may actually feel more "successful" if we are able to transform physical quality to mental quality, although this may be a problem for many individuals who have not attended to the development of intellectual powers during early years. Less active forms of "enjoyment of accomplishment," on the other hand, may also represent a slowing of our neurological "transformers" and "data processors" where we might be able to enjoy more through simpler physical expression, and become frustrated with the forgetfulness, confusions, misrepresentations and energy losses as our minds struggle to "play games recreationally" with complex tasks, large numbers of goals we may try to accomplish, or highly comprehensive or sophisticated mental outcomes we would like to produce. In these cases, a redefinition or discovery of some of the "simpler aspects of life" may allow our minds to "recreate via relaxation," which may be enhanced in some cases with increases in physical encounter in play which requires a minimal level of associated mental explanation, manipulation, symbolization, problem solving, understanding, or analytic resolution.

Our motivation is an important factor in all of the above changes, because we will assign various priority values and meanings to criteria of tasks, our participation and interaction with these tasks, and the outcomes which "materialize" or "visualize"; to the extent that active vs. passive only has meaning as we define the adequacy of "self" relative to the nature of relationship we have with physical space and time, cognitive concepts or ideas, biologic energy saved or expended, and positive or negative reactions from others.

Regardless of our own personal intentions, we must be cognizant of the fact that family members, spouses, friends, etc., often function as <u>dependent</u> outcomes relative to the process or conclusions of our recreational or other types of activities, and frequently base some qualitative components of their life satisfaction and adjustment on the images they have of us as we "behave" or "don't behave" in various ways. As we might move, therefore, to more passive forms of important recreational activity, we may partly decide to do this because of the "pressure" from significant others who "demand" increasingly excessive energy from our "tiring" systems so that the image they want to maintain for themselves can be anchored relative to our contingent behavior. As they notice our transformation to either truly passive and more "simplistic" taking-in-rather-than-"operating on"-reality, or passive physical behavior with more active mental "gymnastics," they may feel we have abandoned them and either increase their demands for more activity, or move farther away from us emotionally to "figuratively" help themselves survive the "loss." We can be very helpful in this "systemic" change process by discussing any slowing, moderation, time-spacing, or self-acceptance process in ourselves as we may retain the same value on our relationship with others but only choose to express it in a less active, but possibly more qualitative way. We may also work together with important people in our lives to share in some areas of movement toward more passive enjoyments and to collectively strive to increase the "defined" quality while decreasing the "actual" quantity of actions or thoughts.

d.   <u>Decrease--High Symbolic--Passive Recreation</u>: Although one condition here has already been discussed as the adverse of the above (<u>increasing</u> high symbolic <u>active</u> recreation), another explanation involves the progressive decline of "recreational" activity in life, as it is traditionally defined as a "creation," development, formulation, or manipulation of various components of our internal or external worlds to the point that the arrangement of circumstances "keys" a "pleasurable response" somewhere in our mental construction of reality that is also physically associated with increases or decreases in neuromuscular and cardiovascular tension. A decrease in passive recreation may mean that we have already decreased "activity," and are aging to the degree that we are moving into a state of being that is no longer generally definable as "recreational," unless we specifically include "restful acquiescence to motivational pressures" to produce thoughts, behaviors, or states of being; or "production" of a passive resting state of "harmony" and perfect "equilibrium" as examples of recreation--which is traditionally not the case in Western society. We may experience or interpret a serious "forfeiture" of traditionally perceived domains of the "viable," "worthwhile," and "venerable" self as increasingly passive states of non-work or non-play seem to plunge us more deeply toward childlike dependencies on our physical conditions of resting metabolism, although this seemingly negative status is possibly more frequently defined by others as somewhat or extensively "pathetic" due to their own fears of inactivity within family and world communities where adequacy is directly linked to activity. As we age and rest, passively, to greater degrees, we may begin to interpret this positively or negatively as dying, or may choose to employ alternate, nonmaterialistic philosophical or spiritual frameworks to perceive ourselves as moving into new states of after-life activity or more qualitative passive "being," or may even materialistically simply accept the fact that our bodies are equalizing and balancing our mental pressures to perform and, therefore, are efficiently using changed biologic capacity to produce a state of harmony between ourselves and other domains of the living ecology, which we had formerly controlled but now must join in a state of equality.

This status sometimes produces our guilt because of the caretaking required from other people, although we must remember that (1) this is a natural part of the life process which we all share as either givers or receivers at different times in our lives, (2) we can continue to meet the needs of others during this state, either in giving them the opportunity to unselfishly love, or to enjoy, at a more mature integrative level, the recollections of our "gifts" of "us" to them in the past which they use positively in the present, and (3) they have a choice not to care for us, and are never forced to do anything in life which they define as negative. Therefore, even if they are ostensibly unhappy with caretaking roles, there is some reward at some conscious or unconscious level which they are enjoying, despite the emotional conflict they may experience.

e.   Increase--Low Symbolic--Active Recreation: For aging individuals who place relatively minimal "identity producing or confirming" symbolism on recreational diversions or amusements, increase during the retirement period may be short-lived as other active or passive pursuits develop a more cardinal role, or the "active" nature of behaviors may help stimulate and energize our mental and physical processes for more productive investment in other interests. These active entertainments may also serve as a form of relaxation from the tedium of more inert or quiescent tasks, although may serve in some ways to "mask" the relatively unstimulating or non-rewarding natures of other activities from which we must escape into recreational endeavors.

Although the direct implications of recreational increases are symbolically diminished, we should keep in mind that maintaining "meaning in life" when work roles decline may require the reincarnation or creation of an entirely new set of aspirations, awarenesses, philosophical beliefs or behaviors with the associated problem of eventually realizing that low symbolic activity is only a temporary "placebo," which could become stale or even frustrating if more primary foundations are not inculcated into our lives. Also the increase in activity (recreational or otherwise) per se may represent an energy-filled escape from more passive and objectionable early lifestyles, which means that symbolic value must be added or revitalized within all forms of activity--with caution, however, that this "finally discovered or actualized gratification" will also progressively decline as some physical capabilities diminish. Major disappointments could create conflict as we are unable to "eat as much desert" as we had hoped throughout a lifetime of deferred gratification.

Family roles may change proportionately to correspond to our increased activity, although misalignments may develop as some members become disappointed that we do not remain "serious" about a sport or hobby, or as others in our lives struggle to understand "what specifically" we are trying to accomplish with changes in active recreational demeanors. Some members, however, may enjoy the opportunity to relax together, and relationships may be greatly strengthened as we finally "let down our hair" after decades of hard work and discipline. In this case, eventual slackening of the pace in the context of a "shared mutuality" with another may result in complementary adjustment of activity level without any serious threats to the "self"--which is presumably symbolized more poignantly in other dimensions of acts or feelings.

f.   Decrease--Low Symbolic--Active Recreation: Although diminution or even total cessation of this recreational scenario may accompany the aging process, major life crises may not ensue since there is relatively little investment of psychic energy in either the "recreational" or "active" nature of these behaviors, which may be substituted for passive activities, or other forms of active behavior through work, interpersonal relationship development/maintenance, or other activities not defined as "play" necessarily. Slowing of this "secondary" support structure, however, may have important side effects in other more patently symbolized life domains, because the active recreation may inadvertently or unconsciously (a) contribute to the general stimulation of neurological activity which may not be enhanced as much via more passive routes, (b) maintain higher levels of biologic health which permits greater "success" in areas of higher identity-symbolizing importance, (c) provide a sense of balanced routine, pacing, familiarity, or person-time-place orientation that builds self-confidence and security feelings to refuse anxiety and fear generated "blocks" to growth in other areas, (d) provide an arena and set of activities within which we can utilize and "massage" our faculties of memory, visual acuity, hearing, intellectual comprehension, vocabulary capacities, attentional variety and excitation, etc. which are all intercorrelated "communicational" devices that must be lubricated and "tuned" as much as possible to contribute to the whole "system" of our bio-psycho-social functioning, (e) remove stress, strains, or other "inhibitors" from mainstream functional areas of our metabolic and motivational lives which otherwise might endure more rapid or pronounced "aging," or finally (f) stimulate or fulfill particular emotional needs in those who joined us in these recreational pursuits, which had a secondary payoff for us as "healthier" people, we're better able to meet our needs for emotional support, intellectual excitation, etc.

As these decreases might continue, we may notice slippage in other domains of life to the extent that higher qualities of symbolism may need to be injected into active recreational pursuits, so that we can motivationally and spiritually "refuel" other valued areas of living through attention to this booster, addendum, or reserve "tank." Manipulated increases in a diminishing pattern may have absolutely no effect if the "slowing" is "biologically" based and "developmental," which can partly be determined by assessing whether changes in our "outputs" (end results of tasks, behavioral accomplishments, "understandings," etc.) actually progressively reflect loss of ability, as opposed to retention of our basic abilities in life which simply require a longer "incubation" period to produce their highest reasonable levels of quality or quantity output. There is some research that also suggests that memory capability is not as "age-dependent" if the aging person experiences variety and exposure to a wide range of phenomena, so that "familiarity" on a broader scale assists in retrieval of information from memory "storage banks"--whereby a larger number of non-symbolic activities, if not decreased, may provide "life exposure" in areas where heightened emotional tension is not destructively invested in areas of predominant symbolism where there is, perceptually, more to "gain" or "lose" relative to behavioral outcomes.

g.   Increase--Low Symbolic--Passive Recreation: In many ways, the development of relaxing and relatively "insignificant" pastime activity may represent considerable psychological growth in counteracting the pressured, success-oriented, and high-energy/"meaningful life" orientations of mass society which all of us, to some degree, have struggled with in life, and which, in some respects, more have contributed to the illness and aging processes through the stress and "wearing out" influences on our organisms. Although some family members may assume this change is inevitable and an example of growing "incompetency" or degeneration, it may actually represent a conscious choice to slow down and "enjoy for enjoyment's sake," and therefore actually represent control and heightened competency and autonomous decision-making. Family members, spouses, or friends may become disappointed as we seem to "drop out of the active picture," not only because they may want more energy and valued active interchange with us as they pursue more highly symbolized life goals, but because they may feel worried about our seeming isolation, "irrelevancy," and loneliness; or be guilty about their inability as "good" spouses or about children to help us "viably" involved in family or community life. The passivity and decreased stress of activities that are not "emblematic tickets to critical states of identity" may, conversely, actually prolong life and enable us to invest productive energy in other areas of personal or family life, although we must "negotiate" with significant people in our lives to help them understand our needs and to agree on areas of "convergence" where high "love" energies from both generations can intersect for mutual emotional rewards. Family members, therefore, should ask us what these activities mean relative to our philosophies and awarenesses, rather than assume anything based on physical appearances alone.

The negative side of this coin, on the other hand, is that the increase in low symbolic recreational activity may represent, for some of us, a gradual relinquishment of important imagery, fantasy, abstraction, or other forms of symbolism within "enjoyment" activities that formerly functioned to help make us feel relevant, valuable, important, and contributing to the well-being of ourselves and others. The loss of symbolic meaning in recreation, of course, may mean that identity-enhancing energy is attached to other activities, and it is also positive because, at least, recreation at some energy and activity level is continuing in our lives or even being speeded up to meet particular enjoyment agendas which represent new growth areas.

h.   Decrease--Low Symbolic--Passive Recreation: One positive scenario in this category is that we have defined a need in our lives for either more activity recreationally, or more significance attached to some or all of our leisure activities and have decided to "get moving" by giving up some activities that have wasted our time or confined our physical and psychic energy.   As we continue to age, however, and may progressively feel dissatisfied with life's "losses" or waning "opportunities," we may only temporarily produce a surge of activity to recapture various "paradises" we believe we have lost or will not attain in the future.   We may, therefore, eventually resume more passive types of recreational endeavors which could be more harmoniously suited to our metabolic age-related capacities and thresholds, although the struggle to grapple with the "gain/loss" conflict in our minds may "force" the assignment of greater symbolic meaning to the more passive activities which existed previously. Family members may become confused or even frightened if passive activities seem "suddenly" replaced with more energetic pursuits, which may be justified relative to legitimate health concerns for stress on "aging" biological systems. On the other hand, rejuvenation of relatively inactive neurons, blood vessels, cardiopulmonary organs, muscle tissues, etc. may provide some inhibiting or corrective bioenergetic forces to combat physical and spiritual "decay" and "degeneration" which may help prolong the positive contributions we can make to our own lives and those of family members. Negotiation and discussion with significant friends or lovers can assist in delineating and understanding the underlying motives and logic of our changed behaviors, and family discussions can also become a forum for significant consideration of various "quality of life" decisions we all must make which certainly are expressed relative to the nature of actions we take, and the meanings which we and others attach to their initiation, duration, potency, and outcomes.

A negative implication within this category is that we have moved from high symbolic activity to a "lesser" status of diminishing symbolism and recreational energy as our bodies or minds have become (or decided to become) incapacitated and inert relative to former physical and mental status. The decline of even low symbolism can represent memory or cognitive "processing" ineptitude, and the concomitant activity regression can certainly occur secondary to exacerbated disease pathologies or ultimate cellular failure in numerous organ systems in our bodies. Hopefully we will have mentally prepared ourselves to understand, accept, and find meaning in what culture has negatively defined as "vegetative" states of being, and particularly concluded important emotional business with important persons or images/phenomena in our lives so that this process of movement or transition will occur with little mental conflict or struggle to hopelessly gain or regain the "illusions" or "realities" of what was "lost" or never "gained" in our lives. Family members will need also to be "at peace" with themselves as they assume predominant caretaker roles for us and can no longer define their own deprivation or satisfaction relative to our actions or the decisions we make in life.

(7) Grandchildren

As many of us age, the advent of grandparenthood can represent the beginning of a "lifetime" of both positive and negative experiences which are directly and indirectly centered on the interactions between ourselves and our children's children. Although "society" generally assumes that these relationships will be rewarding to all concerned and will "naturally" unfold in productive fashion, this is not always the case because there are almost always some psychosocial conflicts attached to growth and developmental changes, and also because parent-child-grandchild three generational relationships frequently are "sprinkled" or sometimes "drowned" with symbolic values and special identity-related meanings which are often not understood or discussed directly. In most cases, of course, this will be a "generally" rewarding experience for all concerned, but I would like to alert you, the reader, to the possibility that you may hold membership in a family unit where problems might occur, and also that all of us should be cognizant of the major potential obstacles so we can help insure that they are resolved in the best interests of members of all three generations as everyone continues along the individual and collective path of growth. Some of the major change-oriented issues will be discussed in the separate subsections which follow:

a.   Parental Trophies (Grandparent Admiration Role): In many cases, grandchildren are planned or secondarily become self-selected "tributes" to the virility and sexual desirability of the mother, the strength and love of the marital union which co-created children, and the adequacy of the male or female adult "child" who continues to need parental approval, which in this case is the approval of the grandparent--for their child--through the symbolism of the grandchild or grandchildren. The degree to which the "little ones" are imbued with this type of representational "tokenism" varies with each family, and may not exist at all in others, although we must be prepared to understand this possible outcome in our own family structures to take greater responsibility for avoiding the negative and destructive role reciprocations which affect our own lives.

In the case of the typical grandparent "admiration" role, we lose our value as multidimensional human beings who contribute to various aspects of the grandchild's growth, because we are not allowed or expected to interact honestly with them as they demonstrate positive or negative traits, and we are greatly constricted in using our emotional energy to help the child learn about themselves from a comprehensive perspective which includes the full range of their singular and interactive thoughts, feelings, and behaviors. Instead, we are usually encouraged by the parents to dote, praise, "applaud" or otherwise unconditionally venerate either the parent or the grandchild to the extent that the drama becomes "syrupy sweet" and "unreal," and we evolve into behavioral automatons or pawns in a "game" which excludes our realistic and qualitative potential--and also produces children who irresponsibly conduct themselves in self-centered, destructive, or irritating ways which disturbs the order and "sanity" of our environments if they are visiting, and virtually ignores our presence when we are temporarily or permanently within the domain where the child lives.

Our task, in these cases, is to use our wisdom and emotional energy to help our children be more confident in themselves as symbols of themselves, and to tactfully decline to use our talents and skills as robotic "yes" men and women which places the grandchild in a "no-win" situation of emotional delusions and realistic emptiness and irresponsibility. We may ultimately become bored or irritated with this recurrent scene, and find ourselves becoming reluctant to pursue visits with the family, or we might succumb and make ourselves actually believe we are performing a valuable inter-generational function in our lives. There are many other contributions we can make, however, in interacting with grandkids, and we also have important needs as people ourselves, which will never be met by our children or their children as long as we remain trapped in tightly constricted and fallow roles as child "worshipers."

b. Parental Persecutions (Grandparent Sympathizer Role): In some cases, unfortunately, our adult female children have managed to gestate children of their own before they have "centered" or focused their own internally satisfying and mature identity "journeys," or in the context of marital or primary love relationships where children become premature "accidents," sexuality and its creative outcome serve other "neurotic"-type symbolic functions, or the family unit is insufficiently prepared and organized financially, logistically or functionally to adequately handle the demands of child care.

In these cases, which range from mild to pathologi-cally extreme, grandparents enter the picture wherein parents feel overburdened, exhausted, exploited, confused, angry, and emotionally/physically "trapped" by circumstances they perceive as beyond their control. The role expectations for grandparents often include "responsibilities" to sympathize with our children's suffering, validate negative attributes of "problematic" grandkids, blame external factors for the unfairness of life, to criticize parenting techniques to create even more justifiable misery and pain, or become baby-sitting "rescuers" for various lengths of time to reduce stress and temporarily "free" our children from their self-imposed constraints. For us, the expression of interest and love for our children and their children must be either withheld or mitigated to avoid imposing "positives" on the scene, it must be narrowly channeled into deceitful and inauthentic patronizing support, or it must be intricately interwoven into symbolic "networks" of feelings and behaviors to the extent that there is very little possibility of ever evaluating its true and effective impact on the giver or any of the receivers. Failures to "play the game" can result in our children's alienation from "uncaring" or "hyper-critical" grandparents; considerable confusion, clinging, or withdrawal from our grandchildren, and general mental and physical exhaustion as we get carried along with the often strong currents of the "suffering" agenda. Our children are typically not as responsive to our "balanced" and comprehensive perspectives on relationship "complementarity" and symbolic interaction, so we might even be defined as interfering, yet we may also feel a conflicting need to get involved to handle our own discomfort with the "unhappy" and "burdened" children we have produced and reared. We, therefore, lose the opportunity to display and practice various personality attributes of our own, including our abilities and continual personal needs to "conceptualize" problems and solutions, use strategies to "elaborate" upon situations to understand them more fully, demonstrate the use of interpersonal "mediational" mental and verbal skills, and capitalize on this need to be involved in a wide variety of stimulating and demanding multivariate situations to avoid aging problems in "underarousal" cautiousness for fear of failing at risk-taking, isolation and alienation resulting in diminished self-esteem, and stimulation of our secondary memory processes and retrieval capabilities (which typically decline in maturing adults) to call on past problem definitions and resolutions-all of which can help us avoid various "production deficiencies" which inhibit various dimensions of our internal or external competence, particularly when we encounter a large number of tasks which might be characteristic of this or other grandparenting challenges.

The dilemma, therefore, is that we can benefit potentially from the stimulation and challenge of trying to help develop a quality grandparent-parent-child relationship which has complex symbolism and negative relationship patterns, yet the very nature of the relationship, in some ways, may prove to be stressful in our attempts to "integrate" meaningfully with our extended families and to use our love and caring in positive ways which are not encumbered by rigid role expectations, and illogical agendas which are confusing and destructive for the relationship participants--including the delicate interaction between parents-in-law and spouses of our adult children.

c. Family Distractions (Frenzied or Organizational Roles): In some family situations, there is little or no direct positive or negative symbolization attached to grandchildren who are born into single parent or dyadic relationships which are organizationally unstable or undeveloped, parents are untrained or otherwise incapable of learning appropriate child-care techniques presently or permanently, the parents are preoccupied with work responsibilities or other necessary/presumed agendas, or the children have special developmental needs or personality styles with which their parents are ill-prepared to cope. In these "disorganized" and sometimes chaotic families, grandparents, especially who reside with their children, often fall into roles as "child behavior specialists" or managers, and spend considerable time with "instrumental" tasks that often are not supported by the underlying family norms, or with pseudo-nurturing activities that ultimately produce more self-centered and unruly children who continue to behaviorally demand control and stabilizing rules/limits to help them feel secure and "honestly" valued.

Grandparents often have to compete with children for time and attention from the parents, which makes everyone feel unwanted, or they witness/exercise crisis-oriented disciplinary tactics which are often harsh, unreasonable and ineffective and generally create emotional discomfort and tension among all involved parties. Consultations from grandparents to their children are often met with "excuses" or "placating" compliance promises, but the quality of grandparental "wisdom" and experience are often lost in the confusion, and alienation/withdrawal frequently becomes the response-of-choice both to reflect frustration and to gain some degree of life-centeredness and peace of mind.

In some cases, grandparents may be "forced" to decline invitations for visits to or from their families, or to encourage boycotts on "children present" encounters which can cause guilt, shame, embarrassment, anger and lonely isolation by both adult factions. Other times, strict rules must be enforced in our homes, or requested in our children's homes, which constrains the potential enjoyment of active and disciplined children, and usually produces resentment of "interference" from "self-righteous" grandparents, which secondarily becomes an emotional wedge in relationships between caring adults who should be functioning as intergenerational "friends." We may also feel uncomfortable with "corrective," "supervisory" or critical attitudes and comments toward our grandchildren, from whom we could otherwise enjoy admiration and loving attachment, and to whom we could render logical guidance, motivating acceptance, and reinforcing reciprocal respect and appreciation.

The solution usually involves some degree of honest feedback to overburdened and confused parents, role modeling to teach them how to parent, support for their frequently deflated self-esteem, and insistence on order and regularity in the environment either to wait for "therapeutic" input to take effect, or simply to provide some controls on otherwise destructive perpetual patterns. Time alone with some grandchildren or their parents can be rewarding, although the typical interactions between them when grandparents are not around usually has a spillover influence in sustained frenzy/exhaustion for the respective participants, and grandparents frequently do not have sufficient time to wait for "traumatic" effects to wear off (withdrawal) in order to enjoy either children or grandchildren.

d. Grandparent Successes (Critical or Pseudo-Supportive Roles): Sometimes, depending particularly on our views of our own life "successes" and our identities relative to the personal and social "outcomes" demonstrated by our grown children, grandchildren may occupy a uniquely symbolic role in our lives as (1) the successes we or our children never were (2) the "corrective differentiations" from our children, as examples to produce guilt and handle our own disguised self-criticisms, (3) the physical confirmations of the lovableness and "adequacy" of our offspring, and therefore ourselves, (4) the sources of love and dependent allegiance among committed "blood" relatives to insure our extended power, "validity," emotional support, and continued activity calendar as aging produces these challenges to our adaptiveness or (5) the relatively perpetual receptacle of our affection, guidance, care or influence to insure our continued "necessity" in life, or to reconcile with ourselves, our children, God, etc. and "pay our debt" through good deeds for any hurts or sins which occurred previously, or for any "negatives" globally connected in our minds to our very essence and being.

The supportive and sometimes idolatrous devotions we "impose" on our grandchildren in these cases usually evolves into a false "maple syrup" reality which puts us in conflict with the healthy "emotional balance" perspectives of our children, or disastrously forms a conspiracy with adult children experiencing dependency conflicts, who also want to experience the "glow" of their parents' unqualified approval. The grandchildren involved may sense overwhelming pressure to "perform" and "please," and resist this control with various types of "failure" or inertia, or become "automatons" of perfection whereby they win the affectional "prizes" but lose big or small parts of their individuality and autonomy in the process. We, as grandparents, may also progressively increase the time spent with our proteges to the extent that our own life patterns and objectives become dormant or "piggybacked" on children's or grandchildren's life journeys, and we may also create description and conflict among the parents who witness this exclusive but artificial and excessive grandparent/grandchild alliance to the extent that they enter an alienated and disjointed relationship pattern with us, seek to exclude our participation in their activities, or less adaptively undercut our authority and emotional linkages with their children through opposing nonsupport or more overt criticism of us as our grandparenting roles.

We can facilitate the handling of this type of eventuality in our lives by insuring we have made "peace" with ourselves and our children prior to the arrival of grandchildren, which includes taking responsibility for our own future "successes" to the definitive exclusion of participating family "role-players." We should also identify the strengths of our children's personalities and allow our own "light to shine" vicariously by observing, enjoying and supporting their parenting behaviors, and additionally realize that the beauty and perfection of our lives will automatically unfold in the natural progression of the grandkids' exploration, enjoyment, and mastery of their world in their own way.

All of life, therefore, may be an interconnected system of "souls," "energies," "emotions" and mental "conveyances" to the extent that the success and accomplishment of anyone else is automatically "deposited in our bank account as well," or is entered into a common community chest which all can admire, and from which each of us can extract "loans" to help us regain faith and confidence in our successes as a simple function of being alive.

In cases where we do slip into patterns of excessive or misguided symbolic attachments to "proxy" grandchildren who really represent us, we can feel positive about our "intents" for them to succeed, and we can also comfort ourselves in the knowledge that we are at least wanting something positive for our "selves" which have been hurt or undernurtured, and we can transform excessive and irrational supports to more sensible, balanced, and still positive forms of admiration from which negative and regressive symbolization has been distilled.

e. Grandparent Failures (Rehabilitative Roles): In some other particular family situations, we, as grandparents, may have been disappointed in the mate selections of our children, we may view our kids as "insufficient reflections" of the qualitative parenting we gave them, we may be resentful of our own life adversities and mistakes, we may be bitter and angry in observing our physical, mental, and emotional "declines" with the aging and chronic illness processes, or we may simply experience grandchildren's personalities with which we are incompatible--any of which circumstances can be translated in our minds as negative indictments or disappointing forecasts for usually innocently victimized grandchildren. This eventuality can also be exacerbated due to the normal irritations of children who explore, test, and fail at many developmental tasks, particularly as maturing grandparents are likewise "associated" with children in experiencing the reemergence of various degrees of dependency (and our children are frustrated with us) and external control/evaluation, and sometimes desperately need examples of "competency" in ourselves or extended "offspring" to help boost self-esteem and psychosocial respect.

Children are often the easiest scapegoats to select to "displace" or "project" our negative feelings because they are least capable of fighting back, and can produce more immediate "positive" performance results through behavioral control and manipulation. These "rehabilitative" efforts, however, frequently emerge only as gripes or complaints about "those bad, lazy, spoiled, selfish, ungrateful or incompetent" kids; or do reach "fruition" as "strategies for personality change" which requires considerable frustrated energy on our parts to "engineer" value and behavioral "reconstruction," which fails because it usually lacks balanced positives/negatives and supportive love.   Grandparent couples can become philosophically divided as pro and antagonists to express their own conflicts, but one or both can easily be defined by the wounded and alienated children as a "grouch, mean policeman, crabby old man or woman, ogre, etc.," which results in more disrespect from the children and sometimes increases in negative behavior and "badness" which is a label the children have already acquired symbolically, irrespective of their actions. The emotional closeness we are seeking, therefore, with ourselves, our children, or the grandchildren is obviously encumbered by this destructive and dissonant deviant/rehabilitator role alignment where "good" is usually never "good enough" and where parents are sometimes forced to push us away to protect their children, and our sense of a priori or ex post facto rejection also alienates us physically and emotionally from important people in our lives.

To handle this problem in growing older in association with grandchildren who can become "indexed measuring instruments" for our success or failure, we must initially sever some of the "dependency ties" to them and remember that "genetic" lineage does not appropriately imply psychosocial obligation to "perform fictitiously as a personality proxy," nor does the term "family" imply that grandparents necessarily have the option to evaluatively assess and behaviorally manipulate "offspring once removed." Some research shows that older individuals are prone to think and problem solve using superordinate and abstract reasoning strategies rather than the less cumbersome and detailed logic demonstrated by younger people, so we must be careful not to use our minds and rich experience to infuse symbolic overlays where they are inappropriate or personally destructive, and sometimes have to relinquish "responsibility" for "successful" family outcomes by being more confident in ourselves, and also realizing that the "visions" we have of life are not necessarily correct projections into the future (for ourselves or grandchildren) but are most validly only retroflections about our past lives which will be experientially, psychologically, historically, and socially different from the future "time" to be lived developmentally by our children's children. In this context, we might even recognize in ourselves some of the negative traits we define in the grandchildren, and assume more responsibility for putting our own house in order before we observe and judge the performance or competency of relatively defenseless little people.

Also, in cases where grandchildren have developed attitudes or behaviors which most of society would define as negative, maladaptive, dangerous, or irresponsible, we are well advised to remember the potent influence we can have as wise and caring role models, particularly since we are usually free of many basic child-care tasks of everyday living, and can have more freedom to develop positive influential strategies to work with young people to help them learn, and to relearn for ourselves, the important human values of love, self-confidence, interpersonal responsibility, etc., which comes when we view ourselves as well as younger generations as lifetime learners who are continuing to grow and develop irrespective of age restrictions or inhibiting social stereotypes and mores.

f.   Grandparent Friendships (Interdependent Support and Growth Roles): The advent of grandchildren in our lives, most positively, can herald the arrival of stimulating friendships with young people, opportunities to extend our "relevance" through "generative" consignment of psychosocial wisdom to new life travelers, avenues of reciprocal nurturance and support, and motivation to continue active behavioral and mental lives to help meet the needs of others and to conform to family expectations for involvement and sharing of collective "energies" to stimulate and confirm the identity and value of the social system.

The change for maturing grandparental adults sometimes involves the reactivation of "mothballed" physical energies and emotional "concepts," and inflamed connective linkages to other people, so that we, and the children, can experience the ego-enhancing richness of feeling depth and symbolic personal/spiritual commitment to life and its variegated conditions of "value." We may initially resist this opportunity because we feel tired, despondent, irrelevant, isolated or manipulated; therefore, we are challenged to push ourselves beyond perceived "limits" in the creation or rediscovery of strengths we can use to enhance the developing personalities who admire us, and to also explore the options available to ourselves, singly, to improve the quality of our own hearts, souls, minds, or bodies for the ultimate qualitative advancement of whatever "life process" we feel existentially resides within our own awareness and sense of "being" or "becoming." We must resist the attractive temptation of superficial and mundane interaction with grandchildren, and almost force our sometimes inactive minds to pay attention, seriously concentrate, intently perceive, and powerfully connect with the dimly lit emerging invitations of children to "engage" them during the critical times they open up and slow their physical explorations in order to notice our presence. We may also learn or relearn the tenacity and assertiveness of reaching out to structure opportunities to interact with our grandchildren, which means contradicting the truth or falsities of "elderly rigidity" through the rearrangement of our schedules, priorities, and especially psychic menus for emotional payoffs from giving as well as receiving. In the receiving department, then, we sometimes must confront the "senior mentor and experienced sage" parts of our mature and adult demeanor to let ourselves become childlike again, so that we approach our little friends with some degree of naivete, simplicity of outlook, explorative open-mindedness, and mental excitement for new learning and growth, which also involves some disciplined practice in memory activation, storage, retrieval, and cognitive integration of new and old ideas, which for many of us may represent a significant but rewarding challenge.

g. Grandparent Irrelevancies (Parent Negotiation Role): Within some of our life scenarios, aging may be accompanied by inceptions, increases, or continuations of our disinterest or lack of emotional reward from relationships with children of any age, where, in some cases, we may not even have enjoyed the process or outcomes of parenting our own children. In the more remote history of psychological and social sciences, this phenomenon would have been theoretically considered a "pathological" avoidance or conflict relative to intimacy, or a sign of personality "disordered" social irresponsibility stemming from some form of childhood neglect or trauma. Today, however, most clinical therapists, sociologists, and adult developmental specialists accept autonomous and individualized adult existence outside the traditional family context as a potentially "normal" condition of psychosocial choice and lifestyle preference, except in cases, of course, where a "neurotic conflict" or personality maladjustment can be confirmed based on careful examination of past history, unconscious motivations, symbolic behavior, and other accepted "symptoms" of relationship alienation.

In the "healthy" side of this tableau, however, our decisions to forego the strains, complications, time commitments, emotional energies, communicational necessities, psychic "payoffs" or other negative characteristics which we attach definitionally to potential interactions with grandchildren usually require some important and very delicate negotiations with our own adult children, and sometimes the grandkids themselves, as they get older. As these developmental communications unfold, however, we may discover new and rewarding relationships with our own children which might translate more immediately or eventually to initiatives with any available grandchildren, or the grandchildren may grow past particular nonrewarding age brackets for us to point that we can recognize rewards or benefits from older children or younger adults. At any rate, the following are major points which need to be made in discussing our preferences, explaining our behaviors, and planning future contacts and relationship interactions with various family members:

1. We should confirm and clarify the existence and particularistic nature of our love or other emotional feelings for our children.

2. We should support the validity and relevance of our children's choices about their own nuclear family and child rearing, and express interest in the rewards they receive for themselves from this process.

3. We should affirm our responsibility to be polite, considerate, and respectful during "necessary" or "accidental" encounters with the grandchildren.

4. We should clarify, in detail, the feelings we have about our own growth, development, preferences and goals which necessarily preclude intimate or prolonged interactions with children, and reiterate that this decision in no way reflects an opinion or judgment about anyone else in life directly, except ourselves.

5. We should provide a detailed "perspectus" on the actions and outcomes we would prefer from our children relative to ideal interactive situations, and also outline the behaviors which they or the grand-kids can expect from us as we "take care of our own needs."

6. We should elicit and even probe for our children's feelings of resentment, anger, hurt, confusion, fear, etc. relative to the position we have taken, and provide whatever assistance we can to help them accept our need to be unique without interpreting it as an indictment of them.

7. We should seek their guidance as to how best to deal with our agenda and preferences relative to the children via direct, indirect or tacit interactions.

8. We should provide regular appreciative feedback concerning the "successes" of parental efforts to help us meet our own needs, as well as identifying areas where improvement might be attempted.

9. We should regularly discuss the emotional reactions of the grandchildren to ourselves directly or to our children as they interact for for or about us, so that any "negatives," hurts, fears, or other detrimental residuals can be corrected or attended to by the parents themselves, or, in some cases, by direct interactions with the children on our parts, which in some cases, to preserve their well-being, may require modifications and changes in our "game plan" to responsibly and unselfishly help children who, in many ways, are not yet able to take care of themselves through cognitive reasoning, ego-defense mechanisms, relationship substitutions, expressions of feelings, or other sublimations or eliminations of the conflicts related to their struggles to integrate personality needs, adult behaviors and social norms.

(8) Residence Changes

The phenomenon of retirement from formal work or full-time domestic roles, the valediction of primary co-residential roles with departing young-adult children, changes in financial status, re-prioritizations of life goals and major activities, and various contingent lifestyle modifications related to normal biological aging and illness--all can independently or collectively precipitate temporary or permanent changes in our place of residence or style of "residing" within new or continuing domiciles. Depending on our "spacial" orientation, perceptions of personal "loco-centric" well-being, security with diversity vs. uniformity, and previous positive or negative experience with singular or multiple residence configurations, we will experience varying degrees of enthusiasm or trepidation in pursuing optional or mandatory reorganizations or alterations of living environments. Some of the most typical residential change "scripts" which impact older individuals and couples will be discussed briefly, along with an outline of some of the accompanying conflicts which may imbue this transitional process with feelings of discomfort, fear, resentment, confusion or consternation.

a.   Movement with Adult Children: Occupying rooms, renovated basements or attics, or newly constructed additions to our children's homes, on a part or full-time basis, can create the following psychological and emotional discomforts that are symbolically articulated through the "associations" of shared physical proximity and pragmatic rearrangement of family social systems:

1.   Children's resentment of intrusion into their physical "life space" with accompanying "assumptions" that their "identities" will be ignored or controlled in the process;

2.   Children's fears of the "unknown" as modification of traffic patterns, furniture arrangement, personal schedules, communication patterns or customary "body locations" represent potential alterations in values, ideas which maintain self-esteem, or perceptions of the meaning of self and others which disrupts our "learned" need for stability and predictability in the environment;

3.   Children's apprehensions about financial "survival" as additional "personages" represent anticipated concomitant expenditures of funds, which activates repressed childhood as well as rationally pragmatic fears of biologic/psychic survival in a "competitive" world;

4.   Children's frustrations that their "self and system-fulfilling" agendas will be altered and the "rewards" will become unattainable due to their responsibilities to meet needs in "competing agendas" which they presume will progressively become more "dependency" oriented;

5. Children's fears of "inadequacy judgments" by others (or their own moral selves) as physical proximity with parents removes "excuses" for diminished love or reluctant caring, and poses "responsibility" dilemmas for the self-serving components of their personalities to wrestle with;

6. Children's anxieties and apprehensions concerning the emergence or reemergence of unconscious, repressed or hidden conflicts with parents stemming from childhood, where still smouldering feelings of anger, resentment, attachment, disappointment, etc. will be activated by recreations of past interactive patterns, and ultimately result in uncontrolled expression and consequent entrapment or alienation relative to present and future relationships with aging mom or dad;

7. Children's sadness and feelings of helplessness in witnessing possible physical and mental declines of valued role models and aspirational heroes/heroines, which represents painful loss of need-meeting resources and symbolic "domains" of the self which the children consider to be empty spaces within their own personality "apparatus" for survival;

8. Children's fears of social "disapproval" and "embarrassing" peer condescensions relative to the unique personality characteristics, attitudinal idiosyncracies, of "deviant" lifestyle patterns of parents who are different from the normative social groups to which the children belong or aspire to belong;

9. Children's anticipated reluctance to experience the strains of confrontation, negotiation, conflictual resistance, etc. as their parents may require home nursing care, convalescent management, "executive" estate advice or control, and decision-making guidance; and resist their children's efforts to "patronize" them or assume increasing authoritative jurisdiction in areas of life where the effects of

"senescence" render us unable to properly manage our internal and external affairs;

10. Parents' fears of loss of autonomous self-government and the symbolic declines in quality or quantity of states of "esteem" or "adequacy" which they have connected to the instrumental and physical assistance to be rendered or offered in various degrees by their children;

11. Parents' guilt about accepting help or "charity" which represents in their minds the loss of powerful social roles of leadership and control, which partly established concepts of parental "superiority" when their children were small, and also induces anger at themselves as they view adult children "taking over" in their places;

12. Parents' frustrations at potentially losing or experiencing alterations in habitual "rituals" of thought, mood, or behavior which are stabilizing and identity-confirming "mirrors" of the self, as they envision "expectations" from others or competition life stylistic agendas from the home "owners";

13. Parents' fears of failure and social embarrassment in overcoming actual or perceived memory, energy or thought inertias to learn new ideas, skills or relationship dynamics for differentiated and more complex social living in a new environment;

14. Parents' concerns that their children will be disappointed at their inabilities to contribute to the quality of a different generation's cultural life, and concerns that the variable life values and experiences learned at different times, from different stimuli and using different conceptual and logical mental styles and strategies will highlight wider degrees of "separateness" and symbolically represent the loss of emotional closeness and connection as a recreation of the earlier "disconnections" of all

previous generation's "escape from the respective family nest";

15. Parents' worries that their potentially decreasing physical and intellectual competencies will be too painful for their children to "integrate" emotionally and that this negative impact will cause various forms of deterioration or lack of growth in the host family;

16. Parents' fears of disappointment in learning more intimate details about the personalities of their children through more intimate connectedness of cohabitation, which makes parents vulnerable to selfish or unkind characteristics which were previously ignored or obscured; and which also produces guilt at presumed inadequate parenting whose interpreted examples may not have been elucidated with less "amalgamated" living arrangements;

17. Parents' cautiousness that they will be inhibited or constrained in various processes of innovation, exploration, or deviation from social expectations or children's family norms, which may stifle their own growth and pursuit of individual self-fulfillment according to personal needs and tastes.

b.   Change of Independent Primary Residence: In some family situations, either necessity or personal preference results in relinquishment of a primary, single family residence, we may have owned or rented for an extended time period usually predating retirement, and often being the "home" from which teenage or young adult children departed the family to begin careers, marry, attend college, "join the service/circus/rock band" of their choice, etc.   Quite often this decision is necessitated by constructing post-retirement finances wherein a less expensive dwelling is purchased or rented, or a smaller home with less burdensome upkeep is desired as our aging process results in physical inability to sustain many forms of manual labor, or simply loss of interest in continuing the preoccupation with home beautification, maintenance, or improvement. Other retiring couples or individuals find the need to relocate for better weather, recreational pursuits, closer proximity to family or friends, or to symbolically make a major change to signal the beginning of a totally new phase of their life journey (which sometimes occurs during or after mourning the death of a spouse).

In each of the above special circumstances, a transition process occurs which necessarily requires psychological and social adjustment, and usually involves some degree of internal struggle with issues of identity stability, loss, symbolism of life goals and destinies, fears of the future unknown, depression over personal "decline," social disorganization, and isolation or existential aloneness in departing from familiar stabilizing surroundings. We can, however, help ourselves and one another within spouse or friendship alliances, by examining the following "check points" and trying to resolve the major question which represents a "psychodynamic" conflict in each area, followed by continued evaluation of the quality of our adaptation and adjustment--accompanied by definitive action on our parts if we discover that we are not generally satisfied with ourselves and our surroundings once the residential change has been negotiated and given time to "align itself" with our personal needs, goals and personality styles:

Check Point A: Am I changing residence because this is the single, most positive alternative and because there are no other better options available to me?

This question is important because we sometimes become frightened, angry, confused, or illogical and make premature decisions for irrational emotional reasons rather than more mature psychological or pragmatic self-fulfilling life objectives. Increasing dependence as we age also predisposes us to allow others to control residence decisions, which sometimes means the outcome meets their needs rather than ours. We may also become mentally confused when internal or external stimuli "flood" our decision-making computers, and the "short-circuiting" which occurs can lead to incorrect or poorly explored selections of "easy" or seemingly "safe" options which appear much different to us when we are re-balanced and making non-crisis decisions.

Check Point B: Am I changing residence to "run away" from something I fear, rather than "walk toward" a future goal I desire?

In some cases, our age-related memory losses and increasing physical incapacities are perceived as actual "slowing" of perceptual acuity confusions in "processing" new information, loss of social status, etc., and causes considerable fear of "destruction" of our "executive control" functions and ultimate "annihilation" of our personal identities--which we can mistakenly and defensively "handle" by "externalizing" the fear and conflict within a physical symbol which can more easily be avoided or relinquished to make us believe we have escaped from the inner terrifying problem. This "irrational" adaptation to declining abilities means we have confused "emotional" and "instrumental" or physical concepts, and therefore, may seek a different residence as a way of pretending we are "revitalized" or "renewed," which may have temporary but probably not lasting energizing and stabilizing effects.

Check Point C: Have I redefined myself as a person who has not "lost" part of her or himself relative to the "external" circumstances which necessitate a move, but has the opportunity to gain something of equal or greater importance?

The financial, health, climatic, or other stimuli to change residence usually "appear" as phenomena lost or relinquished, which means that our minds and spirits can conceptualize the new environment as "forced entrapment," punishment, a "declination learning process," or some other negative "life script" which reduces motivation to grow, destroys many future emotional gains from a new (but not "negative" experience), and set up a before/after comparison where our memories often define the original residence as the more positive experience and "state" of psychological and social being. This illusion of personality loss is derived from childhood misperceptions of the "permanency" of our minds, souls and bodies, and the lack of control we, as children, had over our self-perceptions and individual emotional destinies. We must, therefore, as adults "take charge" of our feelings and make them come out as positive opportunities, irrespective of the social definitions or real physical limitations of our changing circumstances.

Check Point D: Do I have a clear idea about the personal, social or spiritual goals I desire to accomplish relative to my residential change?

If we have decided to relocate due to personal preference, it is always helpful to develop measurable objectives, if possible, to not only insure that we cannot meet these standards without change of living location, but to also serve as a guiding beacon to help us use time and energy efficiently and productively in new residential circumstances. This process is more difficult when we are relocating because of the needs of a spouse, dependent child, or friend with whom we reside, but a necessity for us to insure we avoid anger, resentment, guilt or other conflictual interpersonal feelings which can easily arise when we fail to take full responsibility for our future growth, satisfaction and adequate adjustment in new locations.

Check Point E: Do I have a lifelong and "integrative" perspective about the various residential and other transitions in my life?

It is usually unproductive in the long run to view major changes in life as separate and disconnected units of time, reality, space or psychosocial identity which are not functionally interdependent aspects of our "holistic" growth and learning as we continue to attempt movement toward special and unique forms of enlightenment, awareness, maturity, esteem, wisdom, personal status, goodness, etc. It is important, according to most developmental and psychodynamic theories, for us to understand the past and register its intrinsic "rewards" in our memory bank as areas of learning or improved understanding so that we build a positive motivational bridge to be optimistic about the future, and also so that future decisions will be wisely and correctly guided by simple as well as abstract knowledge of the past, present and future as interactive relative to our total personalities. Our memories are reconstructive and elaborative decision-making processes which can take action, rather than remaining passive, and we need as much practice as possible stimulating our mental assessment and creativity processes by "connecting" experiences with other experiences, and connecting experiences with valued ideas and concepts to help remain biologically and mentally energized, and to insure that in as many ways as possible we progress rather than regress in personally perceived or socially defined destructive ways. Some research suggests that older, more experienced minds demonstrate capability in areas of abstract and "elaborative" reasoning, yet become "cautious" when confronted with complex changes, although the brain increases its capacities in several important physiological ways when we do expose ourselves to complex stimulation, goal setting, and futuristic decision-making. Our memory deficits, additionally, may be partly caused by occurrences in life which are not "memorable," so our organization of new reality in the form of residence changes must become proactive and positive where we also learn something about how we make choices, in addition to making adaptive ones for ourselves.

Check Point F: Are we prepared to become "deviant" in life?

With some residence changes in our lives, we have decided to attempt major "breaks" with substantial attitudes, values, behavioral styles or philosophies of living which are partly "symbolically" represented by our external "shelters," but actually constitute a deeper arterial change, emergence or reorganization of our conceptions of "selfhood" to align the "real" with our expectations of the ideal person we wish to be. This change in various degrees of identity can be frightening all by itself as we explore a portion of inner (as well as outer) reality without prior immersion experience into this "unknown," but life-perspective alteration that can also precipitate negative responses from relevant or irrelevant people in our social worlds which, at best, might constitute only an irritation, but at worst, rejection, isolation or recrimination from family or friends.

In the latter case particularly, we may be required to muster considerable courage, physical stamina, mental toughness and philosophical/spiritual resolve to insist vigorously on our rights to "deviate" from stereotypical or expected "patterns" of living through which others vicariously maintain parts of their own stability and self-perspective through predictability of our "known" worlds. Yet, we may simultaneously want to display equal insistence on our privilege to continue nourishing psychoemotional relationships with loved ones, despite the fact that we may diverge from either mainstream or family normative standards and lifestyle patterns, which others in our lives may not understand or feel comfortable with. Considerable communication to clarify similarities and differences may be necessary along with hard work to fortify emotional linkages which are focused on common human needs and characteristics, rather than on specific or idiosyncratic new behavioral styles which do not necessarily have to threaten the options or preferences of our families to think, feel and behave in personal meaningful ways.

c. Periodic Hospital Residence: The presence of acute illnesses in the less immunologically-resistant aging body, the degenerative recurrence of pathological symptoms of chronic malignancies, and the generalized decline of biologic cellular and organ systems which produce fluctuating needs for supervised rest and physio/psycho-energetic replenishment; all necessitate, for many aging men and women, occasional and often progressively increasing rehabilitative or "maintenance" visits to inpatient medical or psychiatric facilities as adjunctive dimensions of otherwise independent living in primary residences, or semi-dependent domiciliation with family.

The physical and emotional instability and shuffling which typically accompany these movements between conditions of relative well-being at home, and temporary "islands" of physical case and pain reduction, plus associated psychic security, peace of mind, and anxiety reduction are indeed complex and difficult circumstances to endure. The stability and spiritual security of our self-concepts can appear to be nonexistent, random, or negative aspects of life on the "storm-tossed seas" of home-to-hospital-to-home pilgrimages. In these cases, transiency contradicts our traditional lifetime learning about the value of "sameness" of regularity; and the frequent substitutions of various hospital staff leave us even more alone in experiencing variability and sometimes drastic inconsistency in the knowledge that others have about our physical/emotional selves, and in the different approaches which are used to interact with us during "crisis" periods when emotional warmth and comprehensive concern are critical necessities.

Alternating, but slowly degenerating, health conditions can also become "nightmarishly" frightening because of unpredictable and unpleasant discomforts, as well as the disruption of identity-stabilizing routines at home whose outcomes are often interrupted to prevent personal fulfillment or accomplishment, as is the case, concomitantly, with bodies that can appear perpetually unreliable. The absence of "translocational" concepts in many of our minds is somewhat resolved as friends or relatives serve as "crossing guards" to support us before, during, and after the temporary residence changes. Although the mental "imagery" which moves rapidly from physical awareness--to hospital procedure--to emotional perceptions--to hopeful home rehabilitation--and back again to similar or new physical or mental ailments, can produce considerable confusion and even terror in our efforts to find some consistency in either health homeostasis, emotional balance, or external residence or procedural regularity which may easily elude us as we circumnavigate this health care circuit.

As expected, this scenario is very difficult to combat, but we can assist ourselves a great deal by trying as much as possible to divorce our minds from our physical bodies, and to train ourselves to use stabilizing, pacifying, unifying, and balancing concepts about the total "metaphysical self," which we must not allow to fluctuate or vary to the same degree and tempo as exists in the recurrent "ebb and flow" of our aging, acutely ill, or chronically degenerating physical bodies. We can also plan the initiation and completion of various activities, hobbies or projects which are mobile enough (e.g., reading, small craft projects, etc.) to move between hospital and home locations, or become involved in joint mental or emotional "learning" activities with others which can be continued through their presence at our changing locations.

The supportive networks of family and friends can also provide continuity as their love remains stable, but we often need to condition them to refrain from circumstantial talk about "physical things," or false reassurances about "how it will be when we get home," and instead, discuss the emotional and spiritual aspects of living and growing which can become, for all of us, much more stable and lasting conceptual frameworks than we have learned to seek relative to physical or material well-being and predictability.

d.   Permanent Nursing Home Living: Probably the most stereotypical and negatively perceived living arrangement for aging men and women is the nursing home, shelter care facility, modified hospital environment, or private residence which functionally assumes the supervisory, full-time health care, behaviorally restrictive and general "declining health-status" characteristics of regular nursing home organizations. In considering the likelihood that many of us may experience sufficient degeneration of overall biologic or neurologic capability, suffer from excessively incapacitating chronic illnesses, or lose the psycho-biologic energy, spirit, drive or willpower to ade-, quately and responsibly pursue basic living standards and self-care activities--we may, in fact, have to endure the changes and dilemmas of this form of living on a voluntary, family-coerced, or even court ordered basis. In considering various strategies to handle the differentness, comprehensiveness, intrusiveness, impersonality, institutionality, and "finality" of some or all nursing homes, I will first outline the major factors which many residents and human service professionals describe as potential obstacles, followed by another outline of the particular types of personal and social conflicts which may emerge as this transition is selected or mandated as part of our life histories.

Typical Problem Areas or Obstacles of Nursing Home Living

-- Varying degrees of loss of personal privacy

-- Intrusions into personal "space" for health-care regimens

-- Transiency and impersonality of some staff

-- Regimentation due to requirements of "community" living

-- Exposure to some residents with incompatible personalities

-- Physical discomfort of "non-home" institutional environment

-- Recurrent pain and "body violation" of certain necessary medical procedures

-- Lack of emotional stimulation away from family/friends

-- Insufficient mental stimulation with poor "extracurricular" programs in some organizations

-- Loss of personal power due to "administrative" responsibility for personal affairs

-- Energy declines and physical lethargy with limited exercise

-- Restrictions on personal exploration and autonomy with some "on-campus" controls

-- Creativity losses relative to "generic" residential architecture/decorating and building restrictions on personal "living space" manipulation

-- Perceptual "sterilization" with recurrent themes of "illness, decline, death"

-- Social discomfort with inexperienced and uncomfortable temporary visitors

-- Behavioral discrimination due to stereotypes and controls on deviations, idiosyncrasy and originality

Personal Conflicts or Emotional Dilemmas of "Adjustment"

-- Anger and resentment at various intrusions

-- Self-degeneration relative to impersonality and inconsideration

-- General frustration in inhibited life and routine planning

-- Depression, anger, dissolution related to physical decline and illness

-- Fear and apprehension secondary to exclusive bureaucratic control

-- Psychic lethargy experiencing "common" and uncreative environment

-- Spiritual starvation with limited programs

-- Guilt and resignation for having limited or no options

-- Resentment and irritation of nonselective interactions

-- Longing and frustrated hope of returning home

-- Personal self-effacement and abhorrence of medical procedures

-- Emotional emptiness, boredom with limited stimulation

-- Rage and hatred at loss of personal control or power

-- Impatience due to collective routines or limiting restrictions

-- Anxiety relative to experiences and stereotypes of impending "death"

-- Disappointment at "rejection" by family members

-- Confusion relative to change in personnel and procedures

-- Isolation and loneliness with loss of friends

-- Annoyance at discomfort or superficiality of visiting guests

Although many of the above conditions, and the emotional reactions to them, will probably never be fully eradicated either by improved and person-sensitive institutions, or through our own development of autonomous control of our "dependent and entrapped" minds, there are some actions we or family members can take to help alleviate or possibly even alter the negative outcomes which are frequently experienced by us or those we love as we undergo the transition and sometimes painful adaptation to nursing home or other similar types of dependent and controlling environments.

Adaptive Strategies

~ Derive "self-concept" from external "threat"
  -- realize it is difficult to feel whole and complete within "total" and somewhat "foreign" institutions, and get excited about the challenge of holding on to "who" you are with numerous obstacles to re-define your identity.

~ Formulate "internal" rituals and patterned routines
  -- compensate for external behavioral controls on your life by using thoughts and feelings (especially new ones in your effective iconic [immediate] and primary memory banks, and old ones in your relatively stable tertiary memory capacity) to organize your life, combined with written strategies to remember your agendas for growth and self-actualization.

~ Advocate for "participatory management"
  -- remember that your or your family's money is paying for staff and facilities, and actualize your right to negotiate with staff around reasonable, respectful schedules for intrusions, and opportunities supported by management for privacy.

~ Use humor to "accept" what you cannot change
-- try to laugh at irritating bureaucratic insensi-
tivities, changes, or other characteristics rather
than wasting "negative energy" where it will be
ineffective.

~ Try harder to "reach out" to residents
-- accept more responsibility for establishing and
main taining relationships where you gain something from everyone (especially difficult people)
and define your own adequacy relative to your
ability to "care for" some hard-to-reach co-tenants.

~ Unite your spirit and body
-- try to avoid resisting bodily intrusions of medical
and health care procedures by trying to "gain"
something emotional or spiritual from the pain or
discomfort, and try to learn something new from
each "intrusion" you try to "become one" with.

~ Rearrange self-concept priorities ("ipsative" changes)
-- note that some studies show that aging individuals
place high importance on some factors for maintaining self-esteem which are very much related to
conditions causing or associated with (usually
restricted by) nursing home residential status (e.g.,
income and social status, health, social interaction,
marital status, housing, and transportation), which
must be replaced by other factors over which we
have more control (i.e., spirituality, intellectual
growth, acceptance of limitations, etc.).

~ Connect with the external world
-- use the media of T.V., radio, reading, extension
courses, social agency programs, volunteer visits,
letter writing, etc. to maintain a relationship with
the "pulsating" world around you and to mentally
and emotionally "transcend" the boundaries of your
institutionalized residence through your personal
expansion.

~ Insist on stimulation every day
  -- since our biology seems to maintain some of its
     viability through stimulation and exercise of the
     mind and body, you must communicate your need
     for exciting residential programs developed by staff
     or presented by sponsors from the community
     (which you personally can arrange), and exercise
     your mind and body as vigorously as possible on
     a daily basis.

~ Consider some changes of personality
  -- although some traits like social introversion and
     extroversion, openness to new experiences, etc.
     remain relatively stable throughout life, we can use
     the exposure to closely residing "others" to learn
     new ways of perceiving our "selves," and also new
     types of behavior or "orienting" actions and compe-
     tencies which may provide stimulation as well as
     new avenues for personal growth.

~ Build competencies
  -- many research studies show decreases in
     self-esteem related to declining "competence" in
     later years, which means we may benefit from
     finding ways to "build, create, originate, master, fix,
     refurbish, nurture, design, invent," etc. either
     through structured programs of the nursing home
     (crafts, painting) or individual efforts within our
     own frameworks of "productivity" (plants, writing,
     learning a new language, etc.).

~ Accept authority and "envision power"
  -- as we age, some studies suggest we decrease our
     abilities to accept the dictates of authority and
     regulations, but their preeminence in most nursing
     homes suggests that we "reverse" this process to
     define ourselves as strong and capable through (a)
     self-disciplines of "acceptance," (b) understanding
     the indigenous "weakness" of those who use power
     to control others, and (c) retaining powerful

control of our inner selves despite externally conforming behavior.

~ Request "relevant" friendships from family
-- we should not accept the nature and outcome of perfunctory and infrequent visits from family, but should seek more regular and varied types of contact (phone, letters, audiotapes, etc.) plus work together to plan projects, discuss topics, share books, or otherwise develop interactive friendships that insist we are viable resources in other people's lives as well as vice versa.

~ Get off campus as much as possible
-- although there are certainly some physical, mental or even lifestyle preference restrictions on activities, we can assume much greater responsibility to set up opportunities for ourselves individually or groups of residents to attend community activities, participate in social programs, be exposed to visiting friends or volunteers who will sponsor off-campus meals or outings, or otherwise expand horizons--even with the use of lectures or movies on travel, adventure, etc. delivered by experts or university faculty in or out of the nursing home facility.

~ Find meaning in "death"
-- since the frequent exposure to personal declines, degeneration, and death cannot be avoided in most nursing homes, we can help ourselves greatly by learning to see its beauty, connectedness with life processes, and stimulus for our own learning as we approach rather than avoid fellow residents who are dying, and also invite lectures or consultations by spiritual or humanistic experts who can help broaden or deepen our perspectives--including the development of residential "ceremonies" or commemorative activities relative to the pre and post phenomena of anyone dying within the community.

(9)　Relations with Adult Children

　　Although it is certainly necessary to carefully examine the quality of our relationships with our kids long before we reach the 50 or 60 plus age range, it is never to late to turn our attention to this important aspect of our lives, especially since our aging, and theirs, can create new maturational changes and situational stresses in both sets of lives. The needs, aspirations, philosophies, activity interests, social values, communicational styles, intellectual formats, and other specific dimensions of selfhood can certainly change as we compare our present attributes to our ideal characteristics (and factor in our perceived "failures" in life); but self-concept is also part of relationships with significant sources of emotional reward and feedback in our lives, so we also define the self relative to our behaviors toward adult children, their responses to us, and our assessment of the overall outcome of these physical, mental, and "feeling" interactions. Additionally, we know from some research studies that we can also be as strongly influenced by the stimulation of our past and present cohort cultures, as by maturational changes, so the "times" we and our children use as "reference points for personality" may also change either party or the total relationship as it also moves through various phases of world history, and as life changes become part of this person-situation interaction. The degree to which either party, however, is willing or able to change attitudes or future behaviors is a function of the longitudinal quality of the relationship since its inception, the needs of individuals which can be met through the unique character- istics of the other party, and the degree of deprivation each participant feels relative to their closeness with others and personal adequacy in the context of social relationships. Sometimes changes or non-changes can be negotiated infor- mally between children and parents, but in other cases, formal, professional therapeutic assistance may be required, and prove to be very rewarding.

　　In any case, the first step for us, as parents, is to carefully examine our feelings about our children, to hypo- thetically or directly try to discern the nature and intensity of their feelings about us, and to examine the types of behaviors which, on the average, characterize the "functions" of "what goes on when we're together or apart" so we can initially define and categorize the type of relationship which exists. Some common types of parent-adult child associational linkages are briefly listed as follows:

Type 1: <u>Nonexistent</u>:

- behavioral interactions - almost none, superficial

- feelings - neither positive nor negative

- goals - individual, no common agendas

- needs - met alone or by others

- mental connections - mismatched, incongruent

- spiritual sharing - no common dreams of "something else" in life

- instrumental functions - independent, do not need each other

- growth stimulation - no one cares, no confrontation

- bioenergy - flat, no sparks

Type 2: <u>Passive-Dependent</u>:

- behavioral interactions - controlled by one party

- feelings - excessive, starving for nurturance

- goals - stay together, avoid stress, non-individualistic

- needs - met exclusively by each other

- mental connections - close but superficial, forced

- spiritual sharing - very little, relationship oriented

- instrumental functions - highly connected

- growth stimulation - conformity is stressed, loyal connectedness

- bioenergy - associated by trapped, regressive organization

Type 3: <u>Collective Suffering</u>:

- behavioral interactions - offensive, hurtful to one or both

- feelings - disappointed, sad, resentful and angry

- goals - detect flaws, counterattack

- needs - to be victimized, to hurt the other mental connections - suspicious, hypersensitive

- spiritual sharing - strong but negative, "pain-positive"

- instrumental functions - inhibitory, numerous but ineffective "failures"

- growth stimulation - none, negative criticisms

- bioenergy - powerful but destructive

Type 4: <u>Vicarious Success</u>:

- behavioral interactions - "syrupy" and artificially enhancing

- feelings - positive but success oriented

- goals - achievement oriented, pressured

- needs - generally unmet emotionally, symbolized externally

- mental connections - strong but dependent, outcome related

- spiritual sharing - converted to future materialistic gains

- instrumental functions - limited, pragmatic

- growth stimulation - forced, symbolically fearful

- bioenergy - strong but other directed, "content-indexed"

Type 5: Conflictual:

- behavioral interactions - corrosive, combative

- feelings - angry, frustrated, confused

- goals - differentiated, opposite

- needs - excessive but irresolvable

- mental connections - strained, exacerbated intellectualism or exclusively "emotional"

- spiritual sharing - none, used as differentiating weaponry

- instrumental functions - incompatible, used to "display" negatives

- growth stimulation - pretend, accented, nonexistent

- bioenergy - powerful, exhausting, unresolved, imbalanced

Type 6: Mysterious:

- behavioral interactions - tentative, incongruent

- feelings - uncertain

- goals - unclarified, hypothetical

- needs - strong but concealed

- mental connections - exploratory, probing, never connecting

- spiritual sharing - strong but undefined

- instrumental functions - limited, usually with multiple symbolisms

- growth stimulation - moderate, confusing, manipulative

- bioenergy - strong but frequently "by-passing" each other

Type 7: Integrated:

- behavioral interactions - interdependent, matched, satisfying

- feelings - warm, connected

- goals - mutual but allowing independence

- needs - open, clear, outcome-evaluated

- mental connections - strong, continually clarified, congruent in key areas

- spiritual sharing - significant, visionary, practiced with behaviors

- instrumental functions - helpful, not excessive, negotiated

- growth stimulation - positive "cheerleading" plus confrontation

- bioenergy - synchronized, mutually stimulating, increasing over time

Although I have only mentioned a few of the major categories of relationships from at least one perspective, there are some other major typologies that may more closely represent your particular relationship characteristics, and there are certainly numerous additional "descriptors" or sub-categories of the ones already listed to more completely describe their symbolic, functional and operational characteristics. The main point here, however, is that we all learn to make some definitive, "diagnostic," decision about the kind, quality, and degree of satisfaction of our relationships with our adult children, so that we can then proceed to the next step of deciding in what ways the process of our aging may have positively or negatively affected the interactions we do or do not enjoy.

In considering our own aging, there are some significant dynamics of this process which may contribute to the existing nature of the association in ways which do not enhance its ability to grow or become more positive, and also in ways which may cause more healthy "integrated" relationships to deteriorate in their ability to meet continuing or changing needs of all parties as life processes march ahead. The following list, therefore, comprises some of the most problematic contributions of our own aging process to the destruction of more positive components of "good relation-ships," as well as the prevention of greater degrees of "rehabilitation" of our "not so good" connections with adult children. After each "problem" statement, there is also a suggestion "corrective action" to help avert some or all of the negative consequences which might besmirch the continuity, depth, and psycho-emotional functionalism of these important associations.

1.   Problem: We become physically/mentally tired and withdrawn from typical levels of activity.

Correction: Make a concerted effort to step up our efforts at physical and mental "calisthenics" to improve our stamina, and also discuss activity "substitutions" with our kids which they can also enjoy.

2. Problem: Our moods change and we become less responsive to the specific "innuendos," and subtle shades of their emotional states.

   Correction: We must remember the extreme value of our need-meeting function with our children, keep our own moods as optimistic as possible through awareness of our continuing "mission," and try harder to "tune in" to the complexities of everyone else's emotionality.

3. Problem: We begin to resent our children for not "making" our lives any better, and "ignoring" the emotional struggles we increasingly encounter.

   Correction: We not only need to increasingly expand our network of resources to take responsibility for the quality of our individual lives, but should also ask our children directly for some of the emotional help we want--they have a responsibility too!

4. Problem: Our behavioral, thinking, language, etc. styles sometimes change as we age, or do not change to correspond to the changes in our children, and we tend to "miss each other's meanings" and points of view, and sometimes our new or old "styles" become an embarrassment to more "socially conscious" children.

   Correction: We have everything to gain and nothing to lose by continuing to educate ourselves intellectually and culturally, by using the past for our personal benefits but remembering our kids are "rushing ahead" to the future, and keeping pace by conforming to some of their "comfort standards" without feeling an "ego-threatening need" to rigidly assert our "differentness."

5. Problem: Changes in residence sometimes create "distance" in the frequency and even quality of communication, which can ultimately lead to assumptions of emotional alienation and "separateness."

    Correction: We must discuss and "strategize" creative communicational options to maintain linkages, plus work harder in face to face interactions to "get to the emotional meat" right away.

6. Problem: Our dependency on financial or physical assistance from adult children can result in depression, self-esteem problems, anger, or manipulative helplessness/passive-aggressive control, and reciprocal resentment from children.

    Correction: We must openly discuss both sets of feelings and "generalize" the negative aspects by remembering they are "typical" and common human reactions to stressful and constraining situations, which includes assisting each other to remain as physically and "psychically" independent as possible, and also reminding each other that "help is a two-way street where everyone has a chance to be strong."

7. Problem: We continue to "parent" long after our children require this type of "demeaning control."

    Correction: We must remember that functions of the past are not necessarily needed or useful in the present, and flexibly convert some previous social roles to new avenues of association (friend, consultant, stimulator, co-creator, etc.) and openly discuss role changes and functionality with our children--who are also exploring new roles for themselves.

8.   Problem: One additional obstacle which often emerges relates to "territorialism" concerning which residence (ours or children's) is "home base" for joint activities. Typically, parents indirectly believe their kids should "come home" for family gatherings, and this violates their right to autonomy and "residential" priority as well.

Correction: These issues should be discussed with a sensitive ear to pragmatism (who can drive in the snow more easily) but with equal consideration of unique "needs" for "spacial stability" and reference points, especially as emotional symbolism is often attached to the issue of "who travels to whom, and who is in charge when they get there." A 50%-50% balance is usually the best alternative, even when the "older" parties have to work a little harder to hold up their end of the bargain--sometimes this is perceived as a challenge and honor.

c.   Community Opportunities

As each of us experiences various dimensions of growing older, we inevitably compare past and present interaction with our broader external surroundings, and come to some evaluative conclusion about (1) the changes in our perspectives about the city or community where we live, (2) the community's views of us as "changing" participants or consumers of its goods and services, and (3) the quality of our personal satisfaction as a result of the interactive energy exchange between "us" and "it." It is very easy, I must caution, for the isolated older person to make erroneous and untested assumptions about the world "out there," just as the community can "stereotype" aging citizens and close some of its doors through discrimination and prejudicial "targeted programming" which attends to the needs of younger clientele. The challenge for the thoughtful and growth-oriented person, however, is to make every effort possible to begin this assessment process with a healthy self-esteem and self-confidence "baseline" of emotional well-being, so that we "see" all the positives outside ourselves that are truly positive, so we convert as many "marginal negatives" as possible to positives by not allowing irritations or inconveniences to get in our way of happiness, and finally to clearly recognize the "devastating negatives" which represent insensitivity, ignorance, prejudice, and rejection in order to use our energies to change them, plus move past their "temporary" restraints to enjoy other opportunities for self-fulfillment either alone or involving other aspects of the community.

The first step for everyone relative to this person-situation confluence is to understand our basic nature along a continuum from private to socially gregarious/active, with particular reference to the fact that the aging process may prevent an opportunity to change our historical style, which some of us may "hang on to" tenaciously for fear of changing to meet new exigencies or explaining new forms of self-awareness as our bodies get older but not necessarily our spirits and minds. An understanding of any rigid or outdated patterns of self-awareness, plus appreciation of the insidious ways our fears direct and narrow our views of the world will guide us to define the community and its opportunities relative to "potentials" for self-fulfillment, and help identify particular "needs" we have with corresponding "avenues" for satisfaction so our time and efforts in interacting with the community will be more efficient and ultimately more effective.

If we discover any discomfort or "delusional" neurotic thinking which places limitations on what we personally can do, think, feel, learn, understand, or experience, then there is a strong likelihood we will either isolate and feel sorry for ourselves, or "externalize" this conflict and define the community as lacking in its attitudes or activities. This is unfair to ourselves as well as the cities or towns where we reside. We must insure, first of all, that we are "programmed positively" for community activity in general, before we start to identify the specific aspects of the world outside with which we can "match up" needs and services.

The second step, therefore, is to develop an acute awareness of our intrapsychic agendas to be fulfilled, so that an appreciation of our unique needs to develop, combine and enrich various ideas (concepts) which are then assigned outcome values of "being," can become the guiding principle for selecting particular activities outside ourselves to create the inner images we need to ultimately conclude we are valuable, loved, strong, worthwhile, enhanced or positive in some way. "Who I am" (or "Who I want to be") is a preliminary question which guides "What I do" as one step on the ladder to eventually conclude that "I am OK" or "I am better than I was before." Although randomly selecting outside activities is one way of generating feedback to ourselves about the natures of our identities, there is still no substitute, particularly for aging individuals, to do the mental homework to decide what pieces of our "personality pie" are still missing from our historical quest for "selfhood," or what aspects of ourselves must be energized to maintain the image of ourselves which helps us to feel happy, and also encourages us to responsibly reach out to others so they can also feel worthwhile. Although we may be satisfied with our lives and select a specific number of community "maintenance" activities, we are also responsible to charitably help others, and may require the confrontation or stimulation of new avenues of awareness to push us harder to take our benefits and go one step farther in our internal drama of self-actualization to share our love with others.

As a third and important dimension of working on our interaction with the community, we can now learn whether or not we have the ability to develop a systematic network of information and referral relative to any or all community opportunities which exist. For example, we may decide we have not been socially very active in the past, but are lonely now and must become more active "outside" ourselves to obtain some enrichment from other people (Step 1). We may additionally conclude that one segment of our "soul" or "heart" which is essential for our feelings of well-being or fulfillment involves some form of "communion" with nature, "exposure" to the natural elements outside our apartment, etc. (Step 2). But, we may also realize that previous success in fulfilling ourselves with a now deceased spouse has left us grossly inexperienced in knowing how to find out about various community events; we are not on the mailing list of any organization; our friends do not routinely "fill us in" on what's going on in their external lives (we may, in fact, be isolated from friendships, or may have selected similarly isolated "personalities" to confirm our parallel identities and provide "excuses" for inaction); and we do not even have the slightest idea how to systematically discover activities, store the information and access it on a timely basis in the near or remote future, or make decisions using consultations from "advisors" in the community to evaluate the relative merits of various activities and choose the best one to meet our needs.

The important point here is to avoid becoming overwhelmed by the illusive "monumentality" of this project, and to begin, somewhere, to learn how to organize an information seeking, storage, and retrieval system for ourselves. Whether we try various approaches on our own, or seek help from friends, counselors, books, etc., the overall plan generally involves the use of a file box and note cards to describe activities in various categories and retain address information, a list of names of "key informants" in the community who can advise us or provide referral information, a calendar to note times of interesting activities, a planning sheet to "plot" logistical transportation, meal, monetary contingencies (including friends to accompany us), a graphic tree "framework" to "trace" referrals along various branches to construct a comprehensive picture of related activities in various areas of interest, a phone book and "calling strategy" to continually "massage" the outer world to provide us with "clues to the puzzle" of uncovering the less publicized events/clubs/activities. Finally, a documented listing of "don'ts" when we get discouraged and sometimes want to quit the search.

Step 4 entails the development of specific goals and objectives to be accomplished during and at the conclusion of various activities, particularly because we will experience that our "aging process" reduces the "payoff" of some formerly valued community pursuits, so we have to learn to (1) accept a less "extrinsic" reward from our activity and use our minds to make up the difference with "intrinsic" participation or spiritual, rather than physical, outcome, (2) accept less extrinsic reward but continue the activity while substituting another moderately rewarding activity to supplement the positively desired result, (3) select other events or participatory collective enterprises which <u>do</u> provide the full extrinsic and intrinsic outcome within the context of a unitary function or coordinated set of functions in a comprehensive activity "package."

We must always be wary of discovering that our change in physical, emotional, or mental capacity has caused us to, first, view ourselves as "different" individuals, and secondly to <u>redefine</u> activities in the community as having a reduced capability to meet our "new" needs. Even though age, in some ways, changes our physical and biological functions, many research studies show that there is not necessarily a change of any measurable dimension of our self-concept for the following reasons (to name only a few):

(a)   our sense of self is largely anchored by other internal, structural attributes of the self which <u>resist</u> influences of age-related biological influences to create "variance" in "who we are,"

(b)   many definitions of our identity are unconscious and we are unaware of their continued influence in our daily thoughts about ourselves, and unconscious self-perceptions are very resistant to change and are, therefore, stabilizing influences (positive or negative) in our lives,

(c)   there is considerable stability of self-esteem, generally, among older adults, which partly serves as a "protective umbrella" to counteract negative influences of particular body or situational changes,

(d)   some of us possess "personality types" that some research studies suggest are better able to handle and control the negative variabilities of aging changes,

(e)   some older adults have a tendency to fear the evaluations of others, and so hold tightly to perceptions of the "self" from the past, which means, in some ways, the "self" does not become basically different, although maybe more cautious in new "evaluative-prone" situations,

(f) our physical slowing, in some ways, creates greater accuracy
     or competence in activities which now produce fewer errors,
     so the "payoffs" of participation may become even more
     rewarding as we become a better and more "reliable self" in
     the community,

(g) some studies suggest we retain considerable cerebral "plas-
     ticity" in older age frames and therefore continue to retain
     mental capability to derive rewards from traditional activities,

(h) "aging" may be a much more extended period of time with-
     out declines than we realize, with the most rapid and
     pronounced declines at the tail end, but with "perceptions" of
     decline throughout because of learned stereotypes and
     "self-fulfilling prophecies" on our parts,

(i) some studies show that emotions and the affect of older
     people are just as intense and capable of rewarding payoffs
     as those feelings of younger individuals (research subjects),
     and stability of the self occurs because of reduced variability
     of emotional reactions among older generations,

(j) sociability, body image, objective self-concepts, well-being,
     amiability, extroversion, and personal security are variables
     which some studies show to be relatively stable in later
     adulthood, therefore, again, diminishing the detrimental
     effects of reduced environmental payoffs,

(k) changes in our performance in self-concept and behavior may
     have no relation to the distance we have chronologically
     traveled from our birth, but rather to the distance we actually
     are, or perceive ourselves to be, from our death, so that we
     may have a tendency to relinquish present activities because
     we have pursued them a long time, when, in fact, this
     "duration factor" is less relevant than a decline and
     "short-time" factor that will emerge later relative to our death,

(l) our perceptions of negative attitudes in society about "old
     people" are more influential in lowering self-esteem than
     actual events that might impact us (at least according to one
     study).

The point here, then, is that goals and objectives should be defined first, pursued, and then measured--before we make assumptions that we or the activity are incapable of continuing or initiating a "productive interaction" in order to meet our needs.

Step number 5 is the point at which we try to perceptively, comprehensively and honestly assess the nature of the community in terms of the number, quality, accessibility and reward potential of its various goods and services, and also the degree to which each of us may have to alter our "perceptual filters" in order to utilize opportunities of which are unfamiliar, which we have previously defined as negative, or which appear to have adequate potential as useful resources but require more time, effort or creativity on our parts in order to "tap its benefits and make it work" for us. As could be expected, some communities offer fewer opportunities in various categories of interest than others, or spend more time and effort "marketing" particular aspects of "themselves" to enhance their own "identity" (from the perspective of civic leaders, business entrepreneurs, or politicians, etc.) and to respond to consumer demand or monetary potentials. In these cases, some opportunities of interest to us may be obscured or down-played in various forms of advertising or spacial visibility ("off the beaten path"), but we must execute a thorough search and priority ranking of a full range of events and options in order to effectively decide which actions to take to allow the community to help us improve the quality of our lives. Our own ranking of opportunities may directly contradict the "view" the community has of its priorities, so we will probably have to "index" our own listing relative to varying obstacles which may inadvertently hinder the ease of access for seemingly devalued goods or services. This means that a high personal "need-relevant" priority may rank lower than a moderate personal need-relevant activity, if the former one requires more complicated transportation arrangements, is prohibitively expensive, occurs in a dangerous or remote area of the city, etc. We have to avoid, however, the easy tendency to "take the easy way out" and choose a less meaningful activity, particularly as we may make self-doubting or ego-depreciating assumptions about our own decreasing "incapability," or "presume" we will encounter "resistances" which are fears, imaginations, or excuses in our minds. This is the point where we learn about and know our community, and actually establish a "recommended list" of valuable things to do, places to see, clubs to join, organizations in which to volunteer, etc.

The 6th step, in some ways, seems like it should have preceded all the previous points, but actually has very little meaning without first focusing on our individual needs, agendas, objectives and capabilities--which helps us begin this process from a self-perspective of strength rather than "weakness," "helplessness," "dependency" or "vulnerability" relative to the influences of the external environment on our lives.   In step 6, therefore, we evaluate the overall attitudinal and behavioral relationships we have with external "stimulus phenomena, events, environments or influences" relative to our own internal decision-making formula which serves as the basis for our aspirations, feelings of success, perceptions of personal adequacy, and immediate/long-term happiness. The reason for including this particular aspect of under- standing our relationship with the community is to "check out" and critically challenge the process by which we positively or negatively "adapt" or "protect ourselves" from the outside world, so that we don't fall into the easy trap of developing interesting and valuable goals and objectives which could potentially be achieved through various community activities--only to subsequently "sabotage" ourselves in our minds because we perceive a "negative interactive relationship" between ourselves and powerful external influences, like the community (which may be unconsciously seen as a good or bad "parent figure" from our childhood experiences).

In considering the general relationship configurations which can exist (in our minds) between ourselves and the community, some of the most basic scenarios, are as follows:

Person/Environment Relationship #1

External influences are more powerful than we are. We are generally forced to respond dependently and passively to the world's influences, so good or bad results are not within our con- trol but are culturally determined. Our normal state of being is a resting, balanced or "homeostatic" condition; "adaptation" means finding a way to "fit in" to community expectations when we experience the stress of these influences and to handle the anxiety related to our fears of failure (defensive mode). In some cases, the environment is perceived as too complex for us, so we allow ourselves to become "burned out" or overwhelmed yet never give up our "reliance" on the outer world as the "engineer" of our life journey.

Person/Environment Relationship #2

External influences continue to be very powerful. There are strong pressures for us to meet outside demands as our psychic system is stimulated by the "world's" needs or agendas, but we have internal capacities through behavioral and mental "options" to respond to crises or agendas by problem-solving strategies to (a) conform totally but resent it, (b) ignore the environment and learn to accept consequent "suffering," (c) compromise and meet some demands while simultaneously exerting independence to develop competence in more peripheral domains of cultural tradition.

Person/Environment Relationship #3

We perceive ourselves as largely "in control" of our destinies, and the external world or community is an important arena in which our "life scripts" or destinies must be actualized through socially approved "competencies." There are strong pressures from both inside and outside ourselves which drive our systems to seek challenges and create some crises for change, rather than exclusively remain "dormant," and positive/negative outcomes are derived from "efforts" as well as outcomes, although we sometimes need to "defend" ourselves while developing coping strategies.

Person/Environment Relationship #4

We believe we are totally in control of all (or almost all) aspects of our lives, which exist and are measured predominantly as internal loci of "being." The environment exists in its own path of influence which can be an opportunity for our inner selves to publicly display competencies or enjoy benefits, but "negatives" are our responsibility to exclude from awareness in our positive and "balanced" state of being where stresses only occur when we "choose" to experience fears, excessive desires, or irrational ideations. We use the community for our benefit, sometimes feel responsible to change some of its destructive influences, but typically live life first in our own heads, and secondly outside of ourselves.

Person/Environment Relationship #5

In this case we also believe we are totally in control of our lives, but have either "defensively" arrived at this conclusion after being controlled or hurt by other people or events, or "adaptively" have very little need for any external stimulation or payoff to feel safe, comfortable, or self-actualized. We are generally configured in a homeostatic state of tranquility and have little or no need for the outside community, although internal "crises" can erupt when we have sufficiently ignored the world to the extent that social responsibility demands must be exerted on us, or our survival and physical resistance become the unwelcomed burdens of others as we involve ourselves mostly with "doing our own thing."

Although there are numerous subdimensions and variations of each person-environment relationship, the main point is for each of us to remember that some form of dynamic cause/effect interaction between our identities and internal or external influences does exist in our minds, which plays a major influential role in guiding our approach or avoidance to various events within the community. Ignorance of the basic nature of this defined, contingent, interactive connection will leave us confused in explaining "why" and "how" we do or do not get involved in the world around us, and may prevent changes in our "environmental perspective" which could develop from exploration of the past historical roots of this decision-making formula.

Step #7 is the point at which we actually get involved with selected community activities, not only to meet the needs we defined earlier, but also to expose ourselves to possibly uncomfortable or unaccustomed relationships with events, to test out the continued viability of more "internalized" lifestyles which, at younger ages, may have satisfactorily met our needs, but may require reconsideration and alteration as we emerge in mature years as "new" people with a "new" and "changing" historical and cultural age. Our selection of priorities should be perceived as "under our control" and closely correlated with predominant needs for personal fulfillment and competence, rather than representing only expedient or "easy" activities, familiar and emotionally safe endeavors which provide less than optimal satisfaction, or "expected" pursuits which represent the agendas of friends/family/community which we might pursue to maintain dependency relationships rather than meet intrinsic personal needs. We should also be optimistic about our forays into unknown or frightening territory, so that the real "energies" and dynamic benefits of the activities (as interpreted through our mental filters) have an optimal chance to positively impact us, without premature conclusions on our part that the world is deficient, we are destined to lose out, or the only real satisfaction comes from "inside."

We should explore a range of different high priority events to compare their need-meeting potential, and to create varied experiences with the environment to give ourselves a more correct and comprehensive view of the strengths and weaknesses of our surroundings, and to further discover either the skills we need to enhance in order to maximize our gains, the defenses we must remove to allow greater "input" from the community, or the alternate activity options we must choose to more fully satisfy the "selves" which hunger and thirst for emotional or physical stimulation and satisfaction.

Our interactive attempts will also expose us to various "resistances" in the nature or person-controlled operationalization of community activities, which may be associated with the "content" of the activity itself, or stereotyped discrimination relative to different user or "accessor" groups in the community. Either way, we must completely understand all the pros and cons through direct experience so we can effectively and responsibly take appropriate action to change ourselves, other people, (even managers) or the activities themselves, so we and others can use the community to its maximum to help us lead satisfying and rewarding lives.

The 8th and final step only comes into play when resistances or obstacles are encountered which constitute prohibitive blockages to the successful initiation, participation or completion of self-enhancing events for each of us within the community's network of organizations, clubs, entertainment establishments, physical facilities or programs from which we can actively or more passively derive pleasure and meaningful self-perceptions of involved value. In some cases, "benefits" will be reduced by excessive costs, narrow or arbitrary times for utilization, logistical obstacles of travel distance or inaccessibility or engineering/natural design and structure which do not consider reduced physical capabilities or "handicapped" status of many older citizens. In these cases, it is best to initially assume that "insensitivity" results from unawareness of consumer's "special needs" or other priorities in the minds of management or ownership which are inadvertent, but not direct examples of discrimination. Sometimes a letter, phone call or personal discussion with the host organization's leadership authorities can correct obstructions or frustrating impediments, although further action with higher governmental authorities, (consumer protection groups, civil rights organizations, etc.) may ultimately be necessary to pursue reasonable expectations of change.

Other times, of course, we may experience overt prejudice or discriminatory "ageism" which we may initially correct through personal but sensitive confrontation to communicate the offensive nature and deleterious effects of these practices, but we may also need to take more global action again with governmental, legal, civil rights, aging citizens, or business standards groups to bring political pressure, public embarrassment, bureaucratic censorship or litigation to bear as stronger stimuli for action.

We must be prepared, however, for little or no action to materialize to correct discriminatory deficits, yet we may necessarily have to learn ways to "deal with" these problems personally rather than retreat or alienate community systems to the extent that we, and other aging individuals, lose the benefits we might enjoy and need very much. In some cases we may feel it is best to ignore examples of age-related ignorance and concentrate our energies on "moving past" particular points of potential friction with awareness of the hurtful results of fear and ignorance, and resolve personally not to commit the same mistakes ourselves. In other cases, we may define an "educative" role for ourselves and feel that our life has greater meaning as a result of specific interchanges, debates, confrontations, persuasions, etc., whereby we directly attach "humanistically harmful" stimuli as they occur, and either experience an immediate change in people or procedures as a result of our input, or feel fulfilled relative to our continuing efforts to elucidate concerns through the "chain of command" until we have exhausted all possible opportunities to contribute to change, or actually see the results of our efforts. Part of this process can also be a greater commitment to community action, writing, organizing social action groups, lobbying, etc., which should not, however, deter us from continuing to be active in the community to teach others about ourselves as aging but growing people, and to monitor cultural changes to help insure that progress is being made to create sensitivity and caring by all people, for all people.

d.   Relationships with Peers and Friends

Although our non-family social relationships do not necessarily experience any metamorphic alteration as a direct result of aging, it is important to at least discuss some potential areas of stress and types of personal and interpersonal influences, which could conceivably cause changes for the better or worse in these peer associations.

#1   Positive Increasing Closeness: The availability of time to devote to personal relationships, after the relinquishment of full-time employment and child-rearing responsibilities, can be a wonderful opportunity to build emotional structures and "cognitive congruencies" with friends which were impossible or very difficult at earlier ages. Research which suggests that aging men and women demonstrate increases in personal attributes of open-mindedness, honesty, affiliative interest, self-confidence, esteem, relaxed self-concept, humanitarian concerns, social poise, affective ability (men only), self-- awareness (women predominantly), and emotional diversification, (as well as other "interpersonal" characteristics, etc.) also attests to our ability to use these changing capabilities to enhance the quality of closeness with friends. The tendency, also, for men and women to reverse their traditional masculine/feminine gender role "orientations" and to move closer together toward androgogic or "uni-gender" perspectives and cognitive/emotional behaviors also suggests that we may develop non-romantic friendships with people of the alternate sex, plus perform many of the emotional "functions" for people of our own gender which were exclusively performed by their spouses earlier in their lives.

Also, the problems which develop as a result of changed financial, family support, physical health, community opportunity, etc. statuses may provide pragmatic and instrumental vehicles to initiate, strengthen and bind peer relationships to meet survival needs, which may ultimately be extended beyond the materialistic world into "partnerships" to energize spiritual and deeply emotional nuclei of our identities.

Many of us may also reach out to others as we experience the loss of children or spouses through death or family separation, which may open entirely new "worlds of awareness" to which we were "blind" when existing predominantly within the tightly woven and mini-dimensional emotional and cognitive enclaves which characterize many traditional marriages. We may discover, in this centripetal journey, exciting and rewarding dimensions of our personalities through the "reflected appraisals" of others, which not only enhances these new relationships, but also internally creates new "associations" between unknown parts of ourselves which also constitutes a potentially very powerful relationship between "us and us."

#2   Negative Increasing Closeness: In extrapolating, again, from numerous research studies, the cognitive and emotional changes which are associated with aging, and which may push us too close to others in dependent, clinging, crisis management, "psychic survival" or anxiety/fear reducing relationships (for other than temporary respite) are these: loss of social prestige, physical and mental declines, loss of control, increased anxiety and fear, heightened neuroticism, introversion, building depression, decrease in extroversion, more sensitive emotional responsiveness to recent life events (which may be negative or negatively interpreted), decrease in breadth of interests, general and interpersonal motivational declines, heightened hysterical tendencies and hypochondriasis, lowered self-esteem with decreased socio-economic status (men mostly), declining "freshness" and self-assurance.

As spouses or friends die or become less available to us through incapacitating illnesses, and as adult children move away or avidly pursue their own lives, we may desperately seek the consolation of remaining, or even new friends, through efforts to "merge" with them and reconstitute parent-child protective relationships to help buffer the hurt of lost loves, to control fear and anxiety related to terror concerning our future emotional sustenance, and to provide stimulative energy to help us regain the will and motivation to continue living after the dissolution of relationships which formerly provided "enculturated" interpersonal roles to define our identity and sustain our emotional sense of well-being and secure adequacy. Although these relationships may provide temporary shelter or even permanent self-protective dependence, they are ultimately destructive to the qualitative aspects of our internal and maturing/growing "selves" and will typically prevent further appreciation and learning about life, curtail aspirations about positive futures in this or "other lives," dampen or destroy spiritual vigor and energy, remit in antagonism and interpersonal conflict as autonomy is blocked within the relationship, create greater unconscious fears which necessitate more regressive ego-defense mechanisms which further isolate us, and reduce the enjoyment of interpersonal stimulation because of the extensive "work" needed to artificially "connect" the personalities, and to exclude others who begin to be viewed as threats to the "pretend castle" of delusional safety.

#3   Positive Increasing Distance: Because of changes in the "content" of our awarenesses as we age (e.g., interests, role behaviors, attitudes) rather than the more stable "processes" of living and relating (e.g., temperament, style, communica-tion patterns), plus stability, according to some research studies, in self-esteem, autonomy (males particularly), altruism, assertion, competence, unconventionality, and increases in threshold levels for emotional stimulation, we may discover ourselves moving away from some or even all past relationships with peers in an effort to experience more of our individual existential selves without the formerly presumed new or social custom of maintaining relationships "for their own sake" (irrespective of our real need or their emotional payoff potential); or to develop new associations which are more precisely attuned to our current needs and future life expectations. In this context, separation from others does not necessarily mean "distance" from the "self," or from qualitative life experiences which may be capable of comprehensive and meridian manifestation, generation and resolution totally within the boundaries of any individual mind or spirit. Changes in the "closeness" of some friendships, as we evaluate our life histories and document "deficits" or "empty spots" which require remediation for a more complete sense of personal fulfillment, may actually allow us to define specific areas for qualitative improvement which then serve as focal "magnets" to bring us more closely together at a higher or deeper level of meaning, shared reality, or cognitive connection which was impossible without the "time out" or distancing which our "maturity" allowed to transpire. New relationships, of course, can also be constituted which may, in fact, be less "close" than other peer connections, but more instrumentally or peripherally functional in meeting a wider range of needs which are unrealistic expectations from previous or even continuing "ultimately" bonded friendships, marriages, parent-child relationships, etc.

As close friends prepare or actually conclude the "dying process," we or they may need some distance to begin the grief process and to ultimately "let go" of the "physical" aspects of our relationships so that both parties can "look ahead" to new life forms or conditions of existence in the future, and also so that each of us can be independent enough to incorporate and healthily utilize the critical "identity packages" of loved ones as they enhance and continue to interact stimulatively with the needy parts of our inner selves. Never moving away generally means we cannot complete this important separation, evaluation, reconstitution, and growth process because we may be too close to someone else to clearly identify their strengths as distinct from ours, and we are also not forced to "take parts of others inside our hearts and minds" if we have never really become a unified and separate person ourselves. Therefore, continued closeness may result in many years of painful longing for their resur-rection, or self-destructive assumptions about the absence of their qualities because we have failed to individuate and therefore, define and utilize the personality receptacle, which is us, to serve as one residence or resting place, permanently, for the values and worthwhile "functions" served by our friends.

#4   Negative Increasing Distance: The last broad category of possible peer relationships to be discussed here is also suggested by several research studies as a potential direct or secondary outcome associated with "chronologic aging," and the personal self-conceptions and identity-awarenesses which may reflect decisions about ourselves as "responders" to this life conveyance. Pulling away, isolating ourselves, becoming alienated and excessively introspective, rejecting friends, or redefining our needs to exclude other people--are all possibly connected with discontinuities of social roles, negative stereotyped appraisals from others or "society," decrease in positive competency-producing social events, increasing personal hostility, reduction in present/future expectations and aspirations, temperamental fluctuations, lowered activity and energy levels, continuation of past neurotic tendencies, loss of autonomy, and declines in personal appearance, etc.

Any of these phenomena singularly or in concert, along with any other interpretations of our "selves" as helpless, bad, undeserving, suffering, unstimulatable, beyond meaning in life, unnecessary to others, unlikeable, or unable to derive psychic/emotional/spiritual benefit from present expenditures of energy or future aspirations concerning attainment of pleasurable/meaningful/peaceful/victorious conditions of thinking of "being"--can disastrously decide to dissociate ourselves from friends with the possibly incorrect deduction that they are responsible for present or future-expected losses, or that they lack the energy or interest in us to contribute actively and powerfully to "touch our inner selves" or create mutual energy "electro-emotive" vortexes which can break down resistance and stimulate us to seek new levels of satisfaction or life value. Of course, the farther we retreat physically and emotionally, the more inclined we may be to "justify" this decision by continuing the use of irrational and distorted logic, and to thereafter interpret new events or data relative to friendship connections, as confirming the negative and sterile world which we have defined, and must maintain now in our minds to achieve some level of mental integrity and holism--albeit a negative and regressive scenario.

The most important point to remember from all of the above relationship arrangements is that we should each monitor very carefully the various gradients of quality, quantity, distance and functional utility of all peer relationships, not only to insure that we and our friends are doing our best to achieve the highest levels of interpersonal and personal satisfaction attainable through mutual caring and loving, but to detect the earliest symptoms of "system" malfunction, or attenuation which may be caused as we interpret our aging process in any of a number of ways which, in our minds, necessarily or inadvertently defines a "significant other" as a noncontributing entity in our growth or even defensive posture. We should periodically share our thoughts about the importance of quality friendships directly with our friends, and subsequently try to jointly discover specific ways we can "measure" the quality of relationship processes or outcomes, so we and they can reduce any confusions or ignorances which evolve about whether or not the association is "worth the time and effort." This relationship "check-up" method takes special effort, tenacity and courage, not only to boldly and honestly communicate about how we communicate/care/ relate etc., but to resolve to work hard to "fix anything that breaks" within the context of friendships with others.

e.   Junior/Senior Relationships Between Adults

Although relationships with individuals who are younger than ourselves are subsumed as important components of each section of this book, there are some overriding generalities which we should all seriously consider as we attempt, under varying circumstances, to interact productively and amicably with adults from "other" generations and age-related world views. Each of the most important "principles" for us to remember as possible explanatory factors for dissonance, conflict, misunderstanding, or lack of cooperative growth and self-enhancement will be discussed in the subsections which follow. Since the potential pitfalls are the central focus related to life changes for us or younger cohort (generational) groups, we should also keep in mind that another complete set of principles (not necessarily the "flip-side" of the "negatives") could also be enumerated to spotlight the advantages of age-differentiated relationships.   Some of these positive attributes or opportunities can be clearly extrapolated beyond the problem concerns, but other good qualities have unique natures in and of themselves, which may not be concluded as easily from a list of "concerns."

J/S Awareness Issue 1:   The cognitive "styles," cerebration/reasoning procedures, or algorithm "formulas" for solving problems and interpreting reality may have been taught by very different educational and culturally-determined school and family systems for each "cohort" (younger or older generational group defined by time of birth and collateral movement through historical time). When confronted, therefore, with people who truly "think" differently, we may have to learn new ways of using our minds to define and associate ideas, or work with younger adults to discover common "conceptual patterns" or even a new "language of thought" which is not imbedded rigidly within either generational group. Younger people may be less likely to change because their emerging identities are strongly wedded to the choice and consolidation of thought patterns, which are also probably reinforced as the "way to be" through media, emerging technology paradigms, and peers who are struggling to differentiate their independent selves from older "parental" generations.

J/S Awareness Issue 2:   The activity and physical energy levels may appear to be incompatible, partly due to differences in health status and bio-energetic capability, but also because of "learned" physical adaptational modes among health-conscious younger generations as part of "holistic identity," as opposed to equally powerful learning among older generations related to more circumscribed work productivity activity (with diminishing social roles for actualizing this potential) but decreased activity emphasis for more cognitive, emotional or spiritual recreational resting or integration of the nonphysical "self." In some cases, both groups may share a similar focus on events, problems, opportunities or issues, yet approach resolution or competency/mastery aspirations from different self-actualizing activity approaches, although definition of activity "input" to engage with the world may also extend comprehensively to basic concepts of a "world" vis-a-vis activity dimensions. We should approach these differences by defocusing on the approach, and concentrating more on agreement about the nature of phenomena which receive the physical or cognitive stimuli of each group's "action," and share with each other open-minded perspectives and questions about which approach is most efficient/effective, given the need for each cohorts "personal payoff" enroute.

J/S Awareness Issue 3:   Differences in central nervous system, metabolic, cognitive, and other bioenergetic systems between younger and older individuals, plus different self-perceptions of social roles, personality needs, achievement hierarchies and personal "essences" may result in varying types, ranges, intensities and modulated applications of emotions in the context of older-younger relationships. We may interpret periods of emotional openness, closure, stability, change, approach, avoidance, etc. as related to the characters of the relatees (which may sometimes be true), although other variables related to stage of growth, experience with intimacy, environmental pressures, etc. may cause misconnections which can be partly corrected with patience, more open discussions of <u>what</u> we feel and <u>how</u> feelings are <u>different</u> for us or a younger communicant, and common acceptance of the difficulty, for anyone, in understanding and using feelings to bridge the emotional and cognitive gap between people as well as generations.

J/S Awareness Issue 4:   The focal points along various life-span continua, from past to future, serve as anchoring points to help define the function and relevancy of each identity, and can be continually redefined, enhanced, diminished, updated, etc. in an effort to rationalize current behaviors or situations relative to a "factual" (although perceptually "adjustable") past or future. The time space available for past or future visions, plus the number of experiences completed or potentially attainable varies, obviously, if any of us assumes a concrete and linear perspective about "serial" time, so younger people may look more toward anticipated larger quantities of not-yet-positive future "units of translatable identity" which, those of us who are older, may decide to notice more negatives. For example, from a varied large amount of past time--both perspectives, of which, tell us partly "who" we are now and who other people are who relate to us or interdict our "airspace" or "communication territory." The difficulty in merging or sharing viewpoints is initially a challenge of discovering where each of us is gazing/staring/glancing etc. for the "mirror" of ourselves, and then finding the similarities and differences of these nonexistent (past or future) while also recognizing that the only thing that really matters is the action which is presently taking place. We can help ourselves and others a great deal by "validating" the importance of our respective identity-confirming focal points, but also pressing for <u>here</u> and <u>now</u> aware-nesses of our strengths, which are only "illusory" connective tissues to another time, but can fail to materialize <u>right now</u> if we spend too much time trying to discover their presence in the past or presumed incarnation in some mental "tomorrow." <u>Stay in the present with strengths which are mutually defined</u> is the main message in this section!

J/S Awareness Issue 5:   Another major difference which frequently separates the values and viewpoints of divergent heterogeneous generations, concerns autonomy vs. dependency, including the cul-tural definitions of these states of "being," and the socially learned procedures to acquire the "positive" attributes of either condition (or a combination of the two) and to relieve oneself of the "negative" stigmas of "pos-session." Younger generations typically view themselves as emerging toward independence, strength, personal competency and blooming social praise--and away from parental control, school discipline, entrapment of mental ignorance and financial austerity. They have also learned, particularly in Westernized industrial societies, that these desired conditions are attainable through productive work, maintenance of good health and attrac-tive appearance, adherence to personalized values and areas of knowledge, and asser-tiveness concerning rights and opportunities. They typically do not realize that they may only "trade" one form of dependence (on parents) for another (on job, money, etc.), and frequently "transfer" responsibility for their former control to most older, parent-like authority figures of the preceding generation.

Older individuals often experience the same motivational goals as younger people relative to "freeing" oneself from bondage (illness, diminished income, social discrimination) but have fewer "effective" social opportunities and physical/fiscal "tools" with which to pursue this goal, and also have generally "run this race" previously anyway, and are searching for more "mature, enlightened, autonomous" or at least different approaches to accomplish this goal--often within realms of spirituality, emotional enrichment, cognitive "wisdom," etc.

In this light, younger generations, therefore, often fail to see the similarities and "key" their foci on the dependencies and "helpless" conditions of the "elderly," which they avoid as a way of externalizing their own inner fears through social "scapegoating." Older generations, having been stereotyped thusly, can easily feel alienated and resentful of the "punishing" independence in others, and also arrogantly conclude that they, as more mature life travelers, have transcended this stage of development to a new level of autonomy-- which may also be a trade-off of physical and social "independence" for mental and emotional dependence.

In either case, the process of seeking quality, independent, "free" living and thinking is quite possibly identical for both cohorts, but the content of specific definitions of the "state" of existence, and the mechanisms to leave the negative and arrive at the positive, may differ. We therefore, must work hard from both vantage (not disadvantage) points to define the common human struggles and aspirations, and to share with one another discussions of the pros and cons of various distinct approaches, along with recognition of delusional thinking which obscures the similarities which do exist.

J/S Awareness Issue 6:   The importance of cultural ecology and the myriad of influences which shape our perceptions of birth, beauty, significant goals, nature of relationships, function of nature, role of man and womankind, etc. are translated into social, ethical or moral values which represent, quite frequently, vastly "asymmetrical" perspectives for different generations. The events which occurred during our childhood "spongelike," receptive, developmental stages are different for each generation, as are the teachings and role modeling of "heroes" and "heroines" who attracted our attention within the various social and religious institutions to which we were attached as children. The conceptions that each generation developed, which provide "normative criteria" to orient us regarding the meaning of past/present/future, not only define the "tasks" and "tools" of the life-trip, but also form the basis of self-evaluations and identity states which we all ultimately defend and protect as they inevitably come into contact with "other identities" from "other historical periods" which "believe" the world in a different way.

Unfortunately, regarding sharing of human commodities, most of us have sufficiently "fused" with our "relevant" value positions, that even current events are community/world/cosmic phenomena which may have a neutral and non-partisan nature in some ways, are actually interpreted and defined within the context of generational "ex post facto" value concepts so that any current set of behaviors outside ourselves becomes us, and may get internalized within our predetermined positive or negative judgments so we do not, as individuals or collective cohort group members, have to experience as much anxiety trying to integrate patent "unknowns" into our life perspectives. Our value "energies" can also be symbolically attached or assigned to events, so that their "stimulus value" in impacting our lives can be extraneously increased/ decreased/neutralized to make them "fit comfortably" into our mental worlds.

When separate generations, therefore, try to communicate about current events, or about group values directly, the values themselves define, in many respects, what things can be discussed, what outcomes of these discussions are possible, and even how the discussion should be conducted and with whom (as relevant or irrelevant sources of power, new information, etc.). The diversity of experience each generation had in its past, or encounters in its present also highlights different options for evaluation, but it is extremely difficult to determine how number and type of event experienced are "indexed cumulatively" within value frameworks to produce perspectives with varying degrees of "reconciliation potential" with the experience-influenced views of older or younger cohorts. This is particularly problematic, again, because cohort group values even tell us, in many respects, what events to be interested in and which activities of ourselves or our society to specifically ignore as "irrelevant" or "stressful" to our psychosocial well-being. Within the scientific community there is also considerable debate about whether there are "maturational" stages or conceptual capabilities that are commonly shared by each generation as it reaches a particular age-related transition point (which does not help us much in cross-sectional communication between different age levels of society); or whether there is a more predominant, "fixed" influence of current events which dictates many aspects of how and what we think or feel (which would be helpful for us and younger adults if both groups are able to truly and openly "attend" to the present, with minimal "taxonomic" or "lexicographic" influences from our past socialized "selves" wherein we become "robotized" or "automized" by controlling culture "taken in" during specific periods of childhood socialization. The difference here, scientifically and anthropologically, regards the influence of "ontogeny," or the life cycle of a single person, versus "phylogeny," or the common developmental characteristics of a collective species and the particular outcomes of either autonomous "fluid intelligence" or more culturally fixed "crystallized" cognitive knowledge.

The best we, as subjective and possibly "contaminated" individuals can hope for, is to accept the differences in others as sometimes "beyond their control," while trying to discover the capabilities in ourselves and others which we can use to create collective and shared perspectives on present or future phenomena, and to simultaneously remember that what we believe may not be as important, in the grand scheme of life, as how we believe and learn and think.

f.   Political Activity

The nature and extent of any citizen's commitment to work within the legislative, policy making, bureaucratic or community action organizations of local or federal government, is dictated by a complex formula that is not necessarily related to the aging process, although certainly incorporates the phenomena of "time spent in life" as an important dimension. Beside the fact that the frequency, duration, effectiveness or efficiency of our inputs into various forms of the political process may change as we get older (increase or decrease), other factors influence "why" and "how" we participate as voters, campaign volunteers, candidates, lobbyists, committee members, consultants, policy critics, etc.:

(1)   education and socioeconomic status

(2)   previous family values and practices

(3)   political party affiliation

(4)   commitment to social values and altruistic spirit of social responsibility

(5)   network of politically active or passive friends and associates

(6)   the impact of politics on current or former professional or job-related activities

(7)   nature of political activity in our community

(8)   specific issues which represent a political agenda

(9)   effectiveness of citizen involvement in previous election outcomes, policy changes, social projects, governmental structures and practices

(10) availability of various types of rewards for participation

(11) personal beliefs about the "way the world should work" and the emotional value of "action on behalf" of others, principles, philosophies, or values for the future.

Based on the above participatory contingencies, our involvement may fluctuate along a range of "criteria" values that may be stimulated by changes within or between the listed "areas of influence," and only indirectly or coincidentally be connected to our chronologic age at the time we decide to "measure" participation. We may, for example, lead very enriched inner lives of critical thought, analysis, advocacy, disappointment, aspiration, amusement, etc. regarding the political happenings of our town, state, or nation without a direct "cause or effect" of amount of overt behavioral activity; or conversely may exhibit extensive physical involvement to "keep us busy" with a relatively minimal "intrapsychic" payoff relating to a "higher order" symbolic purpose of our actions. Through an examination of our "socially responsible selves" (which some studies say increases with age) and the philosophical values we possess which "connect" us to other people relative to futuristic gains or losses which are "energetically" somehow related to our active thoughts or behaviors, we may discover the political atmosphere as a very "fertile canvass" to colorfully and maybe permanently sketch or portray our "image" as "good, caring, mature, fulfilled, aware, interested, involved" individuals with whatever degree of personal activity fills this possibly not-yet-full cup in our psychic and social lives. In this case, our compensation will come from our efforts at "rolled-up-sleeve involvement," which may not necessarily demand a successful outcome to provide its most substantial meaning for us. Other readers, however, may decide to feel fulfillment only when accomplishments are measured in socio-political contexts, yet may remain excitedly active until the end of one's natural life, engaged in the perpetual pursuit of a qualitative political "win" with which to "notch" one's intellectual, emotional or spiritual weaponry. These pursuits may, in fact, accelerate as we become older, with more free time to devote to specific political projects accompanied by increasingly successful outcomes related to the process of our involvement, which is predicated on a longer life of interpersonal skill-building, world knowledge, intellectual capability, practical experience with social change, quality and size of interpersonal networks for political persuasion and assistance, and increased "correctness of understanding" about political processes which emerges from extended contact and observation of the phenomena throughout successive generations of leadership, cultural conditions, different social problems, etc.

     Another side of political involvement for many of us, however, that may relate more directly to "senior-level" age status can be subdivided into three categories: (1) socially induced reduction of role responsibilities or opportunities, and diminution of performance power, within networks of active political positions, and perpetrated or facilitated by other individuals within those systems as a reflection of "ageistic" stereotypes and discrimination; (2) socially or community-generated closures of opportunities for aging individuals, generally to participate in a full range of political "process," or lack of affirmative action to insure that our special interest perspectives are fairly represented; and (3) negative impacts on various aspects of personal and community life as a result of politically-caused/sensitive legislative policy and bureaucratic implementation which has the initial direct or inadvertent intention of reducing the status or advantages of this particular social group (or improving the status of "competing" groups) or whose ultimate outcome in community action, in fact, limits the advantages or reduces the benefits for any "aged" or "aging" person individually, or for groups of "senior citizens," collectively.

Each of these will be discussed briefly:

(1) Role Decline: This is a social "role discrimination" issue which also occurs in employment, some family structures, and within other societal groups where we must be continually vigilant to assert our rights to maintain social positions where there is no evidence of performance ineffectiveness, and to also have "affirmative action" opportunities to attempt to modify role requirements to elongate our participatory tenure, or to be assigned meaningful responsibilities in alternate political roles whereby we can continue to "be a part," at some legitimized level of organizational need. We may additionally discover that relinquishment of more formal politically active roles within structured networks actually results in greater opportunity for more independent, flexible, comprehensive, spontaneous influence without the limitations that are frequently inherent in the role boundaries which define activities, although we should never make this decision in response to "pressure" to "step down," "slow down" or "redirect our interests," etc. or as a "cop out" when we feel that other roles truly offer less potential, or to avoid the difficulties and stress of "fighting" to maintain our role status within political process.

(2) General Political Isolation: This is typically a more general sociological condition where aging citizens are considered to have "expensive" human needs costing

time, money, or resources which are considered "scarce" within society, or are needed as "bargaining chips" to negotiate with other social groups (businesses, churches, governmental agencies, other special interest factions) to the extent that older citizens are viewed as a "voice needing suppression" to reduce overall stimulus power for social control of some resources.   In other less aggressive situations, older citizens are not seen, necessarily, as a political threat, but are not viewed as a political or economic asset to "win over" to some political constituency, or simply have been assigned devalued social status relative to future contributions to "mainstream" life, and are excluded or not actively included as "relevant" participants in the political life of a community, state, or nation.

In these cases, which certainly occur on a widespread basis, we may be forced to take various forms of proactive or defensive action to not only insure our opportunity to exercise political rights, but to produce various forms of informal or formal pressure or stimulation on their culture to "remember us" as qualitative participants, and to likewise demonstrate some degree of economic and political power as "qualifiers" to "get back in the race." These actions, which can also be personally self-enhancing, can include the following:

a.   organize transportation on election days

b.   develop knowledge dissemination networks

c.   engage in fund raising to produce economic power

d.   meet with candidates to discuss issues, negotiate about votes

e.   establish volunteer groups to support issues or candidates

f.   write letters, newspaper articles, conduct T.V./radio news conferences

g. meet with government/election/political officials to plan great inclusion and participation feasibility

h. initiate and perpetuate personal or "class action" litigation

i. confront inertia among peers through community groups, door-to-door canvassing

j. collect research data and documented evidence of participatory outcomes

k. build alliances with other stronger groups or organizations in society.

These efforts, of course, are time consuming and difficult because their enemy is prejudicial social attitude and selfish constituent power contests, but help may not come from "outside" in sufficient time or amounts to demonstrate an impact on the quality of life which can be enhanced through the informed and active participation of all citizens within a democracy. The challenge of social organizations and personal commitment for political action is certainly a direct responsibility of each member of every disenfranchised group, which has no right to solely blame others for the lost opportunities which evolve in culture, and must take assertive action to protect its own best interests and to communicate with other social groups to help improve understanding and appreciation of the needs and contributions which represent everyone within our multi-dimensional world community.

(3) Negative Social Outcomes: In some, or actually many, documented cases, there is not necessarily a concerted and direct effort by sociopolitical groups or activities to blatantly reduce the political wherewithal of "aging" or any other groups of citizens but the outcomes of politic-ically ignorant/insensitive/uncaring/conflicted decisions may have a negative impact on our efforts to obtain reasonably priced community goods, activate social

service programs, receive competent and timely medical care, receive reasonable financial benefits from social security/retirement/insurance/investmentprograms,enjoy fully the benefits of spiritual development and church/minister consultation, participate in a variety of easily accessed community events, use public and private buildings with relative ease and comfort, secure adequate and reasonably priced public transportation, benefit from various forms of audio/visual/written forms of community information and education, and otherwise participate in community life with equal quality and quantity afforded to every other social group.

In these cases, we may discover that individually and collectively we can use the political system for rebuttal and correction of undesirable outcomes, which means that the process was not blocked or withdrawn from us, but that we had insufficient grass roots participation to (a) substitute more acceptable legislation or policy to result in better outcomes, (b) have early warning of "negative political needs" so that counteractive political measures could have been implemented, (c) involve more voters and other participants to sway critical votes and decisions in more partisan directions for our particular cause.

In any case, we must always be as knowledgeable as possible about the specific as well as general "public outcomes" which emerge within business, social or governmental programs that effect our lives, and encourage as many concerned citizens as possible to be involved adaptively and/or defensively (although this ultimately produces more alienation and loss of power and prestige) as early as possible in the political machinery, so that as many negatives as possible can be averted before they happen. This process ultimately involves coordination, coalition, and understanding among all groups in society, with an underlying philosophy of love and broad human concern which emphasizes that all of us are responsible for each other, and the common welfare can never be achieved until we remove basic fears of "loss" and "differentness" from our emotional "computers" and "vocabularies."

g.   Media and Advertisement

The relationship which any of us develop or maintain with the "content" of messages, the "process" of information delivery, the persons who are directly involved as writers or media "personalities," or the overall community "context" within which the media operates as a "spokes-phenomena," is very much dependent on our degree of "deprivation" or "need" for the reception of various types and amounts of stimulation to our mental/emotional processes, the quality of outcomes gained or lost which revolve around being informed in timely and useful ways, and the symbolism we psychologically attach to the "associations" we perceive as "receivers" of emotional "messages" to our personality structures.

The media, broadly defined, includes radio, television, newspapers, magazines, books, pamphlets, billboards and community signs, and for my purposes, I also include telephone and door-to-door sales solicitations. From the literature on communications theory, we know that each of these forms of visual, auditory, sensory, cognitive and emotional stimulation has a unique "process" or "attention-getting" style by which it enters our "life space" and has some form of influence on our thoughts and feelings, and we also know that each of us is programmed in our "mental computers" with a series of preset ideas or concepts which either need to be confirmed and supported by incoming "data," or which are outdated/dysfunctional and are awaiting new learning to help us change and grow. In addition, many media messages are also "developmental," which means they not only potentially have something to "give" us at the time of reception of their input, but they also direct us to awareness and participation in additional activities or behaviors which materialize either within short or long time frames after the message has been sent (e.g., see this attractive T.V. commercial now and buy this new car later).

In thinking, therefore, about all of the various combinations of what is communicated to us, how the message is delivered, why we "need" to hear or "see particular parts of us reconstituted in the message," the degree of impact on our systems, and where we will conclude the "transaction" relative to potential outcomes; there are several general types of issues surrounding our relationship with the media which have important implications for us as aging biological, psychological, and social beings. Each of these will be briefly discussed separately:

(1) Inflexible Delivery: Many media formats inadvertently are insensitive to the changing needs of aging individuals, and typically ignore impact concerns with size of type on printed matter, speed and volume of verbal communications, clarity in the expression of thoughts or ideas, modification of physical format to facilitate ease of utilization, prohibitive costs or location access to reach "isolated" audiences, color variability for psychic receptivity and stimulation, tonal quality for auditory reception, time of delivery for participation, and reasonableness of extended outcomes to truly involve older participants.

The isolation, ignorance, lack of timely awareness, and noninvolvement which results in the lives of older women and men can contribute to our diminished self-esteem, lack of mental and emotional vitality, depression, and alienation from the nurturing aspects of society as we can progressively feel the world is "not talking to us anymore," and refuses to honestly and clearly invite us to share and participate. We can help alleviate this problem with confrontational calls or letters to media organizations to identify problems for us and other maturing citizens relative to their "presentation" of data, but we can also help ourselves to better utilize existing sources of information by acquiring appropriate prosthetic and corrective devices to boost our receptivity and utilization potential (e.g., hearing aids, eye glasses, etc.), using multiple sources of information as a "checks and balances" approach to get "all the facts," developing personal networks with peer and younger friends to corroborate the data which is available to the community, and also working harder to train ourselves through increased attention and practice to use the media in a more proficient and effective manner (e.g., learning to listen more intently, tape recording T.V. broadcasts, etc.).

We must also remember that media messages and various processes may have important symbolic relevance for our internal psychological, emotional or spiritual well-being (T.V. personality who becomes a "friend," radio music to combat loneliness, books to revitalize "adventure" in our lives, etc.) but it is <u>our responsibility</u> to use them in positive and productive ways to build our personalities, plus we must refuse to let the media become a substitute for interpersonal or community participation, or our own cognitive thinking and self-enrichment which often takes more work as we age--but may provide greater meaning and fulfillment as a human process, rather than artificial substitute which the media can easily become in our lives. We should use media, therefore, to "start our engines," but we should keep them running via our own thinking and feeling exercises.

(2) <u>Irrelevant Content</u>: The quality of the growth and development of any young, middle-aged, or older person to some extent hinges on the character of <u>ideas</u> that are communicated by various media conveyances; plus the sophistication, comprehensiveness, philosophical depth, and socially validated value congruence of the <u>relationship</u> between those unitary ideas or concepts which are perpetrated and supported by the dynamic responses to stimulus input which are encouraged by media style and suggestive nature. In many respects, media "focus" is predicated on relationships that be outside the realm of media control, and actually reflect relationships between economic or political interest organizations in society, and their targeted consumer or constituency groups which are contacted through direct supportive media advertisement, or direct/indirect content and process of message delivery. Some aging individuals are frequently socially devalued as powerful political supportive allies or fertile economic consumers (with the exception of several selected items), the media's placating "concessionary" content often excludes information that is relevant to genuine concerns of those who are experiencing the latter stages of "senescence"; does not contain roles or social scenarios that deal with life, <u>as it usually is</u>, for mature audiences; and lacks provocative style or data which brings to light important issues that apply to intergenerational relationships, advanced stages of the life cycle, problems of aging,

or positive outcomes which could serve as motivational "battery-rechargers" for people who are not socially considered a part of mainstream psychosocial-spiritual life. We are guilty, of course, of gross self-depreciation when we allow ourselves to passively participate in media "exchanges" which are insulting or unclear relative to our needs or capabilities, and probably should be changed with some degree of social irresponsibility for not becoming more active in publicly advocating for higher quality T.V. or radio programs, newspaper reports or editorials, magazine or book content, or other auditory, tactile, or visual stimuli which send messages to us every day as we live, work, recreate, and journey throughout various corridors of community life. In this regard, we should work hard to personally translate and expand the stimuli which are available into thought provoking and energizing issues to build our minds and souls, regardless of the simplistic, incorrect, superficial, negative or innocuous natures of the messages in their original form. Discussing books, magazine articles, T.V. newscasts, etc. with family or friends can help provide an energizing forum within which to expand the ideas which are presented, and more careful selection and attention to only high quality media presentations can help us establish patterns of growth oriented participation within the communications "net," and avoid the regressive "slippage" which can occur when we devalue ourselves through voluntary exposure to low quality communicational input. Volunteering to serve as consultants to various media delivery organizations can sometimes be helpful in creating awareness of "topical relevance" concerning aging groups, although other circumstances may require letters to directors or sponsors of media organizations to communicate to them (become senders rather than receivers) our likes and dislikes, and to establish at least informal "normative criteria" requests for quality "programming" with sensitive social awareness.

We can also, sometimes, become directly involved in media activities by writing magazine or newspaper articles, acting in T.V. productions or commercials, authoring books, or developing a series of public service announcements (public T.V./radio, flyers, roadside billboards, newspaper ads, etc.) which confront the negative stereotypes and neglectful "omissions" of positive role models and life messages which relate to the comprehensive realms of beginning, middle, and chronologic end of the full life panorama.

(3) Offensive "Targeting": In some cases, the media in its various forms of delivery, is far from ignoring or demonstrating insensitive secondary neglect and discrimination of aging populations, but conversely has "selected out" particular subgroups with unique personal, social or physical characteristics which represent "profiles" of (a) potential consumers for the marketing of various products or services or (b) for the public demonstration of selected points of view, criticisms (including human) or unfair/ignorant/stereotyped philosophies which can be either legal and ethical, or beyond the scope and intent of the law and principles of humanistic concern and responsibility. Salespeople, newspaper or magazine advertisements, television/radio solicitations, mailed documents representing a host of "opportunities" or "benefits" for aging populations, or the themes and behavioral messages of dramatic productions/plays/movies/comedic statements or pictures, etc. can singly or collectively function as direct incursions on our civic rights to exist free from correct or incorrect unsolicited commentaries on "states of being," plus these communicative cannonades can prey upon vulnerable emotional needs and precipitate dependent "outcomes" which result in losses of time, money, self-respect, social equilibrium, or faith in the value and useful purposes which the media can serve.

We must all be extremely perspicacious in screening, understanding, and evaluating the overt and implied content of all communicated messages, and become particularly sensitive to our positive, negative, or neutral mental attitudes in response to various types of stimulation (as this helps us grow in self-understanding), plus we should be extremely cognizant of the purposes and reasonable outcomes of various behaviors we perform in response to the sometimes seductive "melodies" and enchanting/demanding "voices" which speak to us with various styles and intents from all parts of the community. Our vulnerabilities, lowered states of self-esteem, loneliness, fear, isolation and heightened dependency on external sources of power and presumedly benevolent leadership can plunge us deeply and helplessly into the pathological "webs" of marketing strategy aimed at capitalizing on our weakest sensitivities--often before we realize the extent of our "magnetized" involvement. This can occur, not only in conjunction with intents to "sell" us products (unnecessary supplemental health insurance, home improvement services, labor saving devices, etc.), but also through the insidious "socialization" of negative ideas about the aging population's incapacities or deficits, and lack of support for the motivational learning which should occur among all age groups to understand and appreciate the comprehensive phenomena of life-span development at all levels and points of its unfolding. We can use each particular form of media input to learn more about the world in which we live (or have chosen not to "live" in a fully qualitative way) and to "check out" our own personal attitudes of self and others, to insure that we achieve the greatest richness of thought and feeling possible by converting any negative "energies" from the words we read or messages we hear, into positive food for thought to encourage us to think in a better, more intelligent, or more sensitive manner in the future.

h.   Consumer and Financial Roles

The reduction of post retirement income for most individuals above 65 years of age, together with rising costs of living, medical care, extended support for young adult children in college or new families, etc., means that substantial changes in financial and consumer roles play an important part in our lives. These changes obviously manifest themselves differently based on our lifelong financial status, capability for continued full or part-time employment, investment portfolios, financial assistance from adult children, extent of health problems necessitating acute or longterm medical and rehabilitative costs, ownership of homes and other income generating property, and the styles of economic living to which we are accustomed. Despite the quality or amount of previous financial planning, and irrespective of our socioeconomic status and crisis events which require economic as well as psycho-emotional types of response, there are several

change-oriented financial and consumer issues which, in one way
or another, effect most of us in later years of life.

Issue 1 - Value of Money: The actual or potential reduction of
assets or the increased unplanned/emergency survival
expenditure of funds causes everyone to give some
consideration to the values and symbolic meanings of the
terms wealth, poverty, have, have not, enough, excess,
security, desperation, comfort, status, freedom, autonomy,
dependence, pleasure, materialism, spiritualism, etc.
Although greater economic prosperity during "productive,
younger work years" may invite the more optimistic
perceptual hemisphere of this "universalist" phenomenon,
it is important not only to view ourselves as responsive
"econometers" to the various fluctuating monetary
calibrations in our lives, but to also remember that our
beliefs about the good, true and beautiful will partly, or
even largely, determine how we interpret or handle the
downs (sometimes ups) of financial change.   Money
coming or going from our bank accounts will certainly
demand certain adjustments in the expectations we have
of particular life pleasures, and will create fairly normal
anxiety relative to surviving with the physically-based
"necessities" of subsistence.   We will all, therefore,
probably be required to decide if we can "extract" some
external symbols of life satisfaction from the inner
pictures of psychological and spiritual wellbeing, without
losing the ability to retain a complete and fully positive
picture of "how adequate we are," or to even substitute
a more illumined and richer mural of ourselves as a
result of having "sacrificed" some material pleasures
learned earlier in life. In some cases, however, we may
not be able to superimpose an "acceptance" or "readjust-
ment" perspective for the values we see as painfully
obliterated or drastically injured.   We may forever define
life's meaning as some aspect of the ratio of economic
gain to loss, and may derive self-actualizing energy from
the "fight" and "quest" to earn or obtain sufficient
amounts of the symbolized self in monetary currency,
products, or services; and may likewise see the self in
resurrected homage relative to the suffering which is

experienced, resented or ignored (but felt) as deficit becomes the symbol of failure which is "defeated" by perpetual, now acceptance, and determined resolution to sustain the mental joust.

Another path, as the reader can easily surmise, is to actually devalue money in proportion to its rate of exit from our lives, or its reversity proportioned inability to correct "negatives," and purchase pleasure, comfort, health, friendship, harmony, etc.; so that a new reality actually gradually replaces a former definition of what ought to be; and we undergo the sometimes awesome struggle of seeing a somewhat illusive or delusive set of circumstances in our economic lives which is incorrect from most external fiscal standards (bologna becomes steak, $1.00 becomes $10.00), but truly represents a new "reality" with unseen parallels and reconstructed logic inside our minds and spirits which elevates other "principles of being" to a more distinguished spectrum of essence and value. In this case, we may partly accept a lesser standard of living as beyond our control, but retain the concept of a former standard or of the notion of "control"--or may relinquish both ideas and believe that the only standard measure is that which is, which cannot be compared to any other parameter, and that "control" only applies to love of self, rather than invest- ment of energy or time in "externals" which have a sig- nificantly diminished value in the holistic scheme of life.

We may even select a third compromise position of historical "retroflection" and learn ways to remember positive aspects of former monetary-related life assets, to place greater priority in interacting with and appre- ciating those material possessions which remain in our possession, and even continue to dream about future life bonanzas, all without attempting to distant perspectives of the "deprivations" we experience presently, or forming attitudes to "enjoy suffering" as a form of symbolic resentment or guilt which would probably also contaminate pleasant "fantasies" about the past or future.

Issue 2 - Practice of Conservation: Another major factor which
affects many of us as financial resources diminish, is the
need to stretch our resources (food, dollars, entertainment, pleasure, Kleenex, etc.) so that the commodities
we need and enjoy the most will have a longer "functional life" for our utilization. We can no longer "take
anything for granted" and have a wonderful opportunity
to, perhaps, view the world for the first time with purely
qualitative "attitudinal lenses" which can teach us to
focus distinctively on the attributes rather than deficits
of things, people, or events in our lives, and to achieve
mental and emotional states of intensified awareness and
profound appreciation of even the smallest "unit" of life's
interrelated "ingredients of fulfillment" at our disposal.
The conservation phenomenon also implies that we
establish an extended, mutually beneficial "relationship"
between ourselves and our resources, and begin to view
a sense of cooperative sharing and commitment to the
extension rather than extinction of "essences of things"
(paper bags, coffee grounds, pieces of note paper) so
that "team work" to presume the significant contributory
"forces" of everything around us becomes a basic foundation of an almost animated associational linkage
between parts of the world which many of us may have
formerly dichotomized as alive vs. dead. A conversational philosophical perspective, in this capacity, may
lead us to even more sophisticated realms of "awareness"
where we might discover interconnections between seemingly one-sided or disparate parts of our micro and
macro cosmos which enhance a fuller meaning of our
existence and the existence of everything else we can
and cannot see.

Learning to conserve also enhances our cognitive
reasoning processes of abstract thinking, inductive/
deductive logic, and general hypothetical planning ability
as we use accentuated consumer skills to understand unit
rather than volume pricing, product depreciation with
wear or normal usage, "extendibility" of various
commodities to boost or enhance the value of related
products (Hamburger Helper), relative amounts of

"nutritional" vs. psychological benefits of food items, and "multivariate potentials" of particular products which allow functional utilization in several domains of our life's needs. We can interact with new or "renovated" personality attributes represented by concepts of life efficiency, perceptivity, frugality, productivity, practicality, functionality, organization, prioritization, evaluation, etc., which many younger people in life never learn, but often use to criticize aging individuals or couples without understanding or appreciating the "intrapsychic" richness which can develop by changing our external and internal adaptations, and making definitive decisions to expand beyond the pragmatic process to achieve greater intellectual, emotional, or spiritual growth.

Issue 3 - Scientific Investment: Changes in financial status can also usher in a need for the initiation or wiser implementation of small, medium, or large "investment programs" to not only save the money we have, but to either obtain more benefits for the fixed amounts that must be expended, as to learn ways to actually earn more money through the international economic community, even though we might only play a small role relative to our capital assets. The process of developing awareness and expertise in "money matters" is, indeed, a great challenge requiring extensive reading, consultations with financial planners/accountants/attorneys, discussions with other knowledgeable investors, and patience to learn the intricate "ins and outs" of the economic system.   It requires comparative shopping and relatively sophisticated analysis of insurance benefits from primary and supplemental policies, differentiation of various interest rates and savings incentives at local banks vs. trust companies, study of the financial histories and projected "futures" of various businesses or stock options, sound evaluation of private or public services to insure that personal costs do not outweigh "measurable" benefits, vigorous analysis of most products we buy to understand our rights for "warranty" and customer satisfaction/ product performance remuneration, and vigilant exploration of cost savings coupons or programs, along with free services which are provided either as customer incentives, or as "legal rights" for aging citizens (e.g., reduced bus or movie costs).

In conducting a comprehensive personal program to become "scientific" as planful and wise spenders, we not only realize benefits in pocketbooks, wallets and savings accounts, but can generalize our skills of perception, analysis, evaluation, reasoning, and decision-making to many other areas of life where we might additionally enjoy this intellectual and emotional growth. We must also develop networks of friends and associates to support these efforts and critique our approaches, which secondarily forces us to "tune up" our interpersonal skills and abilities to achieve pragmatic/ functional as well as intimate relationships to benefit ourselves as well as others. Even though our earnings or savings may seem miniscule within the "grand scheme" of world monetary systems, they are "monumentally significant" to us, and therefore demand the respect and consideration from ourselves and others which places them at the "head of the line" relative to their "intrinsic" value as valid representations of the personality and life-force we bring into the world.

Issue 4 - Legitimized Institutional/Residual Needs: The serious financial plight which many older adults experience as a result of unavoidable income curtailments, medical expenses, or specialized personal care and residential contingencies; or avoidable errors in poor financial planning, irresponsible spending, "anxiety-driven" panics and fearful commitments of monies to unnecessary "life remedies," or neglect of personal health result in secondary costly rehabilitative measures, etc., leaves some of us unfortunately in conditions of "need" whereby we must seek, accept, and integrate various types of private or public "welfare" assistance to sustain our lives and provide minimal levels of opportunity for physical/ emotional pleasure and peace of mind. The solicitation and acceptance of food stamps, welfare checks, public subsidized housing, "sliding scaled" or free physical or mental health care, government sponsored transportation, community reduced rate senior citizen "coupons," public health nursing or home visitation services, church food baskets or volunteer "visitor" assistance, etc., can be a very difficult and conflictual new "consumer" and financial social role for several sad, but relevant, reasons:

(a) society continues to stigmatize and disparagingly evaluate all forms of "dependency" and "nonproductivity" within a narrow spectrum which excludes a comprehensive and truthful view of the whole personality and life process, and also demands humiliating "proof" of these conditions prior to assistance offers;

(b) most of us were socialized to irrationally exaggerate concepts of "independence" and "self-survival," and to maintain paradoxical and confusing definitions of mutuality within relationships which makes us "believe" it is less desirable to "receive," and somehow dishonorable to participate in helping others to give to us;

(c) most of society operates on "fairness" or "equity" principles which posit questionably rational and relevant "formulas" for "earning" social "rights" and "benefits" relative to "time spent" at work or in life, degrees of commitment to the "social order," prior "deposits" of productivity or accomplishment, or attitudes of demeaning appreciation and subservience in accepting the "benevolence" of others;

(d) most welfare and free-reduced cost social services are housed in larger city/state/federal governmental organizations characterized by impersonal, inefficient "bureaucratic" procedures, and frequently offer relatively low professional and staff salaries, along with high benefits for job security and moderate work demands--which means that inferior employees who are protected by the "system" interact with agency consumers in incompetent and uncommitted ways;

(e) society generally places low priority on all types of "welfare" assistance in goods, services, or money, so benefits received are typically insufficient, which perpetuates adversarial and alienated roles between "givers" and "receivers," and fosters resentment and feelings of abandonment by the truly needy--who are additionally "contaminated" in society's view by the poor image projected by those less needy (physically, not emotionally) "manipulators," "complainers," and "cheaters" who also attempt to utilize all systems of social benefit and public assistance.

As some of us experience the irrepressible need to obtain help with basic survival needs, and begin to inter-act with various organizations to "establish eligibility" and "negotiate" to actually receive different types of benefits, the following attitudinal guidelines in the form of affirmative "self" statements may help us functionally and comfortably make the transition from more autono-mous to legitimate recipient/dependent roles if necessary:

-- "I do the best in life that I can, given physical capabilities which I do not fully control, and attitudes/motivations/decision-making abilities which I want to be 'sound,' but are also controlled by current situations, fears, and past learning!"

-- "My thoughts, feelings, behaviors and energies can be a positive force in the world to somehow (even if I don't perceive the process clearly) help others, so it is necessary that I survive in order to fulfill my destiny and help others do the same!"

-- "No one in the world has the right to exclusive owner ship of its monetary, physical, or spiritual assets, or to decide who is 'deserving' of receiving the various 'gifts' of life, so everyone should share every benefit, without limit, discrimination, or accounting of eligibility or appreciation!"

-- "The benefits (or 'welfare') given to me by others are an opportunity for them to grow through goodness, and I do not have to feel bad about this important benefit which they receive as a result of my condition of need!"

-- "Everyone in the world is equally 'competent' and equally 'needy,' and there is no rational or relevant 'scorecard' by which these 'normal' phenomena or states of life can be evaluated as right or wrong, but they can only be assessed in terms of 'degree of fear' which prevents all of us from helping one another unselfishly!"

-- "Anything 'given away' in the world is never lost if we elevate our minds and hearts to a higher level of understanding the 'wholeness' and simultaneous 'nothingness' of the values we impose on ourselves, and the human and biologic processes of life whereby all that exists continues its life in one form or another as a result of seemingly necessary transitions of function and ownership utilization!"

-- "I should want to give freely to others in need, and would want them to accept my friendship and help in order for all of us to live happier lives!"

Issue 5 - Unrestricted "Aspirations": The final point to be made about consumer roles specifically, although there are certainly some restrictions on superficial and material "quantity, quality and frequency" of expenditures or purchased products, is that older consumers may enjoy a degree of selective freedom of product choice (plus personal valuation) which was not possible while occupying traditional social roles earlier in life. In the absence of relatively inexorable demands for children's clothing and food, business or work necessities, home furnishings or accessories for larger families, major recreational endeavors, educational and training expenses, savings fortifications, and mandatory entertainment expenses for peripheral friends or associates, etc.; volitionary option to buy "anything we want" becomes a reasonable reality which can respond directly to our idiosyncratic needs and desires, rather than being "filtered" through the requirements and needs of other aspects/people in life. We may be free to purchase the most trivialized or silly ornament or product to meet an obscure personal fantasy at little cost, or to spend an entire life's savings on a pragmatic but expensive item which fulfills a "dream of a lifetime" relative to function or enjoyment as we define the nature of our existence. In many cases, of course, high costs may preclude ownership or rental of many items, but we are cognitively and emotionally in a less restrictive psychosocial framework within which alternate selections, liberally defined substitutions, or totally opposite "diversities" can be chosen to meet any self-selected need we choose to entertain with a higher level aspirational priority. We may experience some conflict in relinquishing former perspectives on "pragmatic" functionalism, frugality, predominant vs. elective need, conservative vs. liberal self-expression, and selfishness vs. altruism--but reluctance to experience open-ended and unrestrained consumer attitudes and practices to enjoy a nontraditional or eccentric range of options is solely our own decision as many social constraints are lifted with age. Adjusting perspectives about amount of cost relative to "emotional meaning" of projects may also slow some of us down, but we can also learn to feel free and independent as we choose less expensive items, but invest them symbolically with more expensive attitudinal and emotional significance to enrich our lives from a totally self-contained and self-serving attitudinal framework, as long as our desires do not infringe on the legitimate social rights or subjective preferences of others.

i.   Roles in Medical and Mental Health Organizations

The higher incidence of serious health problems or recurrence of acute minor illnesses among aging populations, mental health difficulties which are associated with neurological decline or age-dependent emotional conflicts of psychosocial adjustment, or extensive demands for various forms of physio-social rehabilitation to extend adult independence and optimal functioning as long as possible, create a series of new or perpetuated "roles" for older men and women, as service recipients within various categories and levels of health service organizations. Since these "frameworks" for the assessment of "patient pathology" are predicated on professional and often complex philosophies and taxonomies of biologic/ psychologic human deficit, and are organized internally to meet the needs of staff functionality and performance predilection, the positions and options which impact the beneficiaries of these services often exclude the individual client as a planning participant, and contain various forms of control, discrimination, exclusion, incapacitation, stereotypic assumption, emotional and social redefinition and minimization/deprecation, or personal information consideration which makes productive, cooperative and relatively pleasant participation on our parts an extremely difficult challenge. Although I certainly do not intend to denegrate the laudible efforts and results of most all medical, mental and rehabilitative in or outpatient services, their unique nature as primary or secondary commentaries on the characteristics and outcomes of birth-life-death, and the distinctive and powerful systemic-style which denotes their delivery pattern, often neglects the rights and opportunities of the consumer which must be taken into consideration to insure comprehensive diagnosis of true rather than assumed "disease or health processes," and to encourage each patient to assume a more responsible role in participative management of their "wellness." With this broad cautionary introduction in mind, therefore, we will briefly review some of the most blatantly negative role options and outcomes into which any of us may inadvertently slip or be channeled by the needs of the medical community and/or our defensive reactions to pressure which is exerted for this system to meet its needs at the expense of clients:

Problem Role #1:   "Diagnostic Confirmer"

The lack of scientific research precision, as well as professional interest in gerontology up until the recent past, has resulted in an area of bio-psycho-social life-span development with numerous stereotypical assumptions and hypothesis based on symptoms and clinical observations, but few definitive answers about specific "causes," and even less capability to differential specific aging vs. disease entities as they are uniquely associated with our specific personalities, cultural background, historical learning and genealogy, life experience, and future motivations. With this multicomplex person-problem-situation tableau, and continued health and mental health reliance on generalized "syndromes" of older people from which to derive "reactive" treatment plans which are usually "maintenance" oriented rather than "corrective," each of us can easily fall into patient roles which support the state of knowledge (or ignorance) and traditional "treatment" regimens, whereby the unique case history we present may not be viewed by "open minds" with future orientations toward physical and mental growth, but with "regressive intervention" based on beliefs that there is little hope, "declines" cannot be reversed or really slowed, and that former "diagnoses" of chronic dementia, depression, neuro-anatomical deterioration, spiritual atrophy, etc. are correct, and essentially devoid of any "developmental dynamics" based on a "wellness" or holistic health (rather than illness) model which espouses full integration and functionality of the "abled" rather than "disabled" patient. Our role is one, therefore, of "affirming" the known and being "classified" rather than teaching about the unknown, and participating in a process of mutual exploration, rehabilitation and growth as partners with the professional health community. To avoid this role, we must all be extremely careful about the ways we define "normality" of aging relative to limitations, dysfunctions, disabilities, handicaps, etc.

Problem Role #2:   "System Validator"

This potentially negative role goes hand in hand with #1, and usually occurs in conjunction with today's emphasis on medical and rehabilitation specialization, where each highly technical section or unit of a hospital or clinic can get caught in the "trap" of studying or treating only that aspect of our "problem" which relates to their area of expertise. This is ideal, of course, if the diagnosis is absolutely correct and if no other components of our physical, emotional, or environmental "selves" are connected to a "presenting problem." It is easy, therefore, for our mere "presence" and "authoritative" referral to a specialist or specialized clinic to serve as role-behavior justification for our correct "need" to be there, which consequently means that nurses, technicians, physicians, clerks, etc. may diagnose the problem they are trained to treat, rather than view our severe request more comprehensively through a less restricted, or multi-professional team approach. Our reliance on referrals, therefore, within the health service organization should be tempered with our appreciation of the "self-fulfilling prophetic" validation of problems and solutions, for no other reason than the fact that we and they (specialists) have met on the same turf, which we must remember is controlled by medical professionals who may be inclined to need to believe they are competent, correct, and appropriate resources which are correspondingly matched to each person who is referred. This is not always true and our participation in any particular health service regimen does not necessarily mean it is the right place for us at that particular time. P.S.--If someone is a hot dog salesperson, they can easily assume their potential customer is always hungry for the hot dogs they will readily sell to the "needy."

Problem Role #3:   "Treatment Successor"

An additional role which can be very damaging to us, particularly because services are frequently sought during physical or emotional crisis states of desperation, excessive pain, life turmoil, etc., is that of conforming for the health service, therapist, attending medical "expert," etc. that they have succeeded in their individual efforts to help us and "correct" our predominant problem. This seems like a contradiction of any previous point about "global regressive and deteriorative" assumptions concerning aging clients, but there may remain considerable expectations of alleviating or "curing" prominent symptoms, or at least relieving excessive pain. This is not bad, obviously, as an appropriate medical or mental health attitude and treatment goal per se, but we must be careful not to "conspire" so strongly with "helping" resources that any of the following less desirable outcomes materialize:

(a)   we allow the "passivity" and "dependency" sometimes representing behaviors of older people to cause us to discontinue treatment when the professional, rather than ourselves, decide we are improved or not able to be helped (which is a decision defined as a sub-success by many clinicians),

(b)   our fears and anxieties about serious illness, death, etc. cause us to believe the symptoms are abating when prescribed medication "runs its course" or when medical authority tell us we should be feeling better or demonstrating asymptomatic behavior,

(c)   our lack of knowledge and caution about certain areas of health/mental health problems causes us to agree with counselors or technicians and to "believe" we are improved, when in fact, we are only pleasing someone else upon whom we rely for attention, support, and help during periods of loneliness or acute crises,

(d)   we allow our problem to be defined more simplistically than is correct in order to accept temporary relief of some symptoms or to respond to a narrow perspective of the professional, which ignores a more complex problem requiring more time, expertise, and effort than the health service provider may be willing or able to give,

(e)   conversely, we accept multiple overlapping and potentially contradictory treatments (multiple drugs for example) which satisfies the professionals' need to succeed as a "comprehensive diagnostician and clinical multi-faceted healer," rather than expecting consultations from "separate" specialists concerning "separate" problems, and demanding more coordination, explanation and proof of the potential positive benefits of complex and interactive treatment approaches which are incorrectly provided under the rubric of "holistic" or "comprehensive" health service,

(f)   we fail to persist when positive changes do not occur because we become intimidated by authoritative "conclusions" about the various outcomes of our problems, and we passively accept "decisions" about our well-being which are based on the treatment resources "theories" of etiology and resolution of disease entities, rather than on the actual data provided through our own feelings, intuitions, symptoms and changes in bio-rhythmic or psycho-rhythmic function as only we can know and understand this pattern.

The main point here is that health care is a dialogue between professional and patient, rather than a unilateral "game" played by only one person.

Problem Role #4:   "Benevolence Placater"

In many health service situations, professional staff members, counselors, clerks/receptionists or volunteers have a great deal of interest and sensitivity surrounding the "plight" and "disadvantaged status" of the "elderly," and therefore develop skills and "outreach" attitudes to "attend to" particular age or physical/emotional/cognitive-related "needs" and "agenda" items of their service recipients. Although this form of humanistic awareness, and associated "therapeutic" and relationship-building skills are frequently comforting, as well as helpful affiliates to the successful competition of the primary medical or psychiatric mission, they can occasionally become exaggerated or inappropriately used as subtle remnants of reversed discrimination and "universe isolation" of aging individuals within handicapping frames of reference that suggest "helplessness, childishness, incapacity, need for deferential treatment, excessive vulnerability, or dependency." In these circumstances, which may involve whole clinic-systems or just one interactive example, we may receive numerous overt or "subliminal" self-destructive messages which fail to recognize our strengths, and additionally "suggest" to us the demonstration of <u>real</u> helpless behaviors so as not to disrupt prevailing attitudes to conform self-perception communicated to us by others and further "cement" the probability of obtaining the services we need on a timely basis, as a consequence of "accepting" <u>all</u> the "gifts" which are offered. We can suffer also, by not using our strengths to adapt to difficult, new, or frightening situations, when we are singled-out for specialized "candy-coated" treatment, which also establishes professional and personal norms for possibly dishonest, uncritical, imperceptive or superficial engagement between "real" people dealing with real problems. The commonalities between ourselves and others also becomes obscured when interactions are wrapped in unilateral or bilateral "propositions" about older people, rather than sharing ideas and feelings to uncover non-mythical and unstereotypic "data" which unifies our views of more totalitarian whole life views as integrative human platform--and then deriving facts and propositions which elucidate sub-categories of the shared processes of living. In some isolated situations, as a matter of fact, the "niceties" and benevolent patronage accorded to aging clients can function as a self-supporting smoke screen which prevents professionals from asking pertinent questions or critically observing their clients in order to discover major problems of suicidal depression, mental confusion, pathological loneliness, social support loss, serious undetected physical disease, or other personal needs not clearly articulated by the client who may, in some cases, be too busy responding to the overtures of staff who are trying to be kind.

Problem Role #5:   "Trial Experimenter"

A role which may evolve as either positive or negative includes the aging patient as either a formal or informal participant in various types and degrees of exploratory or trial efforts on the part of health practitioners to test new treatment methods, understand the variable effects of different drugs, isolate specific symptoms through control of various biological processes or concentrated attention to a specific problem area, establish performance criteria to fathom the limitations of biologic or psychologic process relative to natural vs. "under treatment" contingencies, put new prosthetic or rehabilitative procedures or implements "through their paces" to compare the outcomes to previous methods and instruments, or sometimes provide "no treatment" (honestly) or pretend treatment with no active effects (pills with no potent ingredients) to use us as control (non-experimental) groups to compare outcomes with others who have received treatments being studied or to test the emotional effects of our belief that we have received a valid treatment input. This latter experimental situation is associated with formalized scientific studies and patients must be informed about the process, although private practitioners have been discovered "fooling" their patients to help them get better motivationally, or as a process of not providing sound treatment (especially in the psycho-therapy field) to groups who the practitioner and society define as unmotivated, recalci-trant, or hard to work with (minorities, women, the aged, some children, prisoners, etc.).

In any of the above role possibilities, we may certainly benefit from an untried procedure or plan, although any outcomes which do materialize as either positive or negative are always considered "spurious" findings if observations are not contained within a formalized experimental design where large numbers of patients are tested to examine "normative" and "average" out-comes, statistics are employed to document degrees of effectiveness, and all other biologic and psychologic conditions are reasonably controlled or matched or standardized so that there are reasonable assumptions that outcomes are truly "caused" by the intended inputs. We, as recipients of these explora-tory maneuvers, may suffer or "not gain" in the following ways:

(a)   we may endure numerous "stabs in the dark" which raises and lowers hope, with no definitive results,

(b)   we may be given experimental treat-ments because "numbers" are needed to fill research samples when, in fact, other proven remedies are available to help us,

(c)   experiments may be poorly conceptu-alized or executed with few protections relative to side effects, anxiety as participants, stresses of experimental regimen,

(d)   some practitioners may have insufficient knowledge of new treatments or medications which actually have little chance of helping us but they excessively rely on the consultations from sales representatives trying to sell drugs or new devices,

(e)   our failure to respond to the intended effects of "practitioner-valued" procedures may be defined as personal motivational problems which may reduce the concerned care we need later on,

(f)   once experimental results have been attained, researchers or even practitioners, if these have been repeated "null" or negative findings, may lose interest or hope in helping us longitudinally with the targeted problem or others that may be related.

In all cases, we should be careful about accepting any "exploratory" conditions related to health care, which includes treatment by student interns, that may not have sufficient qualitative dynamics to provide the best care and results possible.

Problem Role #6:   "Death-Illness Distractor"

Some research and clinical findings in the area of gerontology suggest that many individuals generally, in western society, are fearful and negatively oriented toward the concept of traditionally-defined physical death, and the degenerative biologic and psychologic processes which precede this outcome in the latter years of life. As a culturally   supported   and   individually "functional" "externalizing" defense mechanism to avoid anxiety in existentially integrating this phenomenon with life's often excessive preoccupation with "youthful" values, elderly individuals can be assigned diminished and undesirable social status as "scapegoats" to isolate the feared "death-demon" from the mainstream of public awareness and personal thinking about the meaning of life. Within the health service professions, where the "dying process" can be correctly or incorrectly associated with the various illnesses or pathologies which define "patient" status, older individuals who are also "sick" or physically "degenerating" may occasionally be ignored, treated discourteously, given lesser attention or priority, receive inferior or unenthusiastic treatment, undergo superficial or non-comprehensive diagnostic or treatment follow-up evaluations, serve as the subject of unkind humor or stereotypical categorization, or even directly receive anger which is based on generic traits or chronologic age, rather than specific precipitating behaviors which in some very specific circumstances might appropriately warrant an angry response from medical or support personnel.

In all of these cases, the possible negative responses or non-responsiveness of others may not be a "personal" attack by any means, but a broad-based discrimination and "pushing away" of a part of ourselves, symbolized in the assumed conditions or plights of aging individuals, which enables younger members of society to define their status as more secure and acceptable through the negative concepts and labels they attach to others who are different.

This prejudicial "game" is not only hurtful as we experience the "exclusionary" coldness or disinterest of others, but can cause anticipatory or reactive retaliations on our part, where we express disappointment toward ourselves by lowering our self-esteem, and/or attack others through obstinance, belligerence, irritability, reduced motivations to comply with treatment regimens or to help ourselves rehabilitationally where we can, or with other behaviors which reinforce the social picture of us "dying" which provides some degree of consistency by reinforcing the expectations of others. Assumption of any parts of this symbolic role to "help others" through exaggeration or avoidance of the "truth" of the illness or death process will always be more destructive for us and for others in the long run than honestly confronting life in all its aspects from the very beginning.

One last caution for all of us, also, is that we can reactively corroborate the "denial" of our "end-of-life dilemma" by assuming entertaining, folksy, cute, and helpless "grandparent" images to partly remove the sharp edge of external condemnation, to endear ourselves to "persecuting" enemies who seem to disrespect us, and to produce valuable behaviors for others to enjoy which provides a sense of value and optimistic meaning to our lives. We may, however, lose additional self- respect with this approach, perpetuate the pre-existing distances between ourselves and others, and add additional fuel to the fire of our "distractor" roles by allowing others to make fun of us in uni-focused amusement diversions which still represent running away from one of life's realities we fear and do not understand.

Problem Role #7:   "Victimized Sufferer"

Although there are certainly other role behaviors or attitudes we can adopt to fit into "systemic patterns" of health care systems, I will only discuss one more major one within the present limitations of space, and the need to cover a wide range of topics in other areas as well. This role is fairly easy for some folks to assume because its exaggerated demonstration of suffering, its flavor of "failure" or hopelessness resulting from accumulations of multiple treatment efforts, and its illustration of exhausting physical and mental fatigue stemming from sustained contact and "recycling" through the rigors of the medical or mental health system of bureaucratic operations, often seems to parallel the "natural" hassles and pains of the various disease and degenerative conditions experienced by aging women and men.

This role becomes functional for many older people for the following reasons, all of which generally do not help us grow and handle the changes of aging very successfully:

-- it fosters attention when we are lonely

-- it gives us control because medical staff are ethically obliged to respond to symptom complaints

-- it lets us blame others for our perils

-- it encourages awareness of problems at an early stage of development

-- it sometimes generates multiple medications and treatments to cover "all the bases" in our minds

-- it gives us a reason to emotionally stay alive

-- it makes us valued customers at health facilities because of the money we or our insurance companies spend

-- it gives us "story content" to discuss with friends

-- it provides secondary support and physical closeness from family and friends

-- it allows us to punish ourselves, or atone for past "sins" as a result of the "pain of suffering."

The hypochondriac, complainer, medication abuser, accident-prone victim, emergency-room pest, multiple physician "hopper," or rehabilitation failure are all behavioral repertoires which can almost seem like reasonable consequences of the illnesses or aging difficulties with which we struggle, although this role becomes destructive when we realize there are secondary or symbolic "gains" to be received, and when we actively sabotage or fail to comply with reasonable and potentially helpful attempts to provide proper counseling, medical services, rehabilitation counseling, or home "survival" assistance. We hurt ourselves by focusing on areas of health which lead to false conclusions by diagnosticians, and by cleverly establishing patterns whereby we contradict or block the possibly helpful services which are provided. Competent health professionals can understandably become frustrated with our behavior and either comply with our demands to try and appease us, or become reluctant to offer services because we are "bad" patients who are not really responsive to competent procedures or attitudes. Many friends, family members or even professionals (with the usual exception of counselors or therapists) will not honestly confront us with our games (especially when physical health is used as the primary "game token"), so we must learn about ourselves in these roles by carefully observing the consternation and extraneous frustrations of those around us, and by carefully and honestly examining our own motives and feelings.

j.   Church and Religious Activities

Any "changes" in our relationships to church activities, religious beliefs and personal practices, or spiritual foundations of life, are intricately connected to the nature, solidarity, and functionality of our religious practices throughout life, with particular attention to the public vs. private, physical vs. mental, present vs. future, leader vs. follower, individual vs. group, active vs. passive (passive is not negative here), concrete vs. abstract, and input vs. outcome natures of our particular organizations of worship/spiritual activity, and the dogmas/practices of the religious traditions they represent.   As in other sections of this book, there are always going to be some changes related to our physical conditions, tolerance, patterns of illness, residential arrangements, financial capability, transportation opportunities, weather constraints, etc. which will not be addressed redundantly in this discussion.

One issue also, which may present numerous "confusions" in assessing our relations to church or religious activities, is that spiritual beliefs may be substantially enmeshed in other types of thoughts and emotions and may not, in fact, be different "entities" at all.   If this is true, then religious beliefs and practices may be governed to a large extent by a full range of influential life circumstance and cultural "directives" which may not be clearly traceable to a separate set of inner perceptions and sensations, or to a more "external" and "transcendental" association with God, "the church," other spiritual "stewards or dominions," or various forms of cosmic or natural "processes" with which we might live our lives in some orchestrated harmonious or contentious fashion. There is also very little research on spiritual or religious beliefs relative to middle or later periods of life-span development, so our discussion here will be very conjectural, and will rely heavily on personal interpretations from each reader.

+   (1)   Active Outreach by Church Leaders: Although many priests, rabbis, ministers, elders, or other spiritual leaders are very active with all "parishioners," some of them increase the fervor of their outreach or responsiveness with aging members of the "flock," particularly if illness or disability has necessitated physical isolation from mainstream church life.

In the case of particularly sensitive, philosophically energized, intelligent, and affirmatively active apostolic prelates, this outreach which may accompany the aging process can be a wonderful opportunity for concentrated, advanced, private, and extremely pertinent learning and growing in one's faith, which may be particularly relevant in resolving or integrating issues related to the holism of our past and future lives, plus formulating the "dying" process into a spiritually growthful excursion through various tenets of one's religious discipline. The application of spiritual and religious concepts and frameworks for explaining and differentiating "reality" conditions and states of "being" is not an easy or rapid task, and often involves some "therapeutic" confrontation of resistances and reluctances, as noted by several research studies which note that aging individuals are typically predominantly concerned about health issues, have confusing perspectives about the meaning of the "declining" years of life, derive little strength from considerations of "after life" phenomena, and live in a culture where death is a topic which is not socially validated as an "exciting" discussion issue and is concomitantly also a minimal "theoretical" concern in many families. With religious leaders who are unskilled (and some certainly are) in the sophisticated and complex process of helping their counselees "work through" and cognitively "struggle" with relevant spiritual issues, this outreach service may end up being more closely related to supportive health counseling; generalized "blessing" and consecration of the "termination" and "rebirth" phenomenon without specific cognitive/emotional infusion into this new "world of being"; comforting of "grieving" family members; an historical chronicle of positive past memories to "ritualistically" give permission for everyone involved to forgive themselves and move on in life, to control social "crises" related to serious illnesses; to encourage aged individuals to conform to guilt-induced social norms and be "gracious" or "profound" about life and death issues; or to proclaim society's "compensation" rituals to help us balance the "negatives" with positives with particular reference to "rationalizing" the value in being old or the benefits previously obtained in life which serve as a retroactive payment for the "pain and displeasure" of upcoming death at some future point in time. These services may indeed be beneficial and helpful at various emotional levels of our personality or family system, but may not be specifically and powerfully related to spiritual identity or religious life--which implies we may need to insist on religious leaders actually working with us on topics and dynamic functions pertaining to religious life.

In some cases also, this outreach can apprise us of various activities or "missions" of the church where we can actively and meaningfully participate, although we must personally evaluate our own resistance to involvement since we may not have sought involvement independently prior to contact by church leadership. The religious goals may, to some extent, be abridged or abrogated if we secondarily get involved because of requests or pressures from authority figures.

+ (2) Active Lay Religious Community Outreach: Many churches and religious communities advocate and deliver considerable auxiliary support and fertile spiritual relationship opportunity through various missions and apostolates of parishioners who are particularly active with peers who are aged, ill, or in other ways isolated from fuller participation in formal church life. Although these visitors, prayer partners, discussants, "friends" in Jesus, or fellow spiritual travelers are not professional clergy, they very frequently provide warm and genuinely effective emotional and spiritual support to help with the trauma of illness or impending death, the sorrows of relation- ship loss, sorting out the mental complications of life changes, filling in during lonely times, and encouraging us in numerous ways to help ourselves through self-motivation, goal-directed prayer, increased activities, emotional catharsis and release, and renewing commitments to God and our respective princi- ples and practices of faith.

In these circumstances, we can forfeit considerable emotional and spiritual advantage by refusing to "open up to love," and allow ourselves to be nurtured within the "receiving" role through acceptance of someone else's positive reflections of the beauty in our own humanity, and incorpora- tion of the "energy seedlings" which honest communication and interaction can provide. We should dispense with "distancing" attitudes and maneuvers like excessive politeness, guilt feelings for needing help, humility and refusal to express honest emotions of anger/ hate/resentment, public displays of religious platitudes and hypocritical zealousness to hide fears and misgivings, or refusal to ask for sufficient visitation or activity time to really "dig" into important matters of life, love, relationships, the nature of God, the meaning of the hereafter, the pattern and function of various life journeys or Karma, etc.

We can also remember that interaction with fellow members of religious groups provides a "stage" upon which we can display, practice, improve, develop or learn to use our religious faiths as operational and visible examples of the basic "essence" of spiritual energy, dynamism, or power so as to further confirm and consolidate our "presence" within various categories of enlightenment or religious "capability," and to also help others learn to use their spiritual gifts through the "receptor roles" we formerly occupied ourselves. Relationships are also uniquely important, not only because they are a "static and fixed" image of more esoteric religious or spiritual concepts or realms of existence, but also serve as a "laboratory" with developmental movement and action by which states of being (according to some faiths) can actually change or improve by becoming richer, deeper, more perceptive, clearer, etc., which involves both people who are part of the interaction.

Relationships with other church members should also be critically evaluated to determine the nature and extent of progress they engender, and to help cooperatively decide how they might even be more helpful in the future.

+   (3) Increase in Personal Participation: The augmentation of available "free time" after retirement from formal employment can be used for increased participation in a host of different capacities within church or religious organizations, or for more extensive or concentrated involvement in personalized spiritual endeavors. These activities can range from assistance with repair and maintenance of church property, or volunteer work in a rectory or synagogue office to "lay ministries" involving cooperation in religious worship services, visitation of the sick or poor, volunteer service in foreign apostolic missions, writing of articles or announcements in church bulletins, leadership or attendance at bible study groups for adults or children, or simply more extensive reading/prayer/meditational lives in private.

This can be a wonderful change for many of us who formerly "postponed" more active spiritual "natures" or interests to pursue other necessary life agendas, and can transform the later years of life into very rich and rewarding exercises of humanity, Godliness, spiritual integrative "wholeness" or demonstrations of good work and charitable manifestations of faith and love.

For some of us, however, the strength and pervasiveness of "worldly" values and "obsessive" demands for "non-ethereal" or "substantive" thoughts and activities which we learned throughout life, can pull us away from post-retirement religious pursuits either because we lost or never gained a sense of "soul" or inner/terrestrial mystical life, or have allowed this part of ourselves to remain undeveloped whereby we do not know how to behave or participate within the religious life of the community. This can be particularly tragic in personal cases where physical disability precludes active real or symbolic journeys to "touch the face of God" (in whatever form we conceptualize the main essence of life), but where disciplined mental and emotional travels through reading, meditation, prayer, reflection, adoration, personal sacrificial denial or suffering, etc. could be utilized to maintain extremely viable and perceptually active spiritual quests. These forms of rudimentary and highly qualitative method-ological "practices" are not easily learned by most of us, and many present obstacles later in life when we might no longer define ourselves as learners, and shy away from the rigors of practice and tenacity which most spiritualists insist are necessary to attain even minimal levels of elementary "enlightenment." The caution, therefore is to fail to use available time to get involved because we are unaccustomed or fearful of religious pursuits, or to become physically engaged but to neglect the emotional and psycho/spiritual transformation process of "registering units" of worldly activity within exchange frameworks of religious or spiritual commodities or conditions of laudable (but appropriately humble) existence so we obtain the full benefit of being active for the right reasons, or sometimes choosing counter balancing "inactivity" or patient waiting or energized observational support to obtain a higher order of spiritual reward, value, enlightenment, or state of grace/sanctity.

+ (4) Fear-Related Reconciliation: The reports of gerontologic research studies plus clinical experiences which have discovered: high levels of "death anxiety" associated with our perceptions of "limited time left and diminishing survival expectations"; the panic some aging people feel relative to suicidal thoughts secondary to depression and isolation; lowered beliefs about "meaningful lives" in the face of illness, loss of status, decreased role functionality, or loss of loved ones/friends; the emergence of unconscious "thanatological" or death apprehensions of loss of "self" or personality disintegration from childhood which are activated by various perceived "deficits" of "maturity"; individual efforts to "arouse" dormant feelings by creating "existential crises" relative to spiritual emptiness; efforts of individuals with deteriorative cognitive dementia to stabilize their progressively confused thoughts by focusing on firm objects or concepts (God, religious principles); rare cases or schizophrenia and paranoi where we become excessively religious, self-righteous an sometimes penitent to handle this conflict; desires to b "rescued" from the "hassles," irritations, stresses or maj crises of life for which we may partly blame ourselves; ar those cases of individuals with lifelong devalued self-concep attempting to achieve reconciliation and rebirth to approa more idealized images of their "personhood"--all suggest th some aging men or women may seek, or return to God, re gion, the church, or spiritual dimensions of their personalit in order to be rescued or "saved" in various ways from dangers or dilemmas which are no longer able to be "worl out" with a full lifetime ahead for the personality construct project to be completed. Experiencing different states oi desperation or need, we may embrace the religions of our past or the spiritual conveyances of the future to earn more

desirable states of "grace," to consolidate the "friendship" and protective support of some "higher power," to immerse ourselves in distracting but praiseworthy activities of religious charity or goodness, or to punish ourselves by unpleasant or unaccustomed "works of mercy" in order to "earn" the right to be free of entrapping guilt over "sins" or mistakes of the past which have not disappeared in our memories over time. In all of these cases, many religious leaders would earmark our increased participation in church or religious activities with some skepticism concerning "proper" motivation and participation to give and receive spiritual treasures from such "selfish" or "impure" ulterior agendas. Other clergy, however, might herald any "return to the fold" as a positive step, and suggest that we become comfortable at first with any protective or reassuring "scapulary mantles" obtained from the faith, and secondarily transform this external warmth to some form of inner grace, spiritual wholeness, enlightenment or oneness with God, which can carry us beyond the superficial or self-serving entry point to a more comprehensive engagement with our particular religious culture. This transformational decision, from one perspective, rests with us relative to particular outcomes, so that (a) failures to achieve piece of mind and soul may cause us to abandon the search or assume a more honest, true, righteous, humble, or otherwise appropriate attitude which may constitute the only open passageway to receive the ultimate and correct benefits from religious practice or (b) success in being "quieted during the emotional storm" may cause us to maintain a "parasitic" connection to the religious "battery charger" or "milk bottle," or produce healthier, self-confident emotional conditions which lead us to seek higher levels of spiritual growth while providing the clarity and relaxation of thought to help us perceive the "truths" of God or religious teachings more clearly and understandingly. We may only be able to make the decision to stop or "go on" based on the ways we feel after some connective "orbital reentry" into church life has been completed. The other alternatives of course to not seeking the church as either an appropriate or inappropriate answer are that (a) there is already full meaning in our state of disequilibrium and we can do nothing additional except experience it presently and developmentally (b) we must do

healthy emotional work first, before we can attempt differentiated spiritual awareness, so we probably need to seek
therapy rather than religion as the preliminary step, (c) we
are already in a state of religious or spiritual existence and
the negative emotions or feelings we experience are necessary
inclusions in the phenomenologic definition of the state of
"being" we must endure or (d) we will lose the opportunity
to benefit in the short or long run from religion and must
find some other form of physical or psychic "healing" in order
to acquire some state of balance, harmony, peace, meaning
or equilibrium in our lives.

Our subject evaluations of any of the aforementioned
conditions will certainly skew our perspectives in ways to
confirm our idealistic and hopeful aspirations, so it may be
helpful to consult with friends, therapists or ecclesiastics to
help us sort out competing motivations relative to different
depths of benefits which can occur at cognitive, emotional,
spiritual or physical levels--which may represent vastly
different relationships between these outcomes and our inputs
based on the unique nature of our religious faith and
teachings.

+   (5)   Horizontal Changes in Beliefs: As many of us age, we use
increasing free time throughout the years to assess the quality
and meaning of the numerous significant life events which
have transpired, as they relate to the satisfaction of
antecedent or consequent relationships which help us feel
secure and worthwhile; and we also evaluate the congruence
or compatibility of these behavioral outcomes, plus our
attitudinal and behavioral "input" actions, with an inner set
of images we have of an ideal "core self" which we have
learned, through socialization and comparison to other
people, is a symbolic representation of some phenomena
which is "good, beautiful, valuable, pure, holy, honorable,
adequate, secure, positive, dignified," etc. This self-evaluation
process is a two-way street whereby particular things we do
create representational concepts in our minds which "justify"
their existence as somehow necessary and desirable for
various levels of our emotional and spiritual survival. We
also possess a set of symbolic categories in our memories

which play "host" to different positive or negative behaviors as they occur, and as they enter each berthing position, the corresponding "good" or "bad" value perspective is "registered" in our minds which pleases us and reduces anxiety if the affirmative "light" goes on, but creates disequilibrium if we accumulate too many negative examples of "who we are." For some of us, the adequacy categories are more "responsive" to physical behaviors, while other people can feel good about themselves more readily with exhibition of particular thoughts, feelings or sensations which do not require external documentation to produce validity.

When we consider religious or spiritual changes in life, therefore, we might examine the set of evaluative categories in our minds and notice that some of them relate more directly to associations with God, or the "hereafter," or states of "being" which we "feel," but cannot register within the ordinary concepts and activities of living on a daily basis. Other "berths" may relate to more socially noticeable emotions, communications, or behaviors which we might be able to distinguish as separate parts of the total self, which balances out the more abstract areas of our spiritual nature. As we age and inspect the relationships between our behaviors/thoughts/feelings and the "being categories" in our minds, we may decide on a "horizontal basis," any one of the following combinations of evaluative perspectives which may cause us to "change" at any point in time during our mature years:

(a)   We may review some previous life behaviors or deci-
       sions from a longitudinal and developmental end point
       retrospectively, and decide they were more "righteous"
       or consistent with existing religious principles or
       doctrines and therefore place ourselves in a different
       and more positive category than we formerly allowed
       ourselves to occupy.

(b)   We may reflect on the past and see behaviors or
       attitudes more cumulatively and conjunctively, so that
       the "highs" or "lows" lose their saliency as "definitional
       guideposts," and "average in" with other less poignant

events of the past or present to provide a generalized perspective of our religious identities, which may change the evaluative framework into which we place ourselves in the here and now.

(c) We may use present experience plus the maturity of lifetime observation and learning to more comprehensively define the "contingencies" within human emotion/motivation and situational stimuli/pressures, which "caused" particular life-phase behaviors or attitudes that are not related directly to our "true" natures. With this "reconstructed scenario" we can therefore adjust our spiritual self-assessments to correspond to a "purer" view of "basic identity" and therefore make "state of existence" decisions in a more responsible, although, not necessarily more positive or easier way.

(d) We may be able to discern a "pattern" of negative or spiritually undesirable behaviors which has remained consistent or even worsened over time, to the extent that we can also identify any emotional or cognitive distortions of positive "reality" or "blindnesses" to the nature, function and presence of spiritual energy or "grace" in our lives--as a focal point from which we can begin to behave, think, or feel differently to reverse the "dark spots" from the past. Any new behaviors which emerge can, therefore, either be defined or compatible with positive categories that already exist but have "waited" for greater "frequencies" of "confirming" behaviors, or new categories can be developed if we previously saw ourselves in a more "deviant" light and expected little in the way of religious, moral or spiritual "successes."

(e) We can use our lifetime of learning to understand that we had various types of positive behaviors or attitudes, but may have been inexperienced or ignorant of the "processes" by which these good deeds could be "deposited" within designated perceptual areas corresponding to states of spiritual goodness or grace, which may signify we have learned to identify and use emotional tools more liberally, openly, effectively or we may have developed greater knowledge of our religious heritages to understand how their principles can be "accessed" to apply more directly to our lives.

(f)   Our life experiences may also have allowed us to "free up," "expand" or even develop new categories of religious dedication, devotion, love or esteem within our minds as a result of knowing more about the teachings of the Bible or our respective church, or we may have developed greater architectural freedom and capability with our own personalities to the extent that we confidently and creatively "permitted" ourselves to be good and valuable in new ways to either find a place for existing behaviors, or to stimulate and push ourselves to work harder in new areas of living to "catch up" with the mental and spiritual dimensions we created for ourselves (and quite probably with the help of God or other spiritual forces).

(g)   Another change sometimes coming with the "wisdom" of age and experience is that we may tend to view God or other deities with either a broader or narrower perspective which results from our extended exposure to their ministrations to us and the world, plus lifelong observations of natural and human phenomena which we surmise are "unrelated" directly to the energy transfers between ourselves and our spiritual leadership "symbols" or "beings." Lengthened "time in grade" may lead us to observe and analyze causal or associational linkages between numerous life circumstances or outcomes of events, which could only be explained as the divine will and "world sculpturing" of a superior power either working through the "natural" dynamics of human emotions or "bio-eco-cosmic" proclivities, or demonstrating totally unexplainable occurrences which we knew were within the powers of our God-figure, but had ignored as a unilateral consequence of divine influence.

In the "narrowing" range, we also have experienced many years of manifested psychosocial-cultural behaviors whose recurrent patterns may ultimately convince us that many or all human "decisions" are substantively "corporeal," and either do not exist within the range of influences of higher powers, or are simply permitted as examples of "free will" which are associated more directly with "result consequences" where the ascendancy of supernatural "capability" does play a major deterministic role. In either case, we are not necessarily "understanding" more about the nature of God or person, but on a "horizontal" plan are using accumulated evidence to separate or integrate their functional relationships, and in this limited sense, do learn more about either entity.

The same type of change in perspective can occur regarding our concepts of life after death, where we may "separate out" or distill our childhood unconscious fears and destructive primordial mental images, from concepts of Hell or Damnation, for example, in order to see each separate realm of existence in its more correct and valid characteristic state; or conversely, we may realize over time that dreams, fears, horrible symbolic perceptions, etc. are really true examples of, and minor or circumscribed doses of the Hell or life without love/God, etc. which occurs at either present or future times relative to our predestined state of birth or "puritanical heritage" or as a consequence of selected "good or bad" thoughts or behaviors of a religious conforming or deviant nature.

In all of these horizontal changes in perspective, however, I do not imply that we attain new conceptual ideations per se, or greater depth of awareness or feeling, but on a lesser plan we use life experience and learning to utilize existing knowledge as movable components of our mental structures, which we can "move around" and associate in different ways (like letters in the Scrabble game) to develop new ideas and awarenesses from existing data which we view from different perspectives. The "wisdom" of "maturity," however, may lead us to incorrectly believe that the manipulation of concepts and ideas actually produces a truer picture or awareness of the world as it actually exists, and that some or all religious teachings and "truths" can actually be interpreted from different perspectives--but in reality the world may exist within a relatively fixed set of principles and definitional dynamics which we fool ourselves into believing we cannot understand without the intellectual ability to maneuver ideas until the correct kaleidoscopic image appears. Our revolution around a stationary object does not necessarily mean the object also moves, although our movement may cause us to believe this is true.

+   (6)   Enlightenment and Depth of Understanding: The final dimension of major religious or spiritual change that can occur, in varying degrees, at any stage of life, is the attainment of depth, profundity, comprehension, perceptive understanding, and other forms of enlightenment or inner appreciation of the totality and comprehensive significance of the "whole" of one's spiritual or religious world and/or intensive awareness and visionary focus on any unitary or specific concept of religious teaching or practice which descends to the greatest depths of integration of our human minds and the basic essence of this spiritual ideation--which, at the highest levels of enlightenment may not even appear to be an idea or separate concept at all.

This form of "vertical" change relates to the vastness and specificity of wisdom which is attributed to the illuminated mental, emotional and spiritual awakenings of "individuals" like Buddha, Gandhi, Christ, religious saints, venerated monks and mystics, and recognized people of superior goodness (Mother Teresa, Father Damien, some Nobel prize winners, great authors of vision, etc.) or perceptive vision. What I call this "higher" form of awareness is different from the "learning" of "horizontal" integrated facts discussed immediately prior, because the cognitive images we formulate actually transcend particular words or factual ideas that might be connected in different fashions, and enter the core of understanding which taps components of our minds and souls which we cannot usually describe to others, and which elevate our emotions to conditions of ecstasy or peaceful tranquility which "appear" to be related to the quality of "oneness" with our religious or spiritual domains. Some critics, of course, may dispell this "fantasy voyage" as simply an escape from the entrapments of mental ideas or emotional burdens by either letting our minds go "blank," or by forcing our emotions to exaggerated "speeds and heights" of activity which we use to "explain" a deepened awareness of ourselves, the world, God, nature, etc.

I believe, however, that momentary or even extended lifetime conditions of "metaphysical" awareness and clarity/ simplicity/comprehensiveness of perspective and meaning can be attained with particular potential for this to occur in later adult years for several reasons:

(a)   older adults are often more experienced in a variety of types of mental discipline, and can use the mind at more complex levels of understanding

(b)   more years of religious study can produce heightened sensitivity to the "meaty" arenas of spiritual significance, which pinpoints starting locations and boundaries for extra-sensory or hyper-sensory psychic experiences

(c)   many anxieties and other burdensome cognitive "clutter" have been removed or conquered through the years, so concentrated and purposeful spiritual meditation and experiential attention can evolve

(d)   older adults have more time to devote to "higher levels" of spiritual practice and can pursue the lengthy practice rituals or training exercises which most spiritual leaders insist is necessary rudimentary groundwork to attain "higher" elevations of awareness

(e)   older individuals may have achieved the earlier developmental spiritual tasks represented in horizontal awareness, so have a more solid foundation for advanced growth and understanding which is not interrupted by the need to integrate and explain some "lower level" facts, principles or configurations of ideas

(f) maturing adults may become more motivated to reach for more enlightened states of "being" because of boredom or achievement of other life tasks, a developmental need to continue upward growth to the most sophisticated types of mental/spiritual exercises, or because of fear of death and the hereafter which stimulates greater effort to perceive oneness/safety with spiritual symbols or to enrich our emotional sensations to "realize" more significance and value in life before the "apparent end" materializes.

One of the major problems, however, for all aging individuals relative to this form of change and "enrichment," is that it may, in fact, never actually occur for many women or men. One view of this possible nonoccurrence, of course, is that we do not "lose" anything if we remain unaware of its existence and satisfy ourselves, to the greatest extent possible, with physical, emotional or spiritual achievements at lower hierarchical rungs of various "developmental ladders." Another human potential viewpoint would disagree with this "incarcerational" attitude, and suggest that birth, life, and death only have relevance if each of us uses every form and volume of energy possible to attain the deepest, widest, highest and most profound levels of spiritual understanding and visionary proficiency possible, not only as an individual personal growth benefit, but also as a religious, cultural or social responsibility to teach others how to also reach their full potentials, and to share the spirit and exultation obtained from these "peak" experiences with other sojourners. In light of this potential "paradise lost," I will briefly note some of the primary reasons which are under our control by which we may negate the highest levels of enlightened awareness and vision from the religious or spiritual experiences of our later years:

-- we convince ourselves that our minds are too tired to do the "visionary work,"

-- we payed little attention to "religion" in younger years and lack fundamental knowledge and practice skills to pursue "advanced understanding," and we feel we cannot "catch up" now, or learn new ideas,

-- we become too preoccupied with health, economic, or other matters and lose sight of our souls,

-- we accept some societal definitions of the incompetence of "old people" and decide we are helpless and incapable of the highest levels of psychic or spiritual achievement,

-- we feel we are "old-fashioned" and judge "metaphysical" practice to be a "quirk" of younger, misguided generations which is impractical for the world of "yesterday" where we still view ourselves to be residing,

-- we are uncomfortable, embarrassed or frightened to learn new awareness or perceptual skills, and become reluctant to ask spiritual leaders or consultants for help,

-- we concentrate on destructive images of death and feel enlightenment will not help or is an illusional "waste of time,"

-- we decide that other people don't care what happens to us, so we confirm their judgments and decide not to care either to "punish them" and feel sorry for ourselves as some form of "glorious suffering,"

-- we notice some cognitive declines in mental sharpness, memory efficiency, and creative insight and assume we are unable to accomplish complex and optimistic goals with our minds in any areas,

-- we measure "life" by the chronologic time of our present culture, and "states of being" by the physical parameters we can see, and therefore, relinquish exploratory theories about other realms of time, space, and "living" which are not supported by practical evidence,

-- we rely too much on the "church organization" and its limited "activities" as the guidon for spiritual life, and fail to muster the independence and courage to go beyond person-mode religious "structures" to the deeper or broader meanings of spiritual identity,

-- we forget about the suffering of other people in the world who are spiritually malnourished or ignorant, and have lost sight of our responsibility to God and fellow humanity to help others grow and "see the light" through our own modeling of enlightened spiritual and religious development.

3. Psychological Changes

Although every one of us experiences a wide range of psychological and emotional changes at various life stages, those alterations that confront us during the mature adult years can be particularly important for several reasons. In one instance, our physical and social modulations may provide confrontational (crisis-like) stimuli to disrupt long-time feeling structures which obscured particular fears or desires, either because we felt satisfied and safe in "matching" feeling states to life activities, or because our routine lifestyles represented organized thoughts and perceptions with controlled energy investments so that unconscious or alternate ideations had little opportunity or pressure to emerge into our day to day awareness. When either condition develops, we may change in the context of trying to handle crises with new emotional or intellectual approaches, or may become more resolved to retain our familiar psychological framework, and expend more effort in the direction of insuring social stability, or discovering ways to become less aware/responsive/impacted by what we might consider more extraneous aspects of physical living.

In other instances, we may arrive at natural or personally engineered "locations" of emotional development that logically "assume" and necessitate the creation or new awareness (for us) of fresh ideas, to stimulate our mind's needs for "differentiation," or new combinations of feelings or thoughts that "authorize" behaviors or energy thrusts which can potentially result in unachieved outcomes or achievements in our lives. In some cases, we may evaluate or present "feelings about our feelings" and decide on the need for greater depth, fervor, clarity, "propitiousness," comprehensiveness, tranquility, etc. as a consequence of boredom with previously attained qualities, or we might define gaps in our life missions or destinies which we are "fundamentally" now ready to tackle, and which may be unattainable without alterations of our perspectives as psychological "perceptual sets" that can now be constructed from previously attained "knowledge," plus wisdom to interact new learning which resides in the future.

Whether psychological changes are responsive to other external conditions, or to inner needs to expand/contract/broaden/narrow, etc., it is important for us to anticipate varying types of psychological stimulus-conditions that may impact us, and to plan ahead to insure that we make the most out of all internally or externally motivated contingencies that materialize.

(1)   Emptiness and Isolation

One of the most difficult psychological phenomena for any of us to explain or deal with is the horrible psychic pain which usually accompanies various types of social losses in our lives. When we are no longer fully engaged in "meaningful" employment or family caretaking, when a loved one dies and our adequacy and importance are no longer connected to this "system" of interactions, when we experience social discrimination and disinterest in our ideas or other contributions, or when our "physiology" becomes unreliable or weak or otherwise "unfriendly" as a complement to our mental images of happiness/success--we may discover psychological feelings of "spaciness," decreased perceived "electrical energy," absence of new ideas or "sparks" to push our emotions into a future "anticipatory mode," disconnection of harmony between "inputs" and "outcomes," serious cognitive questions of the reason for living or for more specific activities, loss of pleasured satisfaction with the completion of projects, longings for company or interactive relationships to fill seemingly "empty spots" in our personalities, and general loss or dissemination of physical energy and spiritual excitation in approach to most life activities. Although no one can pinpoint exactly what transpires in any psychological state, or how thoughts and behaviors are associated in ways that "seem" like they produce sensations in our "hearts" or deep "inner selves" which reside in some special receptacle of "place" within our most profound configuration of the self, we all agree that these "feelings" exist and represent obstacles for many of us in concluding on a daily, weekly, yearly or lifetime basis that we are happy, fulfilled, satisfied or at peace with ourselves and the world.

The solutions to these "emptiness" types of problems run the gamut from rearranging our mental perspectives or adding new concepts to generate external productivity-type activities in what some gerontologists call the "life-events model" of adaptation; to more existential and seemingly "passive" approaches to change only our inner mental realities to make ourselves feel more whole or complete (subjective well-being model). Beginning with the more socially "productive" approaches, I will suggest several psychological strategies to help confront and change the negative emotions we encounter related to feelings of emptiness and isolation. I will conclude this list with more "auto-cognitive" mental perspectives to change our outlooks without necessarily altering the external worlds around us.

(a) Perception of "Activity": One reason we feel empty, alone, or isolated in the context of an orientation toward relationships, is that we view ourselves as relatively powerless in possessing stimulative or energizing qualities to attract and retain other people as significant friends. We also see ourselves as primarily "inside ourselves" and view the outside interactive environment as either frightening, or as a secondary place where the most important dynamics of living do not occur. Interactions with others can be interpreted as a realm of reality where we give up part of our "most special selves" to contribute to the welfare of another, yet we can question whether or not this investment ever "returns" in the form of nurturance or the depositing of "growth needs" in us by other people.

One way to help counteract this dilemma, which keeps us away from others, is to try to view the world of emotions and psychological thoughts as a flexible and movable set of "gains" or "pluses" (never minuses or losses) which occur in abundance in the thoughts or energies of all people, and that we grow by visiting this "psychological supermarket" frequently to select the free items we need for our emotional diet at any particular point in time. The "shopping" occurs through repeated attempts on our parts (food never jumps into the grocery basket all by itself) to talk to and be with other people where our inputs identify the particular psycho-emotional "gifts" or "attributes" other people possess; but the "purchasing" is primarily under our control where we can "take charge" of any thought, piece of knowledge, or perception by others of some value in life--and transfer this "public" benefit to our own psychodynamic system to allow ourselves to be filled or enriched by the "fact" we have obtained.

Additionally, we need to recognize that these ideas, concepts, thoughts or representations of some universal "worth" receive added "energy frosting" (who wants cake without icing?) somehow when they are registered in our minds after coming freshly from someone else who has "consecrated" their ideas with a common human emotional spark that retains its energy if we "capture" it while its power is still active as a result of the nurturing it received in someone else's head. This perspective, therefore, entails appreciation of our responsibility to "pick fresh fruits" and use them immediately, it suggests that ideas and mental processes can transcend particular physical bodies where they are housed, it posits an exchangeable energy field between people that can be added to each idea or thought to enhance conceptual value--but the energy regenerates itself with each new contact we establish, and it finally says that we can never lose anything from this process--but only gain inner fullness with each new psycho-item we obtain.

Empty holes in our psychological system of ideas about the value and significance of life are, therefore, filled with thoughts from others about life, which we change into our newly learned awarenesses, and choose to allow ourselves to be nourished by evaluating the quality and amount of new perceptions which are added to our understanding of the world, where the "quality" is enhanced relative to the human care and love which has been used by "original owners" down through the generations to embellish ideas or thoughts about what was, is or could be.

(b) Interpersonal "Contracting": Sometimes we find ourselves alone and feeling empty, not so much because we feel others have nothing to offer or they have exclusive "ownership" rights of potential gifts (as in the first example), but because our psychological "mind set" sees patterns of relationships which do not contain solid connective linkages of mutual need-meeting responsibility, and our perceptions additionally relegate our role as "negotiators" for emotional satisfaction to a very peripheral or even nonexistent function within inter-personal networks. In these cases, we are frequently "empty" because we have not indicated to others that we need something from them, we often feel that there is little or no joint expectation for us to contribute our psychological strengths, and we lack appreciation of the complex, yet frequently effective, "process" of discussing commitments and emotional roles in an effort to form a "team" to work together for collective emotional satisfaction. In some cases, we fail to conceptualize this association because we feel insignificant, irresponsible or weak, or sometimes have been hurt in the past and do not trust others to "come through" for us. In cases where we do feel some self-worth, however, we lack faith in human "machines" with interconnected parts and cannot "envision" images of emotional "deals," or overlapping feelings that somehow "unite" to form a more solid "whole" than existed before two people "touched" one another with dialogue that does carry a contractual "glue" to provide reliability and security for both participants.

The message for us, here, is to be honest with others about the missing or undernourished parts of our egos, and to simultaneously encourage them to share their expectations of strengths we possess which might be of help to them. We must change our focus from distinct images of separate identities to include a somewhat "blurred melting" of the two together which forms a stronger union, requires continual dialogue to maintain the integration, and yet allows each individual to maintain a separate and whole person for other areas of personal life and growth.

(c)   "Vicarious" Sharing: Another way to rearrange our psychological feelings and focused perspective when we find ourselves in an "emptiness modality" is to view part of our personality make up and approach as "passive" and somewhat "spongelike" in our need to soak up the energies and become enthused about life by carefully and intensely witnessing the activities of others and "vacuuming" their emotional payoffs into our own "needy unfurnished emotional rooms" in our psychological "home." We can vicariously tap into the energies of others by observing movies, attending art galleries, watching sporting events, listening to excited conversations, reading moving novels, attending classes, etc. Although others may expect input from us, or greater growth and pleasure may be possible with heightened investment of external operational "manipulation" or active use and movement of our ideas and behaviors, we can still manage to "believe" ourselves to be filled by "imagining" the presence of external symbolic representations of parental warmth, love, personal value, social significance, etc. (which are "corporealized" in the actions of others where they are deriving warmth and value from life). After attaining this form of perceptual completeness, we may advance our cause even further by defining the "content," meaning, or message of what we have observed in others and either expending energy to overcome our unconscious resistance and "winning" this idea for our very own, or adding other thoughts to expand a unitary "concept" into a multivariate construct at a more abstract level of understanding, thereby giving birth to a growing and developing seedling idea.

The way to insure that this system does not break down eventually, is to remain active as a spectator of numerous different types of "life dramatizations" and to do the best we can to rid ourselves of previously learned, and culturally socialized ideations which, we must believe, subjectively and non-authoritatively tell us that human fulfillment can only come in its most significant format, through relatively equivalent interactions with other people. We must force ourselves to believe that one-way interactions are not irresponsible, that "emotional consumerism" does produce definitive results within the psyche, and that sufficient nurturance can be obtained in this fashion to substantially reduce or avert any negative self-impaired impressions of emotional emptiness.

(d) Existential "Autonomy": The approach which coincides with theory's "subjective well-being" model of adaptation begins with the assumption that the primary and even exclusive locus of human life and its full range of meanings exists in each human mind and set of individualized, selective perceptions which are formulated through controlled as well as extemporaneous "feedback" from the environment of our physical and social existences, and maintained by the self-selected values we place on the active or passive "verbs" of living, the "nouns" to define what exists, and the "adjectives" to differentiate levels of quality. Our happiness and sense of fulfillment comes either from (1) total acceptance of our present condition of "being," as all, and only, that which can occur at each moment of time over which we have little control other than appreciation and compliance with what "is," (2) from our forceful removal of internalized perception of external stimuli and stressors from subjective culture to the extent that goals and objectives are selected from our own array of meaningful events for personal satisfaction, or from (3) our choice of selected stimulus and response interactions with the external world whereby all outcomes are defined as positive relative to our learning from them, and all inputs reflect self-actualization of our right to "engage" the world and produce fulfillment from the energy and "intrinsic pleasure and peace" of "action" all by itself.

Any empty feelings occur, therefore, because we are clinging to delusional or unnecessary thoughts or feelings which remove our power and natural esteem acquired at birth, or because we have "bought into" the socialized concepts of "fear" and "negativity" and "loss" and therefore allow "external forces" to condition behaviors which we do not enjoy and which contain person-made "grades" of various degrees of goodness and badness which, when we fit into "bad" categories, causes us to believe we have lost something (social approval, dignity, power, self-control, etc.).

When we begin to feel isolated, additionally, this is interpreted to mean that we are alienated from awareness of our valuable or "irrelevant" nature and basic existence as non-substantive and changing forms of life energy, and that resolution of negative or alone feelings comes from (1) conceptualizing there is no such thing as "negative," and that all is always positive or neutral, (2) that all we can be is "alone," and that there is no reality to represent "connections" between people or wants except as we "make believe it is there" and (3) our responsibility is to take charge of our minds and formulate only helpful and fulfilling conceptions of a world of peace and harmony, and that we are "filled with ourselves" when we make realistic goals and accomplish them, or make unrealistic goals and enjoy the process of competition with resistance in us and others to accomplish various tasks.

(2)   Depression

According to most research studies and reports of clinical counseling with older adults, depression is a serious problem affecting, to some extent, approximately 30-65% of people over the age of 65, with 10-15% of these sufferers experiencing severe symptoms, and with higher rates for women. This rate may even be higher because some of the symptoms are similar to those of senile dementia (cognitive deterioration and slowing of the brain) or alzheimer's disease, so the problem may be "masked" in some persons who are diagnosed as having primarily physical problems rather than the psychophysiologic-social condition of depression. In some cases, of course, "depressive pseudo dementia" may occur where cognitive impairment and ego-defensive depression may occur simultaneously. Various studies, as would be expected, have linked depression to a wide range of "causative" or associational factors, including worry and distress over physical illnesses, bereavement over lost loved ones (although some studies suggest this type of depression is less severe), poverty and economic constraints, social and geographic isolation from mainstream life, personal and family life stresses, dependency, and a host of others. In thinking about depression as a set of coordinated and seemingly "functional" efforts to adapt to threats to our self-esteem, we must remember that depression is not simply sadness or grief, but is a psychological "defense" mechanism learned early in life whereby we blame parents (correctly or incorrectly) for our unfulfilled desires to feel safe and adequate (as a result of our dependency on them as relatively helpless children for many years). Realizing our inability to meet our own needs and our reliance on "authority" figures to "validate" our positive identity, we decide not to express anger openly to them for fear of their withdrawal or retaliation which we observe through culturally approved parental "judgments" and "punishments" of children, so we try to punish ourselves to correct personal deficits (which "should" have produced needed parental love in the first place) and attack ourselves with ego-deflating (but presumed rehabilitative) denegrating feelings. The more this does not work, the more angry with ourselves we become, because the unconscious "child" in our minds retains this erroneous productivity formula (which parallels learned social "work" roles) since permission for conscious contradictory reality about our strength and independence to enter awareness is never granted because it does not allow the "fearful" person to be irresponsibly but safely "connected" to parents through strong feelings, and would further demand that we face an uncertain outside world which we learned, as children, was potentially harmful to us.

When this devastating internalized feeling of depression attacks on an acute or chronic basis in older adulthood, there are several steps we can take which should ideally accompany formal therapeutic help to ourselves to get unstuck and grow:

Anti-Depressive Step 1:   Refuse to be socially isolated, where depression will feed itself without inter-ruption, and insist on people or some form of external "interdictive" stimu-lation to enter your life. Discuss your depressed feelings with as many other people as possible, and write down/ practice their suggestions for changing your pattern.

Anti-Depressive Step 2:   Remember that the depressive "cycle" is a self-created irrational "game" in your head, only which no one ever wins, but which you can stop at any time--the conclusions and premises of depressive conceptualizations are always wrong!

Anti-Depressive Step 3:   Realize that external events never "cause" depression, and are only associated with it because we choose to make the mental linkage. "Negative" "anything" only exists because we have attached this qualitative definitional label, and we must remember that "we" are not the "social situation," but remain separate/autonomous observers and evaluators unless we freely "choose" to associate ourselves as "dependent responders" to otherwise external and nonexistent events unless we decide to invest them with life forces that control our destinies.

Anti-Depressive Step 4:   Work hard at identifying your strengths, intrinsic "beauties" invested with our birth-right, and basic value/worth/dignity as human beings, with the conclusion that we need no "rehabilitation" from self- inflicted anger because there is nothing of which we are "guilty" in the first place.

Anti-Depressive Step 5:   Try to accomplish positive, self-selected and attainable goals each day, and review your accomplishments before bed at night. Remember that we don't need to be angry with a "self" which is in charge of itself and trying to grow and learn--make every minute count as your positive celebration of you, even if it means accepting life's pains and disruptions and moving ahead despite the hurdles.

(3) Confusion

The difficulties which many aging people experience in remembering facts from the recent or remote past, understanding complex forms of reasoning or manipulation of ideas, associating and perceiving the relationships between different types of information, relating outcome acts or decisions to antecedent linear inductive or deductive mental logic, doing "hypothetical" and abstract thinking in planning future goals, struggling with the unexplained infusion of new and erroneous (delusional, illusional) "meanings" of life events into previously "stable" and predictable thought patterns, or just generally experiencing "fuzzy," distant, "changing," or unfamiliar "awarenesses" of the world around us--all are forms of mental confusion which create psychological as well as cognitive problems in adaptation. The predominant causes of mental confusion, which affect each of us to different degrees, and some of us hardly or not at all, are: wearing down or depletion of neurological cell capability, "death" of various organs which are associated with mental functioning, "infectious" disturbances from various disease activities with various viral or autoimmune effects, debilitating outcomes relating to childhood genetic coding deficits inherited from parents, perceptual problems in reception of information through declining visual/auditory/sensory apparatus, central nervous system "underarousal" and functional slowing which accompanies years of "use" of our biological systems, and attention/interest/preference choices whereby we select to "tune out" various stimuli in our environment--either because we are bored or habituated to it, or are "tuning in" to some other areas of inner or outer awareness. Of course, confusion can also be related socially to our presence in new or unfamiliar environments, interactions with individuals who possess different intelligence abilities or "thinking" formats from ours, communicational or language style mismatches, excessive cautiousness on our part because of psychological fears, or lack of prior experience with particular thought or action "tasks" in which we are currently engaged relative to accomplishment or problem resolution. The above processes which are represented by symptoms of confusion can be called senile dementia, alzheimer's disease, medication side effects, neurological lesions, malnutrition, psychopathology, depression, or psychosis.

In dealing with various forms of mental confusion and differential degrees of impairment, we must all keep in mind that confused thinking is usually not a totally encompassing "blanket" that covers all aspects of our cognitive and emotional process. In fact, part of our mental activity in "observing" the confusion taking place, and typically responding with more "confusion about the confusion," is that we might experience anger and disappointment at this "loss," crisis-oriented fear of the end results of this unpredictable deterioration, and generally lowered self-esteem at declining "competencies" which we previously used to confirm and evaluate the quality of the "self." This perceived progressive disability can also be associated with, or even cause problems of family instability, diminished competencies at work or "productivity" tasks, sexual dissatisfaction, major depressions, increased "awareness" and presumption of approaching "death," reduced self-control and ability to manage one's affairs, actual or feared "institutionalization," and disconnection with the stabilizing and identity-confirming memories of the past.

As we all "witness" and "evaluate" the differences between past, present and idealized processes of using our minds to define reality, figure out conceptual and pragmatic problems, assign qualitative values to ideas, and seek fulfillment in creative and useful functions--we can suffer mild, moderate, or even extreme psychological pain as we apply various "negative" connotations to these insidious occurrences, try to "fight" against the "losses" we believe are materializing, or modify self-conceptions "downward" to "accept" life outcomes which seem to suggest we must occupy some physical and symbolic state of human unworthiness as part of the "culmination" of lifelong "growth"(?). Rather than rebel or give up our search for meaningful lives, partly channeled through our mental "computers," there are some self-enhancing and "rehabilitative" steps we can take to delay, redefine, or improve on some degrees of the various forms of confusion which appear.

(Ways to Deal With Mental Confusion)

#1: Initially with the first signs of onset, seek competent, gerontologic medical consultations for a thorough assessment of diet, brain waves (EEG's), disease pathology, psychological distress, vision, hearing cardiovascular activity and other neurologically-related functions to attempt to pinpoint the problem. It is advisable to obtain multiple opinions about diagnosis and prognosis, and to be insistent that a comprehensive "team philosophy" be utilized to afford you every possible "assessment perspective" plus as many options to improve functioning as possible. Do not be too willing to accept opinions which simplistically relegate problems to "old age," particularly if the medical consultant seems unable or reluctant to suggest "delaying," rehabilitative or reanimative exercises or procedures. <u>Something can be done in almost every case.</u>

#2: Learn about the problems of memory loss, neurological decline and cognitive confusion by reading professionally sanctioned articles, books or self-help pamphlets, and additionally contact community information and referral agencies to learn about the existence of private self-help groups, health-care agency "targeted programs," or university research studies where you can volunteer to participate for educational as well as experimental or service-receipt purposes.

#3: Try to document (you may need a friend or family member to help with observations) the circumstances, times, locations, moods, mental attitudes, topical areas, relationship dynamics, or "stressors" which seem most associated with the majority of confusions you experience. The help of a counselor or psychotherapist may also contribute to "ruling out" or correcting causal factors related to your motivation or loss of interest relative to particular life issues, depression or low self-esteem which has dissipated your physical as well as emotional cognitive energies, manipulative efforts on your part to appear "helpless" when you want attention or feel the need for more "control" in life, social system stresses or pressures which cause confusion as a defense mechanism to "check out" of fearful interactions or as a reflection of overwhelming anxiety related to your social role and significance in relationships with others, or even insensitive persistence of "different" or "unfamiliar" communications from others in our lives who are really talking and thinking a "different language" without helping us to understand and participate more successfully.

#4: Work very hard to <u>accept</u> the inevitable fact that you and many other older men and women in your age range are experiencing changes in "thinking patterns"; and try to avoid interpreting this process as a crisis, which usually compounds the problem and causes greater mental confusion and distress. When we become afraid of an unknown, "disordered," or perplexing "future," psychic anxiety further interferes with logical and planful information processing, and diminishes the cognitive and experiential strengths we do possess, which can produce some positive results of thinking that would make us feel less threatened and

more emotionally secure. We must be at peace and in a state of harmony with our minds, which means "allowing" fluctuation or variability
which we cannot control, and defining this "condition" of our being as
a temporary passage or time-out period which must occur, but will not
directly harm us, and probably will cause little indirect or consequential
destructiveness if we learn to "wait it out" or ask others around us for
help when we feel uncertain or confused. Obviously those seriously
advanced states of dementia will not abate, and we will require
"custodial" support on a permanent basis, although learning to "roll with
the punches" earlier in our mature adult years may even help us to
relax and be more at peace with these final stages of mental
transformation.

#5: By anticipating periodic confusions in our daily, weekly, or monthly
futures, we usually can structure and organize our "thinking lives" to
help "compensate" for many of the mild or moderate "losses" or declines
which occur. We cannot only train ourselves as self-monitors to understand the types of information we forget, or the misinterpretations we
characteristically make, etc. (which also has some therapeutic effect in
helping us feel more in "control" and knowledgeable of our "selves");
but we can teach ourselves "functional" behaviors within modified
"friendly" environments to make coping a much more predictable outcome. Improving "performance" in areas of cognition and mental
decision-making, therefore, can encompass all of the following actions:

a.   arranging our immediate living environment to represent simplicity,
     organization, accessibility of information, logical maintenance of
     data, and planful activities to provide consistency and sensibility to
     our daily tasks;

b.   developing personal "logs" or guidelines to remind ourselves of
     typical stressful events that we "permit" to negatively influence our
     thought patterns, and detailing stress reduction or therapeutic
     actions we can take to control anxiety and calmly "weather the
     storms" of mental declines which disrupt our intrapsychic equilib-
     rium;

c.   taking steps to learn to "rehearse" or practice the recollection and
     utilization of significant old or new thoughts or behaviors, which
     includes using our minds to establish mental discipline,
     cross-referencing memory capability, recollective proficiency

through prioritization and "valuation" exercises, development of energized imagery to highlight facts, language corroboration of conceptual ideations, elaboration techniques, comfortable and organized techniques for exploring and learning new ideas, retroactive "reliving" of positive past events to more permanently "seat" them in current memory banks, and finally, employment of abstract thinking to apply "principles" of past "forgettable" facts to presently "rememberable" events or more recent principles of living ("inferentially derived knowledge");

d.   implementing the comprehensive use of note-taking and written recording and review of pertinent information (along with exercises in verbal recitation and use of "mnemonic" memory aids) to teach ourselves sound practices of information "retrieval" and storage to counteract "processing" deficits;

e.   developing generalized knowledge through current study and educational efforts not only to stimulate dormant or declining neurological functions, but to provide a pool of information to "anchor" us in the present, and to use as "bridges" of experience and "crystalized intelligence" to update past information and supply stimulating energy to our present facts and ideas;

f.   formulating and using "life scripts" or scenarios to denote "attentional" areas of importance to us, and to exclude irrelevant information or extraneous/confusing environmental "noise" to help simplify the range and quality of information we need or wish to remember or utilize;

g.   carrying out mental "simulation" exercises to utilize thoughts or ideas in hypothetical decision-making situations, which helps us improve our knowledge "utilization" skills, plus helps identify behavioral outcome indicators to help measure the successful completion of singular or "serial" forms of mental processing;

h.   finally, developing awareness of the importance of seeking help from others to speak slowly and clearly, to organize their ideas, to test us on recollections, to stimulate and expect us to use our minds, and to not become impatient with frequent questions which we can ask to help "stabilize" us in some semblance of correct/verifiable current reality and to corroborate various "truths" which we may correctly or incorrectly believe to exist.

(4)   Emotional Harmony and Simplicity

In some cases, the physical, economic, and social changes which accompany aging can add excessive emotional overload to the concurrently existing struggle to explore and discover/ rediscover meaning and fulfillment in a life which is "slowing down," becoming "unproductive" according to many community standards, and approaching a "final" destiny which most of us have learned to view as a frightening, painful, sorrowful loss in the physical world we know, and an uncertainty or potential reward in the hereafter. Some of us may fight getting old by trying to increase the frequency of activity to make ourselves believe we are young, or young at heart; we may become frightened and pull closer to familiar surroundings/possessions/loved ones to re-enter the safety of the maternal "nest" or womb. We may attach greater meaning to particular activities, and downplay others to get the most out of our time remaining. Or finally, we may allow ourselves to become sullen, depressed, isolated or confused as a symbolic punishment of ourselves and resentment of the world which has placed us as innocent victims in this volatile life-death conceptual dilemma. In the former cases, our thoughts and attitudes may seem scattered, our activities may take on a pressured or even frenzied nature, or we may rigidly adhere to past or present "principles" of living to make us comfortable and simultaneously exclude any newly uncomfortable "input" about life, which has to be integrated into our concepts of "self" to give assurance of our purpose and value in a full or immediate spectrum of existence. This often represents a discordant array of conflictual feelings which constitute a "formula of life" with multiple definitions of right/wrong, good/bad, valuable/worthless, etc. that have come from many different psychological, social and cultural base camps which frequently maintain different assumptions about truth, beauty, value and quality. These ideas may have been previously amalgamated and interdigitated into a package of coexistence through the use of our illogical mental "gymnastics," and the movement of ideas in and out of conscious/unconscious awareness so that contradictory images would not bump into one another, with rigidity in formulating life rules and contrasts which focused attention on a limited set of "principles of righteousness" while excluding others from behavioral manifestation and concomitant mental reflection.

The "withdrawal" or depressive forms of handling "life-passage" conflicts do not demonstrate disharmony as blatantly, but nevertheless represent our inability to arrive at a picture of the world and of ourselves where both are "good," where previous interactions are reconciled as representing some positive gain (or at least neutral effect on outcomes), and where we are prepared to move into any future "life form" with hope, a sense of completion of previous developmental tasks, and optimism concerning the energies or "influences" we have bequeathed to the world or its people who previously touched our lives.

The message in either "active or passive" forms of struggle to adapt and maintain viability, is that we may fail to achieve varying degrees of simple emotional peace and harmony in the struggles between "good and bad" inner personal characteristics we learned to identify in childhood, and had reinforced or redefined throughout our adult lives; and in the struggles to "match up" inner desirable states of existence or permanent "selfhood" and less permanent but strongly indicative outer behaviors which symbolically tell others (who tell us in return) that who we are is okay. Of course, the search for peace of mind, or ecstasied nirvana, coherent enlightenment has entertained the perspectives of philosophies forever, and has, and will continue to serve as the perpetual "carrot" for all people (including venerated spiritualists, thinkers, and gurus) for all time as we currently know or imagine it to exist. Although none of us is probably Christ, the Buddha, Gandhi, etc., we all have equal right and potential access to psycho-emotional harmony, and can pursue several important growth steps to increase the probability of nearing this goal:

(Approaches to Psychological Harmony)

*   Initially remember that everything we think about is probably influenced greatly by previous socially-guided learning in our childhood and younger adult lives. Remember also that many aspects of society are fraught with oppositional controversy and strife, and that person-to-person, or

person-to-environment tranquility and concord are often
assured only through the establishment of authoritative
monitoring (including punishment of violations) of codified
<u>rules</u> and structured laws.

*   Consider the parallels between "social unrest" and our internal
psychological struggles for "peace of mind," and note that the
problem usually arises when two apparently distinctive viewpoints of concepts of the "<u>truth</u>" relative to "needed satisfactions" <u>collide,</u> and are also "cemented" more firmly when
either proponent becomes fearful of <u>losing</u> status or <u>esteem</u>.
The resolution of controversial "issues" generally evolves when
a third party of permanent or temporary superior (parent-
like) power or status presents a separate "reality perspective"
that (a) either combines the previous alternate conceptions
by modifying each somewhat so that everyone "wins" something, (b) presents a new idea at some higher level of abstraction which changes the "rewards of punishments" which were
previously considered or (c) convince the antagonists that
their "worlds" do not really intersect, and assures them of no
"loss" by re-establishing firm attitudinal boundaries, and
resuming unilateral focus and need-meeting energy on
"self-centered" needs and internal resources to singularly,
rather than cooperatively, arrange necessary satisfactions.

*   Understand that the world is composed of the <u>content</u>
(nouns) of <u>what</u> we think about, and the <u>process</u> (verbs) of
<u>how</u> we think about it, and "act" (behave) to make thoughts
"come true."   In this regard the "content" supports the
"process" and vice versa to such an extent that we eventually
believe or "know" that both "must" be correct interpretations
of the world.   Therefore the most trusted pathway and
guiding light to assuage fears of the unknown and to produce
"competencies" is to control the environment which may be
a potential enemy, or to build individual talents to create
satisfactions for being us. As long as we believe we know the
best of anything, we have narrowed our adaptive options, and
place ourselves in potential positions of discord when new
data confronts us in our interactions with the external world,
or as alternative truth emerges from our unconscious mind
which we created from our own neurological energies, or

incorporated from observations of the world around us, but were unaware of its presence prior to some immediate conflict which stimulated its utilization (like a relief pitcher in baseball).

* Sometimes the ideas or "facts" we believe about ourselves (or others/the world) seem to be "in charge" of our identities, and therefore are assumed to represent, fully, the degrees of balance or personality integration we do or do not experience. The "truth," therefore, appears to be our "childish" minds to inherently signify what "is" in the world, and also how it became significant as though the "decision function" of personality "equals" the knowledge (content) we possess (D = K). This can be misleading as we seek to arrive at new levels of existential harmony in our minds, because we can forge that there is an "executive function" or distinct decision-making "domain" of our personality makeup which can rise above the ideas we possess, to actually control what we believe, to change the meanings of various facts to make them compatible with other important and contiguous ideas we develop, to integrate two or more separate thoughts into an overarching and holistic concept that blends divergencies, or to even "conceal" an incorrect or outdated "piece" of "verity" from total existence in or even outside our minds if we so desire.

* Greater harmony comes, therefore, by "taking charge" of our "subjective" minds; reducing tension between ideas that represent "contradictory" needs by realizing that satisfaction comes from the "process" of deciding, and not exclusively from what the outcome decision (fact) appears to be; and understanding that the creation of new and less narrow or constricting ideas allows the coexistence of formerly disparate "realities" under a more accepting "broad conceptual umbrella" which does not pressure us to rigidly believe any truth as an absolute. We can achieve greater psychological harmony by also realizing that our learned perceptions of "loss" are only symbols and representational images of negative internal psychic states that may not exist in any capacity, except when we believe they exist (e.g., try to measure the part of your personality which actually leaves your body when you are insulted by someone

else), and decide to "validate" their existence with arbitrarily chosen external behaviors (does a kiss really equal the concept of love?). Harmony comes from cleaning out our mental "attic" of ideas or beliefs about who we are/were/might be, which contain resident negative values or energies which presented themselves initially as reactions from other people within various "social" contexts, but do not stand as authoritative analysis or judgment of our inner "psycho-spiritual" worlds.

*   Harmony between the inner personalities we possess who symbolize archaic struggles between independent and parent-controlled dependent children ("Good and Evil") can also develop as we realize that these childhood skirmishes are expanded throughout life to "infect" our potentially compatible and coexistent values and ideas, so that our "philosophical perspectives" become proxy combatants rather than the more frightening "personalities" we envision as inside ourselves. We must work hard to remember that all we can be (most likely) is a singular entity or being who "could be conceived" as totally adequate on the basis of "existence" alone, rather than subdimensional outcomes of separate people we can "become." Our singular selves can integrate a phenomenal range of concepts, ideas or facts in our minds, which only rupture into schism when we give one "notion" a higher priority than another. One dilemma, of course, is how to survive in a world where "productivity," accomplishment, and conformity have material-ized to control a presumed threatening and "passive" environment, and our social and economic survival generally require some prioritization of activities and ideas. The answer to this "roadblock" to harmony is to remember that socially adaptive protocol is possibly an arbitrary, subjective and artificial "solution" to a "problem" which may not exist in the form we envision, but which continues to be defined relative to our "answers" which are perpetuated through family enculturation and societal norms/laws. This lifelong journey to "fit in," therefore, may only be a game we play with one another, where differences have sadly become one of the rules or foundation principles to allow us to play. Psycho-emotional harmony can emerge as we put "society" in proper perspective, and focus more closely on the similarities, compatibilities, and unification of separate thoughts and behaviors, which may only represent different (not better or worse) routes to the same goal--acceptance and love of ourselves and others.

(5) Fear

Advanced age often ushers in a host of both realistic and fantasized fears and apprehensions which not only produce varying degrees of unrewarding cautiousness (which often contributes to corollary negative outcomes that confirm the anticipatory fear), but also necessitate psychological and social "defense" mechanisms to control anxiety, avoid or distort uncomfortable thoughts, separate us from people or situations which we believe are harmful to our tender inner feelings, or "act out" symbolic representations of trepidations by becoming physically ill, manipulating others, acting helpless, fabricating "reality," or "giving up" hope and emotional motivation. Whether the fear is reasonable, or represents unconscious conflict, we still experience psychic pain and emotional distress which can continue for indefinite time periods to the point that "fearful lifestyles" incubate for many older citizens.

The strategy and tactics for eliminating large portions of either real or imagined "anticipatory intimidations or alarms" are generally the same, although deep-seated irrational conflicts typically necessitate more complicated procedures of developmental analysis, confrontation, therapeutic support, and massive relearning about the "self" and its relationship to past, present, or future life events. The following suggestions, however, can provide a basic foundation to attack the germinal ideologic precursors of fears in our minds, plus the more external behavioral "outcome potentials" which produce direct negative results in the form of physical dangers or harm, and/or serve as self-fulfilling prophesies to fuel our apprehensions and make us believe that "emotional malevolence" has also arrived "on the scene."

Anti-Fear Tactic #1:   Talk openly (emotional catharsis) about your misgivings and worries, so that other people can offer emotional support and share common anxieties, and to provide an opportunity for "corrective information" to

supercede assumptions based on our ignorance or inexperience in certain life situations.

Anti-Fear Tactic #2:   Make sure you purposefully choose future
tasks or activities (regardless of whether a
particular event is a high or low priority)
to dispel fears of "loss of control," rather
than becoming involved to please others,
or through inadvertent happenstance.
Personal "power" also comes from planning
the details and specific itinerary of
activities, which we should view as
"beginnings" of personal development
sequences of integrated events, to help
build stronger "chains" of emotional
motivations to "break through" the often
strongly linked "entourage" of frightening
perceptions of physical and emotional
danger and loss.

Anti-Fear Tactic #3:   Research a new activity, person, idea or
philosophy to reduce its uncomfortable
unknown dimensions, and explore our past
lives to recollect similar types of "images"
with which we coped, in an effort to update
our self-perceptions of mastery in dealing
with "unknowns" or "previously-knowns-but-
forgottens."   Knowledge is a powerful
immunization against fear, and the use of
our minds to "supercede" aversive stimuli
by "dissecting" them into smaller component
parts, or "merging" them with higher
abstract goals and principles is an important process of "manipulation" which
reminds us we are in charge of a great
deal of our own reality.

Anti-Fear Tactic #4:   Always remind ourselves that fearful "consequences" exist in the future, and that the
most uncomfortable aspects of "dreaded

outcomes" are actually emotional "domains" which do not actually even exist, and that events (even painful ones) that materialize usually do so without the attached feeling of fear or apprehension. If we can use our minds to objectively explore and hypothesize about potential future dangers, and then return to the present to plan strategies and experience current positive feelings, we will avoid the "rehearsal" phenomena which builds increasing layers of negative anticipations that cause us to avoid or certainly not to enjoy many activities in our lives.

Anti-Fear Tactic #5:   We should also work hard to organize our surroundings in sensible ways to reduce the potential for real negative outcomes (burglars, injurious falls, being alone away from home) through the use of professional consultations (police security experts, fire marshalls to note hazards, etc.), our own checklists to remind ourselves of safety precautions, and the inclusion of groups of friends in some activities that are unfamiliar, or take us to environmental locations where hazards exist (dark streets in crime-infested neighborhoods). We can arrange furniture and objects in our homes to minimize the risk of "interference" with our movements; we can seek the assistance of many free social programs to help us arrange special conveniences or safety devices for residences (special utensils to help arthritic hands use the stove, access ramps to porches, etc.); we can learn special physical rehabilitative exercises to improve balance, hand-eye coordination, leg and arm strength, etc., and we can even take learning courses to help us change or improve our "perceptual awarenesses" of various psychic and physical "realities" to broaden our potential to "see" dangers ahead of time and take necessary, anxiety-reducing precautionary actions (broadening vision scope in driving classes, learning about criminal patterns and motivation from sociologists' university or community lectures, etc.). In these cases, we reduce the ratio between personal competence levels, and environmental demands as risks.

Anti-Fear Tactic #6:   A final piece of advice for use in all previous tactics is to try to become personally confident and assertive in all areas of life. One way to begin is to develop awareness of conceptual, intellectual, spiritual, physical or functional skill vulnerabilities or "gaps" in our personalities which cause us to assume reactive, passive, dependent, controlled or otherwise "inept" postures when confronted with difficult or frightening life circumstances. With an accompanying "problem-solving" orientation about every situation we encounter, we can begin to use newly developed strengths (especially mental and emotional ones) with the confidence we gained as experienced life travelers, and realize that almost every dilemma in life has a solution, and is only frightening when we allow its "aura and demeanor" to overshadow our determination and willpower to survive and "conquer" the real and "assumed" obstacles in life. We need to "risk" failure, of course, to experience most worthwhile outcomes in life, and can even reduce the "trauma" we expect with graduated rehearsals and exposures to various events we feel will overwhelm us if they "catch" us unaware and unprepared (e.g., practicing what we would do to stand up, assess injury, and seek help after a fall in our homes); or trying different assertive sentences to return a defective product to a resistant and belligerent store clerk--(if these were events which "made" us afraid). As an addendum to relinquishing fearful attitudes, we should also eliminate friends from our lives who are timid, weak-willed or excessively direful, and try to associate with those who continually try to build personal and behavioral foundations of strength, self-confidence, and enthusiasm about involvement in all aspects of living.

(6)   Productive Emotionality and Energy

The trials and tribulations of a long life, soured frequently by painful and debilitating illness, the shame of social discrimination, the seemingly perpetual and crucifying agony in remembering lost loved ones, and the often horrifying trepidations of death can produce aging women and men who are emotionally exhausted, wiped clean of exciting and positively motivating feelings, and void of the psychic and spiritual richness which should, theoretically, be the most vibrant and resplendently gorgeous time when seasoned with the wisdom and experience of later life.

Many of us, under the difficult circumstances of the "aging process," assume lifestyles characterized by mundane and perfunctory "maintenance or survival" behaviors. We stop dreaming and "reaching for the stars," and relegate ourselves to roles of passive observers of life; or historians who boringly recount past events which themselves, in the translation, seem to have "died" and lost much of their significance as emotional flames to enkindle a vibrant immersion in the pulsating life around us in the present time dimension.

As in all other areas of this book, I again believe there are important, emotional life-resuscitation steps we can take to control this mostly "chosen" deterioration, and to actually supercede the emotional "power," fertility, and opulence of the middle or even younger adult/teenage years. Some of the most important emotional enhancement practices are noted in the separate sections which follow:

#1:   Intensify Existing Feelings: Many of us are aware of particular positive or negative "thoughts" that cross our minds throughout the day, but we fail to tap into the energy resources that are contained somehow within the inner essences of these emotional symbols, and therefore, we lose the human and spiritual "potency" of being unified more fully with the life "forces" within our souls, relationships and world ecology. We can feel "alive" by taking time-out of activities or other thought sequences to concentrate, intensely ponder, and piercingly feel the comprehensive fullness of a particular happy or sad emotion, and allow ourselves to become lost or totally absorbed in the totality and depth of this experience. This can sometimes be facilitated by tightening our head or body muscles to exaggerate neuromuscular sensations, by using constant eye-gaze at a specific object to see inside its outer appearance, or alternately relaxing and just "dreaming" quietly about a particular reminiscence or fantasy and allowing our minds to "roam" the full extent of the sensation (e.g., ocean waves crashing on a beach we remember from childhood) to "become" each part of the scene and savor its impact on us. We may certainly feel and or even be morose during these "experiential" moments, but at least we will know we are still alive.

#2:   Uncover Previously Buried Awarenesses: In many instances, the course of life events has taken us behaviorally and emotionally beyond or away from previously satisfying "domains" of conceptual and spiritual self-fulfillment; either because we are no longer in relationships which jointly supported particular life scripts; we become habituated and bored with experiences and moved on to try something new (but did not return to some positive aspects of the past); we were forced to give up valuable emotional "territory" due to fiscal/physical or other environmental contingencies; or we failed to fully recognize the positives of the "rose garden" within which we were standing. In any case, a return to significant feelings from the past can be stimulated by conducting a chronological "life review" of specific events, initially (this can be accomplished by reviewing pictures, diaries, visiting old neighborhoods, creating a reconstructed "calendar" or "time-line" of major occurrences) and then "attaching" associated feelings which come to mind or can be "inferred" (what would I have felt while this event was occurring) into the "behavioral scene." The value of this exercise is evaluative, to compare past and present feelings to determine the extent to which our present emotional life is as potent as it can possibly be, by noting the degrees of qualitative difference between at least two different measurement periods. In some cases, we may "believe" that former "activities" dictated particular desired feelings, and we may decide to reactivate components (modified, slowed or altered frequently to encompass current physical capacities or lifestyle contingencies) of goal-directed thinking, planning, and acting to usher in the various sensations of "fulfillment" which our absented behaviors caused to deteriorate. In other cases, we may surmise that current behaviors are adequate, but conclude that they require significant injections of "psycho-energy" to revitalize their function as conduits into the deeper or higher realms of existence. Sometimes we need to "extrapolate" beyond specific acts to envision their broader, more holistic, or more pronounced "generic" life meaning at a world, cosmic, or heavenly level (when I responsibly take out my garbage, I am using energy to benefit the whole of person kind, or when I perform a little dance step in my apartment, I am encouraging all dancers everywhere to "create," or I am fulfilling my highest destiny as a "biologic symphony" to express the nature of God, etc.); and assess the qualitative outcome relative to previous "peak experiences" we have enjoyed in life.

#3:   Discover New Emotional Experiences: It is often difficult or even impossible to "conjure up" feelings we have not pre-viously experienced, especially because the systemization and rigidity of life patterns tend to reinforce existing perceptions of physical, conceptual and emotional reality, and generally protect us from the "unknowns" which could certainly be positive, but may also materialize as negative, conflictual, or frightening emotions which probably irrationally symbolize our "inadequacy, irrelevancy, or emptiness" in life. Quite often the only way to "break open" the boundaries or barricades of our emotional existence or entrapment is to drastically interrupt our "normal" activities to force exposure to unfamiliar stimuli which, in many respects, will carry attached "feeling energies" which will connect to unconscious or undeveloped emotional "potentials" or seedlings in our minds/hearts, or create new awarenesses of open spaces or gaps between existing ranges of feeling where we may interpolate the future presence of a new emotional sensation. The characteristics of people, events, objects, sounds, etc. possess "configurations of reality" (rough, symmetrical, open, closed, confused, circular, etc.) which our minds can translate into similar emotional patterns and energy "graphics/thrusts/emblems/exponents/connotations/ punctuations that we incorporate" into our psychic memory banks and over which we then acquire some form of permanent or temporary proprietorship. Sometimes this takes repeated exposure to the stimuli, along with sustained evaluations of what does not exist in our feeling lives, for us to build a new emotional awareness which did not exist previously. By examining previous time periods in our lives and noting what we did not do (e.g., missing activities), we may question whether or not a potential new feeling might have fit, along with some activity, into the past empty space which may assist us in validating its existence and usefulness in the present. Awareness of the reported feelings and observed activities of others may also alert us to areas of our physical and emotional lives that are absent, and exploration of new activities may help reinforce natural (for others and not us initially) emotions which are attached.

#4:   Convert Negative to Positive Emotions: I have believed for years in viewing my own life, and those of my psychotherapy clients, that particular negative life events which occur during key developmental periods, not only impact us adversely as they occur, but also are consciously and unconsciously interpreted by their "owners" as possessing augmenting, contaminating and germinational properties which cause us to "allow" them to continue to influence (and counterattack) positive emotions throughout our lives. Although some "feeling states" certainly diminish over the healing "waves of time," others become attached to identity as relatively direct symbols of our "bad" or unsavory selves, which we retain as "truthful" documentaries of our "essence" for one of two basic reasons: (a) we have few positive focal points emanating from childhood and would rather have a consistent and strong negative self-image rather than no image, or a weak positive image, (b) we remain emotionally tied to fantasized relations with parents where our "badness" keeps us attached (receiving attention from them actually or symbolically), and is one part of a mental formula for us to "work off" our punishment (of self and others) to emerge eventually from this emotional incarceration as free human beings.

As older adults, these "albatrosses" slow us down, keep us in "neutral," or even move us in reverse spiritually and emotionally in "integrating" and accepting the beauty of all life experiences, overcoming mentally the "physical negatives" associated with aging "declines," and growing into the futures of our respective lives.

I believe, therefore, that previous "negatives" in life should be converted in our minds to some form of "positive," and consequently supported by associated behaviors to expand and nurture the "new identity offspring" into the future. Some suggestions on approaching this "conversion" process are these:

-- One Conversion Approach: Identify facts, principles, values, or perspectives we learned from previous negative experiences, and make commitments to reward ourselves for being lifelong "learners," plus make concerted efforts to use acquired insight in as many different areas of living as possible.

-- A Second Conversion Approach: Realize from some philosophical perspectives that each of us must experience some forms of negative "Karma" in life to not only "balance" our holistic perspective on existence, but to help us appreciate the transiency and subjective irrelevance of many "goods" we define in life. This conversion process actually transforms both negatives and positives by identifying a third dimension which relates to their integration (what "is" and what "is not" existing at the same time) and also serves to control our false senses of superior "authorship" of all aspects of the world in which we live.

-- A Third Conversion Approach: Some people suggest that by intensifying our experiences of pain (physical or emotional), we can actually transcend our present time and space sensations to occupy a metaphysical "space" of euphoric "triumph" or tranquil peacefulness by either "taking control" of ourselves to the point that positive self-control awarenesses and sensations actually dominate the dependencies and fears which either cause, or accompany negative psychophysical stimuli in our bodies; or becoming unified or separated sufficiently from painful or negative awareness that they cease to be differentiated as unique or singularly autonomous/ identifiable from other feelings we elicit.

-- Another Conversion Approach: A somewhat more drastic approach is to decide in life that "negatives" simply do not exist, and that every action we previously or expectantly will take is always the "best" of which we are capable, and that we cannot ever get "better" or become more "righteous" until after we behave and observe the satisfying nature of the consequences. Some might see this as a psychopathic or grossly irresponsible and antisocial framework, but it probably cannot be fairly evaluated by any observer who persists in holding a good-bad viewpoint about life.

-- A Final Conversion Approach: This method involves a compensation and "bartering" approach whereby current "good deeds" can nullify or replace the "less desirables" on the life ledger, and that emotional evaluations will be swayed by the sinning totals or anticipated victors of this struggle between good and evil. The personality, in this regard is viewed in relatively black and white terms and assumes a very concrete and immediate "behavioral" nature which excludes some of the complicating philosophies about holistic/balanced identity, overarching identity states related to motivation and "purity" of intention, and emotional "content" as a foundation aspect of the "self" that "exists."

#5:   Produce Behavioral Indicators: In some cases, we may have developed or reactivated fledgling/frail/sprouting emotions which are not as totally fulfilling as possible, and need some reinforcement system to mirror and simultaneously magnify the image of our enriched "selves" back to our minds, while also serving as irrefutable evidence of the existence and value of our psycho-spiritual sensuousness/ aesthetics and "affective" feeling.   The selection of highly symbolic behaviors can be very facilitative of this goal, by extending the inner feeling, through our skin, into the outer world of physical substances where it can take shape as an identifiable and solid "object" to represent our inner selves. Each action we take as a symbolic emotional "referent" can be exaggerated in its manifestation by slowing, deliberateness, ceremony, excitability, etc. to not only accent its importance as a representation of significant emotion, but also to allow us the time or opportunity to surround its "presence" with qualifying thoughts and corroborative mental "energy" to "explain" it to ourselves as it unfolds.   These behaviors will also produce some form of reaction from the environment which, if positive or negative, can be used by us to reiterate the importance of what we "feel" before and during the act, and can show us, furthermore, that "who" we are and "what" we feel truly makes a difference.

In some cases, however, our actions will be private and not involve other "obviously" responsive living creatures, although there are probably a multitude of wind, sound, movement, quietude "responses" or "non-responses" from our surroundings which "celebrate" our acts but are beyond our present levels of psycho-neurologic perception.   In these cases the emotion can be accented relative to our efforts to perceive feedback, and also our fantasies about types of responses we would like to occur if we were more in "control" of the elements around us.

#6:   Connect Feelings to Higher Level of Meaning: Quite often
in life we are taught that feelings function as "secondary"
associated components of behaviors; that they exist as
"corridors" or linkage "arteries" between present conditions
of emotional pleasure or dissatisfaction to connect various
aspects of personality into a holistic system that "appears"
more permanent and resistant to anxiety and fear; that they
are imbalanced and somewhat "deviant" states of mind that
need to be adjusted "downward" to conform to pragmatic
reality and keep us on an "even keel" (especially "negative"
feelings); or that emotional "peaks" or "highs" pleasurably
exist as "fountains" of humanity, forced temporarily into
heights of "ecstasy" by "earthly" power sources at their base
or point of psychic origin, yet do not connect or couple with
overriding or superior "magnetic" energies which also pull
them "upward" into superior and "nonhuman" realms of
existence.

The latter condition of emotionality is often called
spiritual, "cosmic," fantasy, dreamlike, or supernatural and
usually implies heightened degrees of potency or intensity
attached to emotions as unknown forms of energy, capacity,
endowment, dynamism, "torque," etc., which are not
necessarily related to different "intrinsic" or basic meanings
of the feelings, but more simply to exaggerated aspects of
unidimensional components of the self. In distinction to this
phenomenon, however, we may be able to individually or
collectively (in groups or with the help of God, "natural
forces," thought energy, etc.) identify an "elevated world"
based on various philosophies of life; our unique
perspectives about the "big picture" and the interconnections
between numerous functions, dependencies, and "balances"
of person and nature; "visions" of the "future"; "destinies" of
human life journeys, values concerning quality living and
relating; shared "meanings," "consciousness" and objectives
of people through metaphysical or transpersonal telepathic
communications, etc. Within this "domain of reality," which
most "believers" describe as a higher level of human nature
or as some form of ultimate or transcendent "goodness" or
conflict-free "self-actualization," certain feelings we have at
either heightened levels of intensity or tranquil peacefulness,

can be defined within already-existing categories of value or significance which raises the quality of living to a new and better level of its otherwise normal adequacy. Although some people believe there is a "dark side," hell-like, "nether world" of exaggerated human "badness" which we are also able to attain, the existence of higher states of humanness or "Godliness," or supernaturality are often "alluded" to in culture through many of the arts and iconic spiritual symbols of love, beauty, harmony, victory, freedom, etc. They can open entirely new worlds of thought and corresponding activity which enable us to redefine many mundane sensations with new concepts of righteousness, sincerity, worth, dignity, etc. which have inherent exponents of heightened value or incremental importance so as to transport our "selves" beyond ourselves to embrace "visions" of grandeur of the human spirit and life.   Some of us, obviously, can use this "enlightenment" process to escape responsibility, or to compulsively undo negative acts or unkindnesses, which may have a justification within the grand scheme of life; although many others can genuinely identify heightened states of love and caring and feeling and understanding which are not necessarily "grounded" in traditional cultural or societal norms of goodness or badness, but truly represent other exciting dimensions of existence which permit novel and separate "berths" for various emotions which are sometimes exaggerations of previously existing life perspectives--but may also be entirely different populations of concepts to define life as it has not been known to exist anywhere else before.

We can learn about other worlds of knowing and feeling by reading sociological, anthropological, spiritual, religious, and metaphysical literature, but also by tuning in, or creatively exploring the fullest ranges of our senses and perceptions, to examine the hypothesis that if we remove many traditional and learned beliefs about "what is," and free our minds through meditation and awareness from idea constraints (known "truths") about reality, we may venture into uncharted mental and emotional territories which only free and determined minds and spirits have been able to discover before us.

#7: Develop "Systemic" Connections: The final general approach to enhance the "productivity," defined and functional quality, and stimulative animation of feelings and emotions is to insert them into the interactive context of relationships whereby several "energizing" factors appear to exacerbate, validate and enhance their nature: (a) emotional "content" becomes a shared topic of discussion which occupies time (fills empty places we assume relate also to inner privation) and reduces excessive intellectual energy, which makes us feel "productive"; (b) feelings become a common focal point of reference to "prove" that a relationship exists, and that the "system" has solid foundation girders to help control our irrational fears of aloneness; (c) jointly held emotions cause us to heighten our own neurophysiologic sensations to infuse or "give" our feelings to another as we perceptually use this emotional conveyor to symbolically "enter" the other person's mind/heart/soul to become "one," and therefore achieve a "pressured" state of protectedness and security; (d) expressed emotions are accompanied by physical behaviors which "excite" sensory organs and cell systems and provide a "booster service" to pair psy(mind)chology with biology as a mutually energizing team; (e) the sharing of mutually identified thematic emotions may spiritually enter both participants into some type of "being" state or "graceful" condition where they can experience all or part of the glory/essence/significance of "life" which may exist as either an autonomous or collective phenomena, but which seems to be possible (in my experience) through the combined psycho-spiritual energies of more than one person which "breaks through" defensive and motivational barriers to entry, or which creates a "purer" state of existence because the ultimate goal may have basic interpersonal dynamics as its root.

In any of these cases, reaching out to others seems essential, followed by discussion of our feelings about "us and them," and then mutually "contracted" or agreed efforts to try to improve or enhance the emotional sensations which emerge, which can then jointly be "located" within superordinary domains or dimensions of shared existence.

(7) Motivation

Motivation is a very complex topic to address, or for any of us to fully understand, because it can be associated with a wide range of psychological, sociocultural, spiritual and behavioral aspects of life; and relates differentially to issues of performance rewards, personal goal setting, compensation for guilt or inadequacy, individual pursuit of life destinies, quality/quantity of emotional intensity, conformity to cultural values, human dependency and deviance, production creativity, group pressures and collective "energies," fears and anxiety reduction, religious predestination and "destiny" fulfillment, generation and release of emotional tension, prescribed role behavior in social systems, self-fulfillment and "acquisition" collection, and probably many other input, process, and outcome areas of life. Since I have previously discussed many areas relating to improvement of the quality of inner emotions as distinct entities in and of themselves, the following consideration of motivation will be more traditionally connected to problems in our ability to pursue or accomplish relatively traditional "productivity-oriented products" which reflect the skills, talents, ideas or capabilities of the combined energies of our minds and bodies.

The literature on "aging" broadly suggests that motivation declines for many men and women within some "system" of interconnectedness between external social invalidation and elimination of viable and rewarding "work" roles for older people, personal fatigue and disillusionment in the face of painful and frustrating physical illnesses or declinations, dimmed hope and insight relative to a perceived "shortened" period of life remaining for self-fulfillment and evidentiation of our worth, cultural discrimination which produces "learned" helplessness, or mental confusion and neurological cell loss which topographically prevents logical thinking and planful goal-directedness with integrated effective and efficient utilization of personal strengths. If this "conglomeration" of factors is, indeed, an interdependent mixture of causes and effects, it may be impossible to ever unravel the key and singular factor which we can change, or which can be changed by society to encourage, free, or stimulate our investment of time and effort in pursuit of motivational hierarchies of goals. Assuming that we have personal control over some motivational aspects of our lives, however, there are some steps I feel many of us can take to improve the motivational levels of our approaches to continued "effective" living during our mature years. These are briefly outlined as the following numbered motivational stimulants (MS):

MS-1:   Realize that linear or calendar time is probably irrelevant in predicting any outcomes in our lives, that we are always capable of "beginning," that accomplishments only exist in the here and now for each moment we live so we can always win something immediately, and "magnitude" of achievement is largely our perception which does not require extensive future time to be "important."

MS-2:   We often define "disability" as a subjective gap between our "functional" level of performance and some "expected" and highly valued goal. Physical goals can easily be replaced by mental, emotional or spiritual ones, and there is no commonly accepted "standard" for what is a high level of personal achievement--in fact, some people's "highs" are others' "lows" and vice versa.

MS-3:   Both "thought" and "action" can stimulate accomplishments in our lives, and being "stuck" motivationally in one dimension often means we need to force energy investment in the alternate side of our "whole" selves. The more "familiar" we are with either a behavioral or cognitive approach to living may mean we use this mechanism as an excuse and should practice more with the "unknown" and probably fearful aspect of our personalities.

MS-4:   Motivation for growth and accomplishment sometimes comes in the wake of angry or forceful assertiveness to "free" our independent selves from our internalized guilt-producing perceptions of real, but existentially "non-emotional" social discriminations. We can break loose in some cases by speaking out, not letting ourselves get "pushed around," blowing off steam, and feeling the power of our "personhood."

MS-5:   There are differences between the true nature of problems which prohibit our "successes," and our interpretations and complaints about those problems and the roles we "assign" them relative to our motivation. We should always honestly check out our constraining "delusions" of reality relative to fearful needs to fail or be life's aging "victims," or seek outside objective consultation or therapy to help us "get out of our own way" in negotiating reasonable obstacles in life.

MS-6:   We can sometimes obtain the motivational help or encouragement we need by using our time to assist others with similar problems, which is not only positive action itself, but represents an opportunity to study the ways other people "fool" themselves into psycho-emotional "bondage," which can function as a mirror to view ourselves.

MS-7:   Although many individuals and "organizations" in society unfairly and destructively try to eliminate our functions as trustworthy and reliable citizens, we can help ourselves greatly by seeking and insisting on assuming as much responsibility in graduated-capability areas of our living environment as possible. We generally feel more proficient and adequate when others rely on our judgments and dependable behaviors to help them meet their needs for emotional or physical survival.

MS-8:   We cannot only improve our planning and decision-making abilities, but also enhance our self-esteem, by selecting "intellectual challenges" to help us remember, to push our analytic abilities, and to provide achievement benchmarks as several forms of helping motivation. Books, mental games, discussion groups, school courses, math problems, dictionary utilization, etc., can all help to keep us sharp and hopeful for even more achievements in the future.

MS-9:   One of the biggest hindrances to motivational creativity and activity investment in some people is value and perceptual rigidity which can cause: (a) boredom and stereotyped habituation with unchanging adaptations to life; (b) natural rejection by others who cannot find a place to "fit in," and therefore cease to provide optional emotional outlets for us; (c) diminished capability to interchange physical, intellectual and spiritual energies as aging processes naturally or pathologically close some "achievement" or satisfaction doors; (d) inability to envision and be tantalized by other world or "reality views" which could entice or even voraciously force motivational and energy thrusts; (e) excessive fears which crush the human spirit in their efforts to preserve the "integrity" of strongly held beliefs and to prevent contamination from external unknown infectious stimuli; and (f) self-fulfilling prophesies of negative social reactions, where culture typically defines "old people" as narrow-minded and "hard-headed," resulting in further closure of avenues to gain information, success, and meaningful involvement.

It may be helpful, therefore, for many of us to examine long-standing belief systems and behavioral patterns to determine if "airing-out" or change might provide some exciting new options for dormant energies, and also to use various strengths in the process of studying ourselves and nurturing our "egos" with the warming glow of attention and interest which accompanies self-assessment and change. Asking others to help us "see" ourselves can also be fun and electrifying, plus provide strength and foundation to interpersonal relationships. In the above contexts, we should all be cautioned to remember that general capability for mental and emotional "resiliency" and "receptivity" to new ideas is not rationally or naturally correlated with the diminishing learning speeds, physical slowing, or other "performance" decisions that occur with aging. Also, we should keep in mind that we have ultimate control over personal definitions of "life transition points" which may or may not coincide with physical, neurological, cultural or spiritual "passages" which unfold in their own right. This means that change toward more flexibility can come anytime in life we choose to think, feel, or behave in new ways.

MS-10: In many cases, we lose motivational momentum following actual task-performance failures, not because we are definitively inadequate or lack overall competence, but quite often because we were unfamiliar with the situation or "paraphernalia" associated with our "competence-testing"; we allowed ourselves to become anxious at "anticipated" failures of aging people; we allowed ourselves to become involved with social situations, issues or activities where we had little interest, and therefore did not do our best; or we lacked knowledge and exposure to a particular activity which could have come with more "trials and errors."   We can save many motivational declines, therefore, with persistence, patience, perseverance, and pressure to learn new skills, improve imperfections, overcome emotional obstacles, and develop competence whereby we not only build self-esteem with true positive outcomes, but also convince ourselves that we can do or try even more ideas, activities or endeavors with the hope of similar achievements in the end, or the satisfaction of knowing we continued to try until we reached our natural point limitational termination in any particular aspect of life.   When we get to the end of one trail, nevertheless, we can then accept this and begin work on the multitude of other paths open to all persons in the pursuit of happy and fulfilling lives.   We may have a "functional" age-related deficit in one task performance area, and be functionally very capable in many others, despite what a large portion of discriminatory social values have to say!

MS-11: Sometimes, we can boost not only the direction and intended outcome of motivational goals, but also the "drive intensity" of this form of inspirational provocation, by examining the types and amounts of emotional deprivations we feel which signal short or long-standing self-perceptions of "loss" or "emptiness" that we have been socialized to "believe" can be "satisfied" with the presence of highly valued input activity (trying our best) or particular outcome successes (completing the painting of the house).   Quite often we struggle for years with uncomfortable and gnawing "sensations" of painful emotional hunger or even "starvation," and assume it is the natural consequence of getting old, or do not realize we have any substantial control over its eradication. The "simplicity" of cause-effect relationships between our personal decisions and states of emotional awareness (feeling) is usually obscured by lingering vestiges of childhood dependence where we unconsciously believe "someone else" is to blame for our suffering, and also our "acceptance" of social stereotypes which communicate to us our helplessness, the "arrogance" and inappropriateness of motivational expectations of people who are "over the hill" (this of course comes from people who are climbing irrelevant hills and don't know it), and the futility for aging generations to improve emotional health because there is little "time left" to accomplish results which stem from motivational changes.

Motivation concerning our needs for "relatedness" or growth, or even basic physical survival, are a function of personal perceptions of our strength as controllers of our selves and the environment, previous and expected "outcomes" in the form of interpersonal closeness or individual harmonious peace and satisfaction, the values we place on particular dimensions of living and "being," and the personal costs of time/effort/change which we feel are necessary as we change thoughts or behaviors in life. Although many times we settle for less happiness if we have to work too hard to obtain it, an awareness of our degree of dissatisfaction with the feelings we have chosen may help to "tip the scales" in favor of more motivational energy, especially if we perceive ourselves to be approaching "crisis" levels of emptiness from which we fantasize we cannot recover.

MS-12: Many research studies show that aging women and men tend to relinquish the values and efforts invested in obtaining "extrinsic" or external/material life achievements or rewards, in favor of searching for inner satisfactions or "intrinsic" spiritual or emotional "meanings." If some of us lack acceptable levels of motivation, it may simply mean that we have not yet reached this point of "developmental" transition, and therefore remain locked in a cognitive and emotional struggle to get "blood out of a turnip" which is of diminishing personal value (former extrinsic rewards) and have not yet shifted perceptual and valuational focus to our "intramural" endemic selves. We may revive motivation when we "get on board" with the normative trends of our particular age cohort or social group and learn the "fine points" of human development from a different focal point.

In other cases, some of us may have decided to retain more external symbols, artifacts, and philosophic orientations of "selfhood" of personal adequacy, but may notice motivational depletions with aging because we have not "re-strategized" achievement tactics to account for uncontrollable changes in social status, and/or physical/mental functioning. We may become motivated in this context when we become "smarter" players in the "games" and life journeys leading toward external rewards, so that "compensational" plans and techniques enable us to revise need-meeting approaches, without alteration of the personally satisfying end products.

A third category of people who notice motivational losses relative to life "rewards" may be unable to choose either inner or outer "carrots" of pursuit, which may reflect neurotic-type conflicts about our basic ability and competence as "choosers," rather than reflecting anything about the specific nature of the outcome "choice." In related cases, we may have temporary crisis anxiety because we require more exploration of various new or old life values, and may be best advised to try to remain patient until factual evidence of personal preference "catches up" with intuitions or social/peer pressures for us to change philosophical orientations.

MS-13: A final motivational quagmire may result when we have excessively internalized many of society's negative "myths" about the differentiation between "young" and "old" people, to the extent that we "tell ourselves" we are "outcasts" from the mainstream of human living, and we further conclude that this "extrapolated" status reduces otherwise obtainable options and retrospectively suggests that motivational efforts on our parts are relatively futile.

We should always clearly discern the commonalities we have with all forms of natural life, so that we continue to envision a full cadre of "choices" for internal or external need fulfillment, and concomitantly refuse to allow the opinions of others, who define "difference" out of their own fears, to cause us to alter self-perceptions of personal choice and motivational strength.

(8)　Generativity

The concept of "generativity" in the behavioral and social science literature refers to the aspects of adult development and growth when each of us assumes responsibility, and also derivespleasure and a profound sense of emotional/spiritual meaning from awareness of our influences on the world, our families, and communities, and younger generations to whom we would like to impactfully "pass on the torch" of positive citizenry and life-quality.

Because each of our lives is so very different, and platformed by varying philosophies, values, behavioral patterns, and socio-cultural "journeys," it is difficult to generalize about the specific nature of any individual's sphere or particular type of influence as a socializing agent, teacher/mentor, friend, leader, guide, philosopher, helper, benefactor, etc. Nevertheless, there are some guidelines which we can all use to begin the process of assessing the "what, where, when, how, and how much" questions we might periodically or regularly have about the developmental functions we have performed for other people or situations in our lives. These various "approaches" are not listed in any particular order, and can be used singly or in concert to examine or access by sources of traditional and innovative information to give us the greatest possibility of learning how our lives have been significant, plus improving specific types of influence in areas or with people we care about.

First Approach: Direct Questioning

Although our friends, spouses, children, or colleagues some-times become a little uncomfortable with the honesty and self-revelation necessary in this technique, it is one of the easiest and most direct ways to learn if we have had a significant impact on others. We should not ask a "yes" or "no" question because of the embarrassment this sometimes causes others, and because everyone politely gives the affirmative response, but we might inquire about the ways our thoughts, values, behaviors, or lives in general have helped significant people in our lives to grow, learn, change, understand themselves better, or appreciate and love us with greater depth of feeling. We might inquire about contrasts in ideas which created dilemmas before our input helped to "clear things up," areas of emotional blockage which we might have assisted in emancipating, or philosophies which now make life seem more sensible or vibrant which had not come to fruition prior to our involvement as teachers, consultants, confidants, advocates, "confessors," etc.

Second Approach: Artifact Inventory

Another way we can more precisely measure the successes or accomplishments of our lives is to list the significant possessions, property, gifts, symbolic belongings, inheritances, assets, fixtures or other vested interests which we or others we care about utilize and also note the specific ways their life has been more beneficial or meaningful as a direct or even inadvertent result of our contribution in bringing about the presence or facilitative circumstances for these various commodities. We might compose the "before" and "after" pictures or recollections in our minds, and draw conclusions about alterations in "quality of life," or even project into the future about the full range of benefits "to be" accrued as years go by (e.g., a child's college degree where we assisted financially or with emotional support). We might even go back to the First Approach, and ask relatives or friends about the meaning of gifts or other "collectables" which we provided to show our positive feelings and to help with continued growth and change.

Third Approach: Provocation Challenges

There are usually numerous occasions in our relationships with colleagues, family, or friends when any of these human "barometers" can demonstrate or show us "who they are," partly as a result of our influential modeling, teaching, consultation or stimulation of their thoughts and feelings. Unfortunately, they also regularly behave in ways which produce measures of their own internal self-influences, or show the effects of their relationships with other people, so we cannot always be clear about the specific effects we have had in influencing or helping to shape the course of their destinies.

One way, however, to produce some evidence of our "finger-prints" on their hearts, minds, or souls is to periodically "engage" these significant others in discussions which allow them options to choose, or to suggest "problem" or issue resolutions which encompass several different "competing" perspectives, one set of which might represent the particular point of view or life philosophy which we have espoused or "taught" in the context of our relationships with others. As we and others discuss controversial, but important life topics, we can sometimes see ourselves "mirrored" or "echoed" in the conjectural reasoning or decision-making processes and conclusions of others, and even, on occasion, be surprised by the extensions of our "original" ideas into more comprehensive, sophisticated, efficient, precise or functional frameworks which shows that our "children" or creative inputs have grown up.

Although this provocative approach may seem like a manipulative game, it is really a learning and growing exercise when we also participate, and use the opportunity to "check out" our own current vs. previous philosophies, plus learn new ones and their rationale from our former "students." In childhood, our learning was primarily characterized by acquisition of "facts," but the best measure of adult growth and generativity is through the assessment of knowledge application, synthesis, and integration.

Fourth Approach: Study Imbalances

The social science theorists and practitioners generally tell us that major changes or significant events in our lives are connected, causally or consequentially, with disequilibrium or disruption of the static and balanced "systems" of thought, feeling and action which we all develop and maintain to control fear and assure calming predictability in life. When we age and find ourselves "removed" from previous "mainstream" work, community or family roles, there may be relatively extended periods when "nothing happens" and exciting disruptions fail to earmark the energy we might expend in trying to "influence the world," where returns to harmony and quietude (especially if the resulting state of affairs is different from where we began) signal that a major event has occurred which is so stimulating that a "rest" is needed to "recover."

By reviewing our past as well as present lives in search of recollected periods of disjunction, we may remember extremely potent and volatile experiences which, at the time, appeared pathological, destructive, irritating, confusing, or demoralizing--yet be able to recognize positive developments or outcroppings as a result of our involvement--which can only be seen clearly now from our present vantage points. "Crises" from the past, which our unconscious minds have sternly told us to forget, may emerge in our discerning and evaluative conscious awareness as important generative "victories" which caused us to change our opinions about important issues, rearranged relationships which benefited over time, created awareness of conflicts which we have helped to resolve in ourselves or others, or presented initial opportunities to "test out" various strengths and adaptive responses which have now become fairly routine components of our personalities.

This study of "imbalances" from the past can remind us of our "natures" and "destinies" as different types of "influencers" on the "resting" components of the environment, and might even compara-tively suggest disruptions for the future which we "should" initiate in order to perpetuate our meaning and significance in the world--to let ourselves and others know we are still "alive and kicking."

Fifth Approach: Bearing Witness

Another method of assessing the "effectiveness" and impact of our lives is to utilize the help of a colleague, partner, friend, therapist, minister, etc. who will listen, as well as provide analytic/integrative/summative/projective feedback, while we discuss all or part of our life history, and reflect on its meaning and value in our lives. This descriptive and investigative "histo-chronograph" helps us to build a developmental sequence of growth stages for ourselves where we not only can view and appreciate, in an organized way, the construction and recurrent enhancement of our personalities, but also "tease out," with the questioning and summarization of our assistant, some of the important influences and contributions we have provided for others who touched our lives along the way.

We should be as detailed as possible in reconstructing salient memories and happenings as they occurred in reconstructed logical, or previous serial time perspectives, which our witness should listen intently and perform the following duties to help us truly understand and appreciate our "cumulative selves":

a. ask us why we made particular decisions and how this was beneficial, in some way, for ourselves and others;

b. inquire about what we learned from some experiences, and how the facts, principles, styles, or attitudes we acquired have "helped us to help," or more effectively care for others in our lives;

c. highlight the "positives" which we may not see within the mundane, traumatic, or just "hazy" tableaus of the past, plus "reframe" or alternately interpret every negative event or emotional "stain," to expurgate and pasteurize any continuing assessments of "failure," so that we can discover the "good" in all our actions or developmentally learned consequences of actions;

d. give us praise and credit for our accomplishments and contributions of the past, and suggest similar or even innovative ways we can continue to influence the course of ongoing life in the future;

e. communicate pleasure and enjoyment in simply sharing a life history, and make some commitment to learn and grow from this vicarious observational and integrational role;

f.   summarize major points and interpretive conclusions which can serve as a foundation from which to proudly review and appreciate the past, plus connect these past successes to values, emotional feelings, philosophies, or other intrapsychic dimensions of our present personalities so that material phenomena can be somewhat or totally "transformed" into mental images of the "self" which become permanent fixtures in our psychodynamic "homes" for the soul.

Sixth Approach: Personal Awareness

In some cases, we can appreciate the more spiritual or philosophical contributions we have made to life by sitting down alone and enumerating the predominant values or beliefs we hold, recording the wisest "truths" we have learned, documenting those aspects of society or culture which are "wrong," irrational, or unfair in our opinions, and summarizing our perspectives on the overall purpose and meaning of life itself.   Although we may not have directly articulated all of these philosophical or spiritual credos in a direct way, or cannot ostensibly elevate specific examples of societal change or veneration in our honor, we can certainly feel confident and distinguished for being a person "on the right track," and remember many of the Eastern and Oriental "Karmic" philosophies which clearly say that positive thought or energy has a very real and lasting impact, not only in supporting the "enlightened" life forces in others, but in helping to create a general fertile cosmic environment where all forms of living matter may share and benefit from the "good vibes."

If we act on emotional insights and creative aspirations through prayer, worship, meditation, art, music, drama, writing, etc., then our generative influences may have a secondary, symbolic or "inferential" stimulus value in connection with the "booster shots" added to our initial inputs through receptive spirits, an appreciative God, happy concert audiences, or just "passers-by" who notice a beautiful flower on our porch that we loved and nurtured with enthusiasm and hopefulness for the very core value of the "living phenomena of being."

Seventh Approach: Retreat

Although there are many other techniques which can be employed to help each one of us "realize" our worth as contributors to successive generations of fellow life travelers, the last one I will discuss is sometimes necessary when "all else fails" to produce discernable proof of the talents we display and the "gratuities" we render in the present as well as past. Oftentimes our own activities and behavioral processes are replete with positive injections of stimulating energy or edifications within our respective social networks, yet we become habituated and almost anesthetized to them, and eventually take our importance for granted, or assume it is simply "normal routine" within the daily spectra of surviving on this planet. Nothing, of course, is "perfunctory" unless we choose to divest life's "flower" of its petals, fragrance, and ultimate function; and therefore compromise to some, or a great extent, the exhilarating triumph which comes with each sunrise, and grows with anticipation of a new dawn when we go to sleep each night.

To heighten this appreciation, it is sometimes helpful to temporarily withdraw from regular activities, suspend many of the functions we incorrectly feel we "have" to perform, or alter the sequence, style, context, intensity, or demeanor of those health and safety and sustenance behaviors which must continue. Withdrawal or retreat, of course, disrupts homeostatic or balanced systems and allows us to experience the reverse impact of our absence as a way of simultaneously illustrating the functionality and possible importance of our presence. We may gain realization of how necessary we are to the lives and personal repertoires of other people around us, and even appreciate our own inputs by noting the emotional losses when these routine, but maybe important behaviors are discontinued.

Retreats or changes in active to passive patterns for brief or even moderate periods can also provide rest and rejuvenation from other overwhelming responsibilities which may be very rewarding in lessened amounts, or when pursued with sufficient rest and recuperation following "down" periods of stress and physical/emotional strain in our lives.

In any of the previous self-examination situations where we discover insufficiency in our "generative" influence on some aspect of quality living, we can use the informative data as a springboard from which to launch new efforts to have an impact, if we feel this is necessary to boost self-esteem and enhance our overall feelings of worth and human value. In some of the cases, we can continue questioning significant people in our lives to determine special "needs" they have, or suggestions about ways we can help them with personal struggles, growth interest, emotional conflicts, disturbed relationships, future aspirations, religious or philosophical "questions," etc. Also, we can use parts of our "null" findings to stimulate thinking about our values in life, the sufferings of other people in the community, social changes which should be instituted, political candidates who should or should not be elected, etc., and commit small, medium, or large portions of our physical or psychic energies to social or spiritual tasks to begin "making a difference" in our lives and those of others around us. It is never too late to volunteer services or contribute ideas and skills for the betterment of someone else, and we can all, regrettably, be assured that someone "out there" is lonely, in pain, frightened, needing love, deficient in some skill we possess, or capable of contributing something to our lives if we reach out to give them a chance. The important point about "generating" positives for the future is that each specific word, thought or action can be viewed as a totally whole and complete transaction between ourselves and God/others/our egos/our hearts, etc., which can be scaled at the highest parameter of human caring, and remain as a permanent testimonial in our minds and the memories of those we help for all time, as we perceive it.

(9) Major Psychological Pathologies

Since many readers may be fearful of "developing" major or "life threatening" mental health problems, and may likewise lack information about seeking help, I will briefly address this important topic at this point.

Initially we can all be relatively assured that serious problems with psychosis, suicide, drug/alcohol abuse or addiction, schizophrenia, major depressions, or crippling disorders of character or personality are restricted to an extremely small number of aging men and women. Although statistics and samples studied vary in the literature, most agree in all categories of serious "pathologies" that percentages for men or women do not typically range beyond 7-10% for these syndromes, generally, although some symptoms (e.g., occasional confused or delusional thinking) do accompany many physical illnesses or neuro-deteriorative processes for the aging population as a whole.

In most cases, older adults who suffer from mental disorders or serious social/psychological maladies (drug or alcohol abuse, criminal behavior, etc.) have had experiences with these problems much earlier in life, many of which represent continuing childhood conflicts which are typically never fully resolved for any of us who have experienced particular traumas or deficits in early parent-child relationships. Of course, the presentation of symptoms in later life can be related to social problems of isolation, cultural criticism and neglect, personal loss, financial declines, physical pain and disability/stress etc., but these "stressors" are generally not "causal" of previously absent mental illnesses, but contribute to the reactivation of conflicts or the hyperactivity of symptoms which were previously programmed into our conscious and unconscious mental "road maps" for adapting to life. Major psycho/social pathologies are also characterized by a complex and intricate set of inner decisions, values, distorted perceptions, functional formulas, ingrained fears, and defensive patterns which are generally resistant to change and permanently affixed to our cognitive processes of defining ourselves and others, and adjusting to the stresses which we encounter on a daily basis. In almost all cases, people do not suddenly "snap," "go over the edge" or precipitously become mentally ill because of unitary, or even a chain of current stressors, where there has not been a previous history of recurrent struggles and "structural/consitutional" deficiencies in basic content and process of healthy emotionality and logical thinking.

In cases where an older individual has had a history of mental or social problems, and currently suffers from active symptoms or constraining defensive or compensatory behaviors (e.g., staying in the house with a phobia of open spaces); or if anyone else feels they are "developing" a problem with logical thinking, false beliefs, depression, "chemical" abuse, irrational fears, false sensory perceptions, excessively rigid behavior patterns--a more paramount concern is the unavailability, inaccessibility, or incompetence of treatment options to help with these problems which definitely can be improved, ameliorated or occasionally eradicated in older populations.

Many family service agencies, mental health counseling services, or hospital in/outpatient care units remain prohibitively expensive in view of "psychological" coverage gaps in insurance policies; they do not provide transportation services to help older patients regularly attend appointments, and frequently are not staffed with trained geriatric psychologists, psychiatrists, social workers, etc. with expertise in handling the unique interactive therapeutic styles of older generations or fully understanding the particular natures of mental health problems in aging populations. Older clients, therefore, frequently receive conservative "stabilizing" drug treatment without growth oriented psychotherapy individually or in groups; they receive "supportive" counseling to quiet symptoms but do not dig into "causes" of problems (usually with the incorrect assumption that older people cannot grow or have little "time left" to enjoy improved status anyway); or they are substantively ignored and typically drop out of the treatment system which is unconcerned or non-responsive.

In defense of mental health counseling programs, however, another problem is that many older individuals who truly need some form of assistance do not utilize programs which are accessible, fail to discuss "special needs" related to finances or transportation for which solutions may be feasible, feel they are not worth helping, drop out of real treatment when a good therapist correctly begins to uncover uncomfortable or difficult feelings or "secrets" which must be painfully dealt with for change to occur, or feel they can handle the problem independently.

When we consider, therefore, the real need for mental health care for some of us, and think about the bureaucratic or personal obstacles which constitute barriers to the improvement of emotional and psychic life, there are some very simple rules which we should all follow to insure we are achieving the highest quality of thought and feeling of which we are capable, and that we access the necessary social and psychological services to help us grow:

-- Immediately notify a mental health professional, wherever you can find one, as soon as any disturbing symptoms arise concerning your thoughts, feelings, or behaviors.

-- Use the "information and referral" system in your city, along with consultations from local professional societies or national institutes of health or mental health to locate pertinent service centers near you that have qualified geronto-therapeutic staff.

-- Never allow finances to become an obstacle, since all facilities will ethically provide some form of service during "emergency" or "crisis" situations, especially hospital or mental health clinic emergency services.

-- If you are unsure of "safe" or "normal" patterns of drug use, alcohol consumption, or behavioral patterns, take courses in university settings, read diagnostically comprehensive self-help or health maintenance literature, or see a counselor to "check you out."

-- Always insist on therapy or weekly growth oriented counseling when you need help, and never rely totally on "drug treatment" by a psychiatrist as the only intervention provided. Therapy should minimally occur once a week, for at least one hour of time each session.

-- Never let the sun set on suicidal thoughts, serious alterations in your reasoning abilities, unconcern for your daily health and welfare, sleep disturbances or major weight loss, etc. because all of these problems are serious. Tell someone every time you think about killing yourself or giving up!!

-- Always believe it is possible for you to change and grow--never take second best concerning your viability and capability as a human being.

-- Complain publicly to whomever will listen (elected officials, radio announcers, newspaper columnists, social agency directors, attorneys, leaders of self-help groups, etc.) about any gaps you experience in mental health, psychological or social services, and make specific recommendations about ways your special needs could be more effectively met.

-- Develop supportive networks of family, friends, church volunteers, etc. to help you "work through" crises or recurrent psychosocial problems, and keep them currently and completely informed of your status, regressions, or progress.

Chapter 3

The Future

Introduction

Although none of us controls, unequivocally predicts, or maybe even understands time which "seems" not to have arrived yet, it is important, as history accumulates in our socio and psycho-chronographic memories, and in our "physiometric" sensations and changing capabilities, for all of us to arrive at some enlightenment about our present identities as they relate to "that which is to be." Each of us, of course, will approach this task with a range of difficult frameworks, which include various quantities of the following perspectives: physical well-being, problem orientation, economic and material gains and losses, emotional richness, interpersonal stability and mutual stimulation, social significance role functionality, mental growth and learning, psychic harmony and peace, spiritual commitment and triumph, reconciliation and suffering of loss, resolution and acceptance of the past, fear or uncertainty about the unknown, decision-making and preparation for surviving family members, stimulative enticements of productivity, enjoyment of leisure, repose in disengagement, etc. The quality, therefore, of that part of "future time" which we are privileged to experience depends not only on the specific theoretical or "life explanatory" orientation we utilize, but also on the flexibility we have in modifying or changing valued beliefs which become state or dysfunctional, and the degree of intensity or favor with which we manifest our conceptual beliefs in personal action and psychic/physiologic/spiritual sensation.

This chapter, therefore, will discuss various areas of belief and preparation about the years, months, or days ahead for each of us respectively; with a particular emphasis on suggesting methods and perspectives to make these "dreams" as rewarding and meaningful as possible.

Loving Relationships

The social image of "older" men and women, perpetuated by "culture," younger individuals, and even those of us with more advanced "mileage," frequently characterizes a lonely existence following the death of a long-loved spouse; absence of meaningful relationships with adult children except for occasional "politeness" visits; reluctance to reach out and build new interpersonal structures because of physical and logistical constraints, and pessimism about the "payoff" of commitments with "time-limited" futures; the absence and inappropriateness of sensual or sexual energy in relationships with companions who provide "company" for us, and general lack of excitement and animation within the few "social" activities which exist to primarily "pass the time."

Although this bleak and depressing description does not apply to many mature individuals who are happily and actively involved in relationships, and provides incorrect suppositional evaluation of "single" men or women who spend considerable quality time and "self-actualized" lifestyles essentially alone--there are, nonetheless, large numbers of "suffering retirees" who are presently, and maybe permanently "doomed" to experience much of life in austere and sterile aloneness, and who may actually prefer the sensitive emotional "bonding" which accompanies close interpersonal relationships. If we discover in the process of aging that we are more isolated, lonely, independent, or excluded from intimate social relationships than we would like, or if the "connections" we do have are "stale" and void of nurturing, warmth, and goal-oriented energy for growth, the following pointers my be helpful to move us "off center" with an "action mode" to improve the quality of our emotional lives with significant other people:

Relationship Tip #1: Any positive experiences or highly "charged" emotional "sensitivities" in present associations do not erase, violate, betray, or minimize the quality of previous relationships, which we should continue to keep alive in our hearts and minds forever, by using the strength and knowledge gained earlier to enhance current or future relationships we develop. The childhood emotions of fear, guilt, dependency, and compulsive narrow-mindedness are the "culprits" which prevent us from falling in love again, because of assumed loyalty or dedication to the memories of deceased or absent spouse, lovers, good friends, etc.   There is certainly something very valuable to learn by experiencing the "pain" of loss, but healthy personal growth demands that we "go on" in our lives to grow in new and even more qualitative ways by using all previous life occurrences as foundations upon which to build new "superstructures" of caring, learning, and enlightenment. We are also socially irresponsible by isolating ourselves from others who might also be lonely and need the "salvation" of human fellowship and passion, and who may never love again unless we, personally (being possibly in the right time and place historically) take action to "connect" with them.

Relationship Tip #2: When we're lonely and feeling victimized by life itself, it is fairly easy to assume that potentials or probabilities of new relationships are extremely limited in a world where we "appear" to be the only inhabitant. This is quite obviously a reincarnated childhood "delusion" in a world with billions of people who are basically just like you and me, and likewise, very much in need of relationships to help them progress into this "fearful future time" which most of us view with uncertainty, skepticism, and apprehension. We must all remember, with "concretized" certainty, that every human being who lives (according to every theory or philosophy of psychological health and adaptiveness) needs and can benefit from some degree of emotional stimulation and reciprocal caring from other human beings, and that personal attitudes or behavioral styles which suggest otherwise are usually examples of disguised fear and anxiety based on other persons' questions about their own adequacy, rather than any form of "predicted deficiency" about us.

Our biggest problem in "casting relationship nets" into the world's bountiful "gardens" of fertile humanity is either <u>fear of rejection</u> (which must be interpreted always as one of two falsehoods which obscure the underlying positiveness of human nature); (a) other people push us away because we are a "significant force" of which they are frightened, or (b) we behave in objectionable ways because we have not yet discovered our beauty and strength) or <u>disillusionment about</u> the "<u>payoff</u>" of working hard to make something happen for ourselves. In the second instance, our "laziness" can generally be interpreted as either (a) the recollection of childhood "failures" which were interpreted incorrectly to us by fearful parents, (b) diminished perceptions of our own personal "efficacy" in influencing the world (usually resulting from relationships with parents who infrequently allowed us to "win"), (c) incorrect self-perceptions of our ability to be patient and defer gratification while working for positive outcomes (also usually a ghost of childhood where life was so uncertain that we hungrily wanted everything immediately) or (d) our lack of information and ignorance of various ways to build information and referral networks for ourselves by using telephone consultations, mailed "activity" or resource documents, and personal linkages to lead to other avenues of access to opportunities for relationship building which includes opportunities for us to connect with adults, older or younger than ourselves, plus children, orphans, lonely prisoners in jail, shut-ins, pen pals, etc.

Relationship Tip #3: Very often in seeking new relationships, or maintaining existing ones, some of us became frustrated when others "seem" incompatible or do not appear to be "like us," and we may likewise withdraw from associations where "differentiation" creates anxiety, discomfort, confusion, disagreement, or conflict. As we try to discover "harmonious" connections with other people, or lament the sometimes increasing disjunctions in long-standing marriages or friendships, the unavailability of age-similar or value-compatible, etc. prospects often results in disappointed withdrawal, or we may uncover individuals who are very much like ourselves but become bored and stagnant when this "mirror of self" reflects the same picture day after day and lacks the ability to stimulate our mental and emotional capabilities, even though this type of "balanced" relationship may appear to be a safe and cozy nest within which to rest and relax.

Although tranquil and non-demanding liaisons between people are extremely beneficial to nurture and protect some aspects of our personalities, many studies interestingly observe: (a) improvement in health status (using many different indicators of measurement) within contexts of "heterogeneous" social relationship environments that generate the stimulation of cognitive and emotional "complexity" (rather than similarity); (b) higher levels of intellectual performance among older research subjects when they were required to utilize intellectual/psychological "strategies" to adapt, through problem-solving to different relationships and situations; (c) higher personal preferences for diverse social experiences as an index of life satisfaction from an "active" rather than "passive" perspective; (d) higher levels of overall functioning and personal/environmental mastery in more differentiated, challenging, creative situations where there are greater expectations for individual stimulation, variability, and responsible problem-solving to meet personal needs, as opposed to childlike dependency where conflicts are minimized.

In planning growth for present relationships, therefore, or initiation of new linkages with other people in our lives, we may discover much more psychophysical energy and stimulative satisfaction by sometimes relating to people who are much different from ourselves (e.g., teenagers with Mohawk haircuts, torn jeans, and chain-covered leather jackets) and actually add dimensions of "reality" which push and challenge us to think about exciting new ways to "believe" or dream, and we may also note increases in our physical adrenaline and mental "electricity" in relationships where both parties have to try a little harder to "connect" and understand, as opposed to more sedentary dyads where there is nothing left to learn or explore because two people have merged to become a safe, but possibly uneventful "one."

We can also probably benefit a great deal from learning to be more open minded and flexible, with the underlying philosophy that there may be little to gain psychically and emotionally from simply convincing ourselves perpetually that we know all there "is," and that real quality in life comes from attaining one level of understanding and then, for psychosocial "safety" reasons, maintaining that unitary belief forever. In this case, the predominant questions for those of us who become rigid and stubborn with increasing age are these:

a.   Is our rigid belief system really helping us grow and become better, stronger, brighter, at anything?

b.   What do we think we are afraid of and how can we prove it exists?

c.   What will we really lose by assuming more flexible attitudes and behaviors?

d.   Have we really tested out the difference between new and old ways to comprehensively prove that one or the other is better?

e.   Is life so perfect now that we absolutely must not abandon the values and beliefs which have helped to place us in this psychological, social or spiritual domain of "perfect ecstasy?"

Relationship Tip #4:   As each of us looks to the future of various types of relationships, an important question should always arise about the capability of each array of "experiences" to reach their fullest degree of qualitative depth and emotional significance, which also includes the direction, strength or velocity of their "movement" toward various goals and objectives to elevate the participants singly and collectively to new or more solidly confirmed states of satisfaction, pleasure, morale, significance and life meaning. Relationships can be "going somewhere" in their ability to stimulate more openness and exploration of hidden feelings or emotional struggles; the pressure they apply to participants to gain more knowledge/skill or mastery in areas of living which might ultimately enhance self-fulfillment and our options for healthy "self-aggrandized" social achievement; the "richness" and "sensory power" of peaceful or intense emotionality which comes from shared human love and appreciation of the full "life" within us; or the more "materialistic" outcomes which are achieved through the coordinated talents and ideas of two or more people who work together to produce successful vacation trips, social parties, works of art, mechanical inventions, beautified or renovated homes, or just ideas and dreams which could not occur with similar quality, if attempted unilaterally.

This suggestion to push new or old spouse, friend or family relationships to their fullest extent does not imply that we become obsessive-compulsive "overachievers" who are never content or at peace, but that we may vastly improve the subjective and highly internalized "life force" in our hearts and souls by using "interpersonal vehicles" to facilitate or produce "expectancies" of enhanced quality of life, and for some of us, to substitute for the lost productivity roles in the social order by providing a place and purpose for energy investment value assignment, and maintenance of high moral.

Relationship Tip #5: An important dimension of every relationship which retains our interest, enthusiasm, desire for perpetuated closeness, and "psychic" energy, is the psychophysiologic sensual or sexual tension which evolves as two people discover their mutual attraction, which is partly based on emotional "electricity conductors" that signify desires for secure "unification"; sharing of "life forces" to combat fears of the nonhuman unknown "cosmic world-void"; and self-reflected ego satisfactions which we displace, through affective ties, into feelings of caring for someone else. Although we may be personally uninterested in traditional physical sexual expression with special male or female friends, or we conform to predominant norms for exclusive heterosexual contacts specifically, there may, nevertheless, exist a foundation fiber of appreciation and covetousness to experience and "narcissistically" enjoy human sensuous stimulation and "significance" (via the neurological sensations of physical touch or sensory perception) of any "self" reflected in the cultural value we place on intimate human interaction.

We may also wish to heighten our awareness and celebration of our "being" through the excited and tantalizing "connectedness" of hetero-gender interaction, or "autoerotic" self-stimulation through massage or masturbation, as an additional approach to creating "heightened" experiences of relevance, "aliveness," and functional importance in caring for ourselves or others.

The classic studies of Masters and Johnson, Helen Singer Kaplan, and others clearly denounce many myths of inappropriate, deviant, displeasurable, or even impossible sexual and sensual enjoyment in the "latter" years of adult life for many individuals or couples, and many thoughts and sexual counselors advocate for the continuation of sexual interest and activity on a permanent basis, as long as the conceptualizations and activities remain pleasurable for all involved parties.   The slowing and decreased sensations and responsiveness which occurs at different rates for each of us do not, therefore, prohibit a meaningful "sensual" lifestyle, but only suggest that we learn to adjust mental expectations and behavioral outcomes so we can enjoy pleasures which are available, without becoming frustrated or disappointed that desires, acts and experiences do not remain identical with the sexual/sensual "performance threshold" we believe we established in adolescence or adulthood when we assumed that our sexuality was manifesting itself in satisfactory or even "peak" dimensions.

All future relationships, therefore, should be replete with every imaginable form of symbolic and actual sensuality of coordinated mind-body self-fulfillment, so that we "tune-up" and utilize all facets of our psycho-physical "machines" to retain memo-sensational and conceptual (fantasy, symbolization, pleasurable awareness) viability as long as possible, and also use sensual tension increases, followed by cathartic "resolutions," as a way of controlling excessive frustrations and learning to relax through the antecedent technique of neuro-psycho-physiologic exaggeration and expansion through exoticised channels of exaggerated or embellished human interaction and expectation.

Philosophical Centeredness

The opportunity to have lived a long and experientially full life, accented by numerous occasions to analyze success failure and "all points in between" and to retrospectively oversee various stages and processes of human growth and development, perches each of us on a pinnacle of poten-tial awareness and understanding of some, many, or even all aspects of human life--which is certainly one of the most phenomenal "happenings" with which we are acquainted. Although most of us do not purport to be great philosophic "wizards" or "enlightened" lamas, and probably will never be publicly "canonized" for discovering major "truths" about life, love, and happiness/sadness, we are, at the same time, the sole proprietors of the fullest and most comprehensive reality which our individual minds are capable of perceiving, and we may have "taken in" sufficient world data in our life time to actually have some major "answers" which we have not yet formulated into a reconciliatory consummation and culmination of life's pursuant anxieties and exploratory destinies. Also, the images in our minds may existentially represent the "totality" of all that can exist, which has never been truly "external" from our thoughts and mental/emotional symbols, wherein the world "out there" has only been an illusion or identical representation of our selves--which simplistically means that there may have never been anything to know or learn, except that our minds and souls <u>are</u> the world, which does not exist anywhere outside our anxiety controlling fantasies--so that the "answer" to life's mystery, is that we are it and not it, and, in fact, there never was a real "question" in the first place.

Although these issues are certainly ultra complex or ultra simplistic for our understanding, we should realize the important philosophical role we can, and probably should, exercise in our histories, and further appreciate the unique vantage point we have toward the end of our known life continuum, which may allow us to either manipulate the vast relevant information we have collected, or become exhausted and overwhelmed with its complexity and irrationality to the point that previous positives and negatives cancel each other out, and we are left with some form of brilliant awareness of the mental, simple, peaceful, or nonexistent existence of "it" all.

The notion of philosophical "centeredness" in subtitle of this section of the book, means that we have the wonderful <u>opportunity</u> as we mature, and maybe social/spiritual <u>responsibility</u>, to put "two and two together" from a "seasoned" and "encyclopedic" orientation to integrate heretofore conflictual, adversarial, unsettled, or anxious dimensions of our "egos," to possibly rest in harmonious states of pleasure, fulfillment, accomplishment and reso-lution--when we conclude that 2 + 2 = 4, 0, or you don't need to add any numbers together.

We can possibly "center" and "unify" our beliefs about the overall value and significance of our contributions to an "improving" humanity, the growth which emanated in our lives from various "losses" as types of suffering we endured; the relationship between "goodness" and "badness" in our lives (or society) as a reflection of some overriding principle of human dignity or vulnerability, or as a balanced "scale" of some sort to alert us to their similarities or provide greater learning about reasons for their differences; the inherent value of other's contributions to our lives as a growth and developmental necessity for all interactive parties; the functionality of balance and structure as opposed to/or integrated with crisis and disorganization as resultant outcomes stemming from basic human strivings or innate capacities; or a host of others (seemingly dichotomous, "multivariate," contradictory, mutually exclusive, or antagonistic "pros and cons" of life) which have left corresponding "schisms" in our belief and thought systems which signify "unknown futures" and are typically symbolized with anxiety and rigid personal "defenses" to make ourselves artificially "live with" pieces of life's puzzle which do not naturally seem to "fit" together. Our lifelong knowledge and accumulated wisdom may help us to study and understand complex or obscured "principles" by which the world or human nature operates so that we can reach analytic conclusions and more closely approach ownership of ideas which help to merge, integrate, expand, contact, or even eliminate other concepts which trouble, or have troubled our inner most expectations of harmonious linkage between all or at least many parts of our typically adjudged "complicated" world.

Social Commitment

One set of theories on aging says that "maturing" adults are gradually eliminated from, or perceive themselves as increasingly "dysfunctional" within the social productivity "work force" (including supportive traditional female roles of child care and home maintenance relative to male employment away from home) and consequently "disengage" from mainstream cultural activity and responsibility to establish to new forms of balance through assumption of "passive mastery" activities, increased introversion perspectives, general declines in stimulative interests and desires for social validation, and relinquishment of many assertive "social justice" and "human rights" demands in the face of environmental "encouragements" and barriers to perpetuate the isolation of "unproductive" and differentially opinionated older "job competitors" from the young work forces striving to establish "social position and status."

A second theory of "subcultures" adds to the disengagement perspective by suggesting that aging men and women "ban together" to protect themselves, collectively, from intergenerational conflict and social discrimination, and also to achieve greater personal satisfaction and fulfillment through friendships and associations with those who share "historical perspectives" and current activities/interests which are "indexed" for the energy and capability "declines" of aging neurophysiology.

While the above two theoretical perspectives are manifesting themselves partly in the development of diminished self-esteem, low morale, mitigated productivity and various psychological fears and apprehensions among many "disenfranchised senior" citizens; the "ruling" social order is also neglecting many "human compassion" responsibilities through the continuation of negative stereotypes, overt social discrimination and abnegation of many personal dignities, and perpetuation of subtly destructive circumstances or unavailable opportunities for older people to maintain a fuller range of choices and facilitative options to participate in all social and cultural activities.

This model of life, which includes critical interactive junctures between individuals and the environment, suggests that satisfactory "adjustment" is the product, "systematically" of coordinated and interdependent "need satisfaction" that results when both factions assume affirmative action and growth-oriented perspectives for the optimal development and achievement of desirable and compatible outcomes from both people and social institutions. In contradistinction to an "existential" model of individual well-being where each "self" is the center and sole "domain" of "actualized potential," a systems, role theory, or interaction model of life events suggests that persons inside and outside various cultural groups have specific responsibility to improve the "correlated" functioning of both aspects of psychosocial living. As each of us, therefore, assumes differential vantage points in moving out of roles in some systems, and into positions in others, we may have an important responsibility and social commitment to not only share our thoughts and feelings about the negative impacts of life transitions and adjustment of any group of citizens who may have changing needs for participation and productive "engagement" in life, plus a challenge to work with older people and social institutions to help correct the "ills," ignorances, inconsiderations, and irresponsibilities of each.

The silence and lack of involvement of men and women who understand the pain and suffering of social "irrelevancy" and who have felt the horrible "sting" of prejudicial unkindness, results in continued ignorance in all sectors of society about the powerful relationships between environmental and personal inputs and outcomes, and robs concerned social planners of valuable wisdom and "field-tested experience" to help them appreciate the special and common needs of older people, and to conduct effective interventive activities to produce change, and facilitate equitable reconciliation between the "old" and the "new" as they should complement the missing parts of each to produce a more effective whole.

We may decide, therefore, to help ourselves and others who age and experience "losses" of esteem, opportunity, social appreciation, and participation by working on volunteering in any of the following social action areas which relate to all aspects of human potential and community development: civil rights movements, political candidate support, legislative lobbying, urban renewal projects, counseling for life transition problems, mass media public awareness campaigns, journal article education, remedial learning and skill development programs, social activity programs in helping agencies, visitations of the sick or "shut-ins," retraining and consultation for second or third career development, participation in national or local associations for retired people, consultations to various companies to develop useful products and aids for aging citizens, social protests at discriminating businesses or community activities, organization of self-help groups to stimulate interest and energies for all areas of personal growth and learning, expanded education in schools and among educators about the full developmental life-span, participation in medical or social research projects to help build knowledge and theory about aging, etc.

The development of personal social commitment philosophies, along with dedicated and tenacious follow-up activities not only provides an effective way of caring about our own quality of life, but helps us use valuable years of remaining life to help others, and cultures us in general to develop potentially lasting attitudes and practices of human welfare and love which will possibly stand as symbolic monuments of the worth and value of our lives, and help make some of the pain we have all experienced a meaningful and useful experience when the energy is transformed into various dimensions of human concern.

Ecological Safety and Control

Almost every study detailing the problems and emotional conflicts of the primary aging phenomenon, or secondary reactions of maturing individuals to prohibitive, limiting, ignoring, constraining, discriminating or complicating environments suggests that personal control of "self" as well as situational contingencies is an extremely important loss for many men and women as they leave their "relatively" powerful and autonomous roles of middle age and struggle to make the often difficult transition to more dependent and at least physically limiting aging roles.

Factors such as environmental predictability and associated personal stimulus control, situational responsiveness to manifested personal competencies, positive perceptions of health status irrespective of real "functional" capability, resource "deficient" environments which challenge the problem-solving and strategic analysis skills of those trying to "adapt," psychological needs for "activity" and expressions of emotions, and self-perceptions of inner "authority" and tranquility when faced with control by others or externally authoritarian organizational systems--all seem to be somehow related to perceptions of life satisfaction, personal and social security, higher moral, and general sensations of worth and dignity as human beings.

In continuing our journeys through the latter years of our lives, it seems important for us to attain as much control and directional jurisdiction over internal as well as external factors which can conceivably exert negative or contradictory influences in our lives as a result of the seemingly natural conflict between the destinies of our human spirits and physical bodies; and alternate "paths" of molecular configurations and energy properties of inert objects (furniture in our home which remains stubbornly movable due to mass, density, gravity and function) or social systems seeking to meet their own unique needs for balance, freedom from conflict, and productivity.

In the case of internal control, which has been discussed numerous other places in this text, it should suffice to note that this is accomplished through philosophical centering; development of emotional freedom from childhood dependencies; fulfilling destinies of generativity; reconciling with past conflicts or mistakes; achieving security through spiritual awareness; transcending learned productivity compulsions; acquainting ourselves with the impermanence, subjectivity, and invisibility of human thought and values which, when they represent differing perspectives, always create some form of conflict or crisis; pursuing new learning to master ourselves and our ignorance of the vast unknown structuring relationships to meet needs and to represent collateral, shared foundation agreements, and celebrating the basic worth and beauty of the "human" condition and "spirit" irrespective of its social definition or behavioral configuration or function.

In the case of ecological or environmental controls to insure our safety, the regularity of planned activities, the stability of "artifacts" to help anchor varying memory capacities, the continuity of human respect, the timely reception of needed goals and services, and the availability of stimulating and motivating opportunities which are planned as serendipitously allowable; the following pragmatic actions may be useful at different times for all of us to develop and maintain control over various aspects of our psychosocial lives:

Plan 1: Legal Security

We should all be fully aware of our constitutional rights; prerogatives for legal redress and compensation; opportunities for lawful and jurisprudent advocacy; contingencies for developing funding inter-personal contracts; and personal privileges for privacy, property protection, product performance guarantees, professional service competency, and refusal to enter unlawful agreements or pressurized/ discriminatory/misleading contractual arrangements in all areas of our living.

We should discover reasonably priced or free public legal services, meet regularly with an attorney who will remain appraised of our "case" and life situation, learn about legal self-help or educational classes to help senior citizens learn about, and use the legal system, and maintain an organized system of records to supply "proof" and confirmation of all significant transactions which affect our lives. In addition, we must be knowledgeable and assertive in conducting personal business, and utilize "as needed quickie" phone consultations to law offices, university law schools, public defenders officers, civil liberties and human rights advocacy groups, etc. to check our own progress as we become involved with formal or informal contractual service providers--consumer/client/ patient relationships. We should never allow ourselves to be coerced into any decision to spend money, sign contracts, participate in activi-ties, or behave in any new way unless we are fully certain of potential consequences, and have had the opportunity to protect ourselves legally from any negative intended or inadvertent outcomes. We should also be "streetwise" to the necessity of obtaining effective "guarantees" for all products or services we purchase (which includes free service, insurance supported "treatments" etc. which are all still paid for by "someone" who should be protected), and learn to ask questions about various types of "recourse" we have to obtain complete, correct and competent benefits from people or organizations with which we negotiate.

Plan 2: Residential Facility

The conduct of happy, stress-free, physically comfortable and mentally stabilizing future lives depends partly on the control we exercise over our physical living space, because its degree of systematic organization, rationality, accessibility, privacy, security, and aesthetic decorum partly symbolizes the internal conditions and status of our most intimate and special "selves," which is confirmed when there is high correspondence between our intellectual and emotional intents, and the outcomes we experience in our daily world of activities.

Many of us naturally become frustrated when (1) bodily movement is restricted by furniture style or positioning or limiting architectual design, or unavailability of handicap--sensitive access properties in buildings; (2) our self-esteem and independence are diminished in the shadows of excessive or unfair activity restrictions or mobility rules which do not represent individual capability "indexing" (i.e., nursing home norms); (3) we become frightened and confused when we have not planned our living space to allow predictable availability and structured patterns of use of various products or necessary "tools" (e.g., medicine, organized food shelves, access to emergency phone numbers), or when we do not maintain organizational memory charts or notebooks to "keep us on track" in sequentially conducting daily activities, or where sufficient staff and nursing support are unavailable to help us during "marginal" periods of adaptation; (4) we become angry and disorganized when we lose or misplace important commodities which are not able to be safely or routinely stored or shelved due to unavailable organizing furnishings or storage arrangements; we experience humiliation and disillusionment when our privacy is violated by intrusive organizational staff, neighborhood confusion or noise, interruptions in routine by uninvited guests, salespersons, or organizational norms or inflexible operational hours and services availability; (5) we feel infantile dependence when we live in environments that define our needs, interests, values, preferences, or capabilities without including us, initially in responsible advisory or feedback-providing roles for program design and implementation; (6) we may experience cultural discomfort or disappointing absence of stimulation and growth potential when forced to reside or interact with other groups of people with whom we are either excessively or insufficiently compatible ("homogeneous" or "heterogeneous") intellectually, socially, spiritually, physically, etc.--depending on our own needs and goals for establishing particular types of interpersonal relationships; and finally, (7) we may become depressed, bored, inattentive, or inept in environments void of stimulating color and design characteristics, lacking sufficient lighting or fresh air, or otherwise exhibiting drab, unexciting, dilapidated or dirty characteristics which reduces our pride in human existence and the aesthetic qualities of successful growth environments.

We should all assume active roles, related to all of the above situations, to not only clearly and openly define our needs for comfortable, organized, and rational living, but also work equally hard within the immediate social environment to help plan and negotiate necessary and equitable match-ups between resources, management rules, personal desires, environmental outcome demands, and individual "input" capabilities.

Plan 3: Personal Protection

As most of us know from tragic newspaper reports and "horror" stories from friends, "older" people frequently fall into acute or even chronic roles as "helpless victims" of criminal acts of theft, burglary, vandalism, assault; or "white collar" crimes of fraud, bunko, or other manipulative schemes involving deceptive product sales, high pressure contract negotiations, bank account withdrawals, erroneous charitable donations, exorbitantly priced advanced funeral misrepresentations, property or "land deal" shams, etc.

Aging men and women are also particularly susceptible to the dangers of fire, gas explosions in ovens, electrocutions, or other serious home/workshop accidents because we tend to "forget" some of the "basics" of sensible and safe use of machines, or the security protections to avoid fire hazards or accidents; and because "unsteady" physical conditions easily lead to perception errors, dexterity deficiencies, forgetfulness, or poor planning for the safe use or storage of dangerous commodities in residential or work environments.

Finally, we also experience periodic medical or health "emergencies" which are secondary to real and legitimate "crises" which our bodies and minds undergo, but the "process" of accessing proper emergency aid and experiencing these services is frequently complicated or unnecessarily deleterious or disorganized because we have failed to plan ahead, or establish a system to handle emergencies as part of the overall phenomenon of <u>taking</u> as much <u>control</u> of our present and "future expected" environment as possible.

Although many of us insanely insist on learning the "hard way" from ex post facto disastrous outcomes, there are some very simple and useful personal control techniques we can use to help avoid (not fully prevent in all cases) the occurrence or exaggerated negative effects of these serious personal safety situations:

a. Regularly contact the Public Information Officer of the city/state police, F.B.I., fire department, or health department to receive any literature available on personal or home security, emergency procedures, or "precautionary" planned living to keep you knowledgeable of preventive as well as reactive options. Home visits and on-site inspections are usually part of these community services--especially for police and fire protection.

b. Maintain a current, accessible, and comprehensive list of emergency phone numbers (including neighbors who can help), and ask a trusted and knowledgeable friend or family member to help you "rehearse" routine reactions which you should take for each type of danger or emergency situation that arises.

c. Learn proper security measures to protect home and property, and to correctly use and store dangerous chemicals or other products, and take a course (offered in numerous community organizations) in self-defense and danger awareness/avoidance to help "deflect" the forcefulness of personal assaults, accidents or other mishaps which might occur. Also, regularly conduct physical fitness activities to be biologically and "mentally" able to "think straight," withstand falls or crisis psychophysical emotions, to "appear" less frail to would-be aggressors, and maintain sufficient stamina and strength to help yourself during emergency or escape situations.

d. Take courses and do reading in emergency medical procedures and lifesaving techniques, and instruct friends or others close to you in the utilization and timing of any skills necessary for them to apply to you during emergency health crises. Also rehearse these procedures and provide written instructions for treatment of poisoning, cuts, burns, bruises, shock, heart attacks, choking, anxiety attacks, shortness of breath, etc., so that you or others can regularly study the often single steps that may someday save your life.

e. Seek consultations from police officers or directors of important community activities (banks, stores, utility services, home repair shops, etc.) to learn about all possible fraudulent or manipulative crimes which are typically perpetrated against aging men and women, and also understand fully the precautions and defenses which are necessary and most successful in avoiding, resisting and exposing criminals or unscrupulous predators upon senior citizens.

f.   Finally, learn to be assertive and say "no" when you mean it, and to control conversational interchanges so that you insist on complete information and clarity in all discussions, or are comfortable in announcing your intent to "think about" or "research" a topic before making a decision. Also train yourself, without feeling guilty, to refuse to answer the door if you feel unsafe, to hang up on obnoxious phone solicitors, and generally to refuse to be insulted, manipulated or "pushed around" by anyone who does not have your safety or best interests at heart. Do not act like a naive or stupid "old person" and be wise to the harsh realities of many seamy sides of the world today so you will be able to avoid or quickly extract yourself from potentially dangerous or physically/ emotionally threatening situations and pursue activities which you decide are most conducive to your best interests.

Plan 4: Public Services

As part of the "human need-service provision," "ecology" of our respective communities, numerous "necessities" of life are "purchased" by the citizenry at large, through various forms of equivalent or skewed democratically evolving tax or free-for-service "contracts" for food, clothing, public utilities, information, entertainment, protection (which we have already discussed), property maintenance, financial services, etc. Unfortunately, the policies, "program" designs, and products of these myriad services are typically controlled by "affluent" and powerful political or bureaucratic leaders/administrators; and are philosophically and financially "sponsored" by constituent groups in the community whose financial and political wherewithal are opportunistically used to meet the best interests of the "who's who" factions in a city, state, or nation to earn or save as much money as possible for themselves, to produce public ego-enhancing visibility relative to good deeds, or to insure selective advantages of qualitative product availability or service provision relative to their particular lifestyles and living conditions (e.g., better street lighting, police protection, trash pickup, etc. in richer neighborhoods).

The retired, "elderly," poor, minority groups, women, some rural residents, the uneducated, and other "lower status," politically and economically powerless groups, therefore, are usually excluded from having significant input and consultative equality in service planning, and consequently do not often receive products or services that are geared toward their unique needs, available at reasonable or flexible prices, offered in a timely fashion, or planned to include specific user characteristics to facilitate the acquisition and successful completion of "interchanges" between people and products so that the special needs of special people are truly met.

We can assume some degree of control, or at least provide confrontational attention to our best interests by becoming more verbal, public, persistent, clear, and productive in our "polite and caring" criticism of services we do not enjoy (few T.V. programs of interest to older adults), those we need but do not have (public information about community activities for seniors, special repair services for wheelchairs, etc.), or those we have but do not need or want (supermarkets built in quiet neighborhoods where bus service is adequate for us to shop in "industrial" areas and return to peaceful residences).

We need to announce or provide lists of desired food items to local grocers, talk to bank officers about innovative financial programs which might assist us in meeting particular needs related to "aging" customers, advise local repair shops of the needs we typically have and encourage them to develop the proper expertise or maintain necessary "parts" to properly attend to our service requests, identify the types of recreational facilities we would benefit from the most and share these desires with city planning officials, etc.

Although we cannot and should not dominate the public arena with our own idiosyncratic agendas of life satisfaction, we can certainly all be more responsible in making our needs known, and in criticizing components of our ecology or environment which insult us, fail to provide stimulation, control democratic options, or just "miss the boat" in really understanding what we, as older citizens, need or want to help us lead happy, safe, and productive lives.

Mind-Body Integration and Stress Reduction

One of the most obvious phenomena of our extended growth cycle is the gradual almost imperceptible change which occurs in both our bodies and minds, coupled with some of the more pronounced crisis "breakdowns" we typically experience in physical health (heart attacks, strokes, serious-slowly healing injuries from accidents) and the sudden "awareness" trauma of accumulated mental incapacity when we foget something extremely important, "blank out" momentarily in a conversation, or become confused in situations, or in ways which represent atypical patterns of our adjustment to problem-solving or novel "demands" on our "integrative" cognitive capacities. These "regressive" type changes are often difficult to "explain," rationalize, understand, "balance," assimilate, etc. because they are occurring in two connected but also very separate human systems; they are "proceeding" at frequently different (although sometimes parallel) rates, they are also offset by growth changes in both mind and body as we develop capacities we have neglected previously, and finally because we can easily use mental psychological defenses and symbolic logic to distort or rearrange or remain unaware of any or most of these changes as we continue our movement throughout life.

In addition, we experience some stresses in our "mature" adulthood which, as noted throughout this book, are often very different or differently perceived from earlier years, and these mini-crises or irritations are also examples of failure to integrate and coordinate various competing thoughts or valued perceptions in our minds, which can sometimes affect our bodies as well if we exaggerate the problem to the point that its attempted resolution has to "spill over" from mind to body, or if we have a personality style developed from childhood whereby we "select" various organ systems to symbolically represent the conflict, in which case our minds and bodies are integrated, but in a collusive form of destructive psychological entrapment.

In either of the above cases, there are some very important approaches we can take if we experience dissatisfaction, chronically diminished morale, anger and resentment, or other forms of "maladjustment" related to the ideally "friendly" and compatible "partnership" between our minds and bodies, or between disparate components of cognitive ideologies or perceptions which prevent otherwise pleasant sensations of mental peace, psychic tranquility and overall personality harmony:

Integration Approach #1: Probably the most ideal philosophy to use, with the longest lasting results, is to view "deteriorative" (as we know it at the present time in this culture) change or stressful irritants as "normative" conditions of existence both inside and outside our systems, over which we have very little "corrective" control, and which seem to represent an overriding "life process" that parallels other inhabitants of our natural cosmic world which has some sort of "master plan" wherein current medical and "productivity" philosophies to counterattack and slow or change this "journey" may be "artificial tamperings" with the eco-social-spiritual domains of comprehensive existence.

Although this theory of "natural progression" seems (and maybe does) to represent an equilibrium, balance or "continuity" theory of life, our mental adjustment to it generally contradicts our socialized learning to "overcome" problems, succeed and "conquer" obstacles, fight off laziness and inertia to be "productive," and "compensate" for losses or weaknesses by improving or bolstering capabilities in other areas over which we exercise more personal control.

In adjusting, therefore, to the inevitable, which should be viewed as positive because it represents life's "blueprint," integration comes when we change our productivity orientation to adapt feelings of unity and "fluidity" with the "ebb and flow" of physical/mental change so that our expectations are always existentially reinforced and corroborated by what is currently "happening" or occurring in our psychophysical "selves." We retain a mental and physical "growth" orientation by learning to experience and contemplate the peaceful coexistence of the two factions, and to regularly readjust our minds or bodies to the tenor of the alternate part of our selves, so that we try to fully enjoy the maximum or minimum energy output, whereby these qualitative scales are increasingly predicated on their compatibility and unification. For example, if we jog or walk more slowly today than yesterday, our minds should contemplate and concentrate on the pleasures of movement per se, and our movement should speed up or slow down as our mind (during a walk, for example) in concert with the mental movement we are also experiencing.

There is, of course, a special complication and difficulty when we experience physical pain or distress, which for many aging women or men, can assume horribly distracting and seemingly inescapable tortuous proportions. The best we can hope for, here, are approximations or gradients of "acceptance" of pain through the Eastern spiritual traditions of transcending physical sensation. This is done by inexorably intense mental concentration and fusion with the core of the painful body part and nerve sensation to the point that we dare to make it worse by fighting against it, and also to the extent that we can use our minds to so intently "envision" its existence that it may actually "go away" or "lessen" because we have "disengaged" its mental booster or amplifier by becoming so connected to its essence that it ceases to exist as a separate entity/concept/sensation from all other signals or non-signals that surround us. These types of techniques certainly take years of hard work and training by psychic, meditational, spiritual, therapeutic, holistic experts, but can be partly aided through the introduction of medicinal tranquilizing or narco-anesthetic drugs which help reduce pain and bodily discomfort to manageable limits.

In the case of environmental stressful irritants, the process of integration is one of "centering" our minds on their own thoughts or on positive bodily sensations (rhythmic breathing, relaxed muscles) and removing our bodies (physical behavior) from immediate contact with stressing stimuli (leaving a room where noisy chatter is frustrating) and uniting both factions of the self in a concerted effort to exclude all external disruptions, and to achieve harmony by "listening" to the organized life processes and non-processes (neutral rest, non-thought, or forced activity) of ourselves and allowing them naturally to discover their own level of adaptation to each other --- NOT TO THE EXTERNAL WORLD.

The above unification of mind and body approaches necessitate the relinquishment of all external criteria or standards or values of adequacy which are part of the "social" world, and relying solely on the rhythms, patterns, directions, movement or adjustments of mind and body to themselves and their own criteria of "work" and survival initially, followed by alignment of each to the other through some mental and physical concentration until they are so closely fused as to jointly "select" their own direction and state of activity or rest.

Integration Approach #2: This theory and procedure is probably less desirable and longitudinally effective than its predecessor, but still constitutes a form of integration, although generally restricts the continuity and stability adjustments to the mind alone, which then retains its "conflict" orientation to our physiology but dominates and controls the variability and "deviancy" of undesirable physical sensation and activity by overriding its influence and reducing its qualitative priority within the comprehensive scope of our identity "domains."

In this approach we decide on a consistent self-image or identity-concept of "who" we are and "what" we believe, and maintain "stability" of this system by continually thinking old or new thoughts which either contain our "selves" in "tightly woven" patterns, or extend our mental "territory" by finding innovative ways to expand or extrapolate ideas which do not contradict the basic values and premises of our "base of operations." When it comes to changes in our bodies, we have several options. We can predominantly ignore the physical parts of our "personhood" and develop standards of achieving or more "passively being" which involve only desirable thoughts and formulas for consistent thinking and logical reasoning; we can view our bodies as antagonists which provide conflicting stimuli that must be controlled mentally, and therefore redefine "negative" bodily actions as "positive" aspects of our growth, or force mental images to become so pronounced and intense that they "drown out" the opposing sensations; or we can force our bodies to "corroborate" mental expectations through performance "outcomes," which must be converted to "degree of effort" rather than "absolute achievement" as aging naturally produces declines in many physical competencies.

We maintain the regular patterning of these personality "traits" by frequently not attending to, or validating that any part of "us" is changing, and by insisting frequently that we are the "same" person we have always been although the "unreliability" and "deviancy" of our physiology may be even exaggerated to "hold in place" the solidarity of our thoughts which must be strong to offer resistance. Body and mind, in this case, are either integrated as polarities (weak mind vs. weak body) which are observed, evaluated and controlled by our superior "strong mind" which finds the weaker "children" together in a system of predestined vulnerabilities which provide "opportunity" for our cognitive strength to emerge victorious; or the mind is given paramount reign and the fluctuations of the body are relegated to a status of virtual irrelevancy.

Stress reduction, from this standpoint, is viewed as a process of "abstraction" of mental symbols, values, and images to higher levels of importance so that the competing values which precipitate our anti-stress reactions are redefined as less significant than other awarenesses or goals, or provide an analytic challenge to study and understand their casual origin through the "distancing" which occurs through assumption of "higher order" evaluative mission or prerogative as part of pragmatic survival or intuitive and intrinsic learning for its own sake. Stress is removed when we mentally decide it does not exist, and unite discrepant value positions in our minds to the extent that "no contest" continues to exist between subordinate ideations, or the "contest" is an expected occurrence which allows activation of a highly trained "problem resolution system" which we "know" has a high probability of accomplishing its goal, partly because we have decided in our lives to exclude some aspects of "reality" which we cannot reconcile as having power over our lives, or which have powerful influences that can be channeled into a more "holistic spectrum" where larger numbers of compatible relationships between differing ideas are possible and where the "name of the game" is always to discover some way of turning "lemons into lemonade."

Integration Approach #3: This is the least effective among the "adaptive" methods of trying to develop some form of "amicable" and balanced relationship between the mental and physical "worlds" in our perceived life space so that changes in either one in any direction do not register a "tilt," failure, "hopeless loss," crisis, or "identity destruction" "print-out" in our mental and neurophysiological "computers" to the point that further regression occurs in the alternate area of living as well.

The "compensation" formula is different from the previous win-lose philosophy, as we envision a "buddy system" between mind and body whereby weak members of the "team" remain "valued" partners and participants in life's journey for us, but require extended efforts from other stronger "comrades" to "make up the difference" relative to outcome values and criteria of physical and mental performance. When we become physically incapable in one area (specific athletic skill, for example), we can compensate for this by improving our capability in a substitute set of muscular or movement skills, or we can change "tracks" completely and use our minds in a more desirable, useful, energetic, or "successful" way.

In handling stress, essentially the same plan evolves whereby we feel "depreciated" by a particular social problem, worry, environmental irritant, relationship dynamic, etc., and instead of reconceptualizing the problem, centering on ourselves, or directly overcoming (even destroying) the stressful feelings, we again compensate by saying to ourselves: "I am really trapped, upset, or hindered by this particular problem, but I can make up for lost time, energy, or positive feelings by working harder or longer, or more effectively in another area of my life so that I can regain positive self-image feelings by not noticing my weaknesses and demonstrating my qualities in some other realm of existence." We generally must suffer whatever pain is inflicted by various stressors, but "gain valuable ground" later, or sometimes simultaneously with extended stressful living situations by our own or society's measurement of alternate "examples" of competency.

The reason that this approach is the least desirable however, is partly because we often maintain allegiance to "external" standards of competence and personal adequacy, which changes socially as we are often displaced or ejected from reward-producing cultural roles; and also because this approach represents a child-life form of compulsive and manipulative bargaining (with parents initially, and ourselves secondarily) where we make deals to be good in one area because we have been bad in another. This retains a schism in our personalities (not schizophrenia or "split" personality) between right and wrong, successful and unsuccessful that never lets us achieve full autonomy or self-respect for a 100% positive and lovable human identity.

The compensation plan also progressively breaks down as both mental and physical capacities naturally diminish and we eventually cannot "keep up," and also because of excessive "wear and tear" on stronger "team players" who eventually become exhausted and sometimes resentful from "carrying the load" for the less capable elements of the team.

Materialistic Symbolism

As we think about the important thoughts we wish to possess in our future "treasuries" of personal fulfillment in life, and the memories we desire to retain or build to fortify a cohesive, positive, satisfying image of ourselves to either meet the standards of some external authority (e.g., God, natural order, family "tradition," etc.) from which we will personally interpret or actually receive future rewards, or to serve as foundation cornerstones of "philosophic relevance" to guide desirable social or interpersonal actions--we should give important consideration to the artifacts or material possessions we have from our past, or should acquire in the future to represent who we are, where we have been (in our minds and hearts mostly) and where we have yet to go, to be more fulfilled or satisfied with ourselves. The symbolic meanings of physical possessions can be extremely functional as foundation reminders of the core beliefs and principles upon which the basic quality and significant "essence" of our lives are predicated, and they can also push or beckon us to demonstrate particular behaviors (or avoid negative ones) which help us to create and maintain healthy relationships with important other people in our lives, and to <u>define ourselves</u> in specific ways, so that the parallels between ourselves and the characteristics of our symbolic material referents or "proxy selves" confirm the destinies or statuses we need to maintain for psychic equilibrium, spiritual enlightenment, and future aspirational "hoping" and "expecting."

Some examples of specific symbolic "functions" of material possessions, or even non-possessed objects or events in our past or present (e.g., a certain building in our home town, our recollections of the Great Depression, etc.) are briefly listed as follows:

#1. general aesthetic beauty, sensory pleasure, the value of nature as the "natural beginning" of all objects, the significance of our "perceptual" abilities, the beautiful connection between "observer" and "observed," the importance of creativity in enhancing the quality of life;

#2. functions in life and purposes of acts or thoughts (e.g., vase is to <u>hold</u> flowers, mind is to <u>hold</u> ideas), interdependent relationship values, causes and effects, "thematic" goals for future actions or ideas, intricacy and worth of thoughtful "design," efficiency and effectiveness as criteria of quality living;

#3. dynamics of relationships between phenomena, symmetry and balance in life, meanings of various "shapes" of things/people/ ideas/values, "dimensionality," various "forms" of idea or image communication, figure-ground (foreground, background) relationships, separateness vs. integration and wholeness, "spacial" configurations of life phenomena;

#4. attributes of people and emotions (rough, smooth, soft, etc.), simplicity vs. complexity of identity, characteristics of change/ movement/activity (rigid vs. flexible), the natures of conformity and deviation, similarities and associations between separate aspects of feeling/living, energy aspects of life "forces";

#5.   aspects of time orientations, particularistic vs. universal "scope" of action and viewpoint, measurement principles, amplitude/power/velocity aspects of human or nonhuman life circumstances or objects, magnitude/depth and volume aspects of life, proportionality, limitations and capacities as evaluative foci, emptiness or "nonexistent" as components of reality, safe vs. fearful perceptions of power/strength;

#6.   communicational style and facility (e.g., giving, receiving), continuity and segmented identity, mediational aspects of interchanges or associational life linkages, principles and processes of "transfer" or movement "between," clarity vs. confusion as compatible and conflictual beliefs, aspects of clarity of meaning, characteristics of idea organization and outcome consequences;

#7.   relativity, subjectivity of viewpoint, issues of control of opinion related to raw perception vs. value-laden learned perspective, stability vs. change as life "processes," unity vs. interconnected wholeness, integrity and coherence, the role of symbolism in life, mystery/intrigue/the unknown and excitement, "expectation" as a mental proposition;

#8.   achievement, role of rewards in life, relationship between effort and outcome, the value of success vs. failure, the meaning of possessiveness vs. relinquishment, ownership and sharing, inner as opposed to outer definitions of the world, the meaning of production and consumption, receiving vs. giving, the interpretation and value of having or viewing life as concrete vs. abstract, wanting and desire as functions of motivation and qualitative existence.

Although I have only mentioned a few of the most important principles (at least to me), characteristics, or "demeanors" of life which we can perhaps understand more fully by studying the "natures and functions" of various possessions or activities with which we associate ourselves in life, there are certainly many more aspects of what we hear, see, smell, taste, touch or perceive (think or feel about) which can be translated into similar or different properties of ourselves, so we can learn more about the abstract and often illusory and unclear natures of us by understanding about the "natures" of objects around us which, unlike thoughts, feelings or sensations, we cannot "envision" as easily.

There is probably a very good and information-rich reason for every single artifact we possess and equal significance in our efforts to learn "who" we are relative to the "things" in life we do not have or do not want. Many hours of interesting and growth-producing hours can be spent individually or in groups of family or friends to observe our environment and to "translate" its characteristics into meaningful symbolic dimensions of our personalities and orientations to all aspects of life.

Perpetual Learning and Intuitive, Experiential Wisdom

Although most studies generally indicate that the "peak" of our learning (remembering, solving problems, reasoning abstractly, planning future inte-grated goals, etc.) occurs between late adolescence and early to middle adulthood, there are numerous older individuals who strongly believe in, and benefit from concentrated, serious, energetic, routine, excited, continuous, and applied formal or informal learning about a wide range of subject areas which relate to both "pragmatic/practical" as well as "abstract/esoteric" purposes in living. Although the intended goals or purposes of our learning are as different as there are unique personalities who participate, we should all be cognizant of the fact that the approaches we individually use in the process of learning or educating ourselves to overcome ignorance or accom-plish other objectives, plus the qualitative outcomes or end results of our efforts are dictated, in many important requests, by the following: our culture, socioeconomic status, our community's orientation to learning and the availability of opportunities for cost sensitive education/organized experience/training, the cohort or historical group of which we are a part, our previous learning and education levels, the ways we were socialized in our families to view learning, the types and rates of neurophysiologic "decline and deficit" we experience, nutrition and health related lifestyles, the characteristics of our living environments which facilitate or hinder pursuit and retention of "learned phenomena," whether or not we learn facts vs. processes of "how" to learn as this affects future educational building-blocks, our verbal/reading abilities as they are related to the use and acquisition of learning, our personality types as they provide foundation platforms for responsibility/autonomy/perseverance/self-confidence/behavioral control in "negotiating" learning tasks, pressures from the environment or from significant relationships in our lives to learn or not learn, opportunities and rewards in our social worlds to implement outcomes of what we have learned, previous "success or failures" in formal or informal learning situations (plus current level of anxiety in testing our abilities and honestly confronting our learning "inadequacies"), our level of morale and motivation as we deal with all areas of the aging process along with choices about learning, our perceptions about intellectual "compensation" for other "declines" in our lives, the nature of specific criteria we use to measure our own learning and the effectiveness and reliability of these "indicators of adequacy," our subjective perception of our own status educationally and the extent to which we feel we have "changed" or can change in the future, and undoubtedly many other "variables" which affect our lives.

In view of the above factors which influence "why" as well as "how" we learn, we must also remember that learning probably always occurs in every human or animal life no matter what we do, and that many of us may be fully satisfied with our levels of "understanding" of ourselves and others, and may not need or desire to become more "seriously" or formally involved in pursuit of educational attainment. It is, however, interesting to note that involvement of aging men and women in formalized continuing education programs, as noted in most all scientific surveys, is extremely low (near four or five percent and represents extreme deviation from the degree of involvement of other "age brackets,") despite some "conducive" enticements of life savings to spend on education, more time available, fewer social or work obligations or worries, reduced costs for many programs to return to school, although "older" people may be more involved in private or self-directed learning for a whole variety of reasons which are not yet fully researched or understood. Nevertheless, many of us may be interested in learning well into the final days of our lives, so I think it will be helpful to point out some of the valuable goals which we may select to serve as "vehicles" for continued involvement in the learning process.

< LEARNING OBJECTIVES >

LO #1 (Learning For Its Own Sake)

In some cases, younger or older people seek formal plus informal opportunities to learn simply because the challenge and excitement of mental "discovery," and titillation of neuro-sensory cognitive organs provide a feeling of vibrancy, "aliveness," self-actualization and personal growth. Although the facts or thinking/reasoning procedures acquired certainly translate into "advancements" in social skills and task accomplishments, the primary "achievement" relates less "pragmatically" to feelings of personal "expansion" of awareness, growth of opportunities to perceive the world in increasing varieties of ways, and advancement of personal freedom and autonomy (defeating the "dependency" of ignorance along the way) as new and fresh ideas replace some of those which have become stale or boring.

A certain degree of "magical" or "fantasy" dreaming may accompany this "intrinsic" learning which can be interpreted as a "soaring of the human spirit" beyond its "dormant or baseline" capacities through the heroic act of attacking any mental inertia we have, and pushing our minds to the outer limits of their capacities--which may produce a form of aesthetic or spiritual "high" as this mental trip progresses mysteriously into unknown recesses of exotic or forbidden cognitive territory.

LO #2 (Attaining Spiritual/Psycho-Emotional Enlightenment)

The outcome benefits of this learning orientation are sometimes very similar to those of LO #1, although the "location or sphere" of validation or measurement is "celestial," "heavenly," "eternal," "God-like," and seems to belong to a special other-worldly place which seems to exist gloriously beyond the skies, or within the deepest confines of our innermost thoughts or soul-like awarenesses. There is some degree of dependency for many of us who optimistically rely on rewards from a "Heavenly Host" or "Master Builder/Architect," where the reinforcement contingencies are sometimes related to learning as a form of reaching and searching for the "God" inside or outside us, but other times, the reinforcements are more closely tied to the more formal religious facts, or less formal spiritual or humanistic "principles" we acquire to directly assist us in conducting holier or more righteous personal and interpersonal activities within the "here and now" framework of daily living.

Spiritual enlightenment is a form of learning which sometimes encompasses the attainment of insights or visions of abstract and exalted "supernatural" or "ultranatural" "discernments," which represent heightened "sensations," victorious "attainments," "frenzied" emotions, monumental "tranquilities," cosmic "expansions," voluminous "longings," etc. that ultimately provide a personal evaluation of security and expressive/creative/fulfilling movement toward a majestic goal which, retroactively, attests to the basic value of the learning act itself, and affirms the utilitarian value of that which is learned and becomes part of memory as this "substance" instills hope and optimism for concrete or "apparitional-visionary" rewards and accomplishments in the future.

LO #3   (Developing Wisdom)

As we approach "advanced tenure" in our informal roles as "world observers," we are often expected by younger family members, some peers, and community groups where we assume senior advisory functions, to possess seasoned wisdom and experiential/intuitive knowledge of the intricate and complex workings of human and social relationships, counterbalanced by our assumed equivalent clarity of vision concerning the simple truths of qualitative human life, love, growth and survival. These external pressures are also fueled by our own internal desires to "put together" consistent plus divergent "sets" of our historical experience and observations, with the integrative and explanatory "adhesive" of deduced/induced theory or abstract reasoning so that life will retrospectively begin to "enflavor" a meaningful continuity, sprinkled with stages or even moments of significant learning which we and others (through our wise tutelage) can benefit from as pain-avoiding and achievement-producing guidelines for effective and efficient future being.

We may, in this regard, be drawn to more formal learning activities involving serious encounters and analysis of philosophy, religion, sociology, psychology, political science, or anthropology through public lectures and private study; or we may less formally enter into extensive and often difficult/exhausting periods of self-reflection, personal analysis, interpersonal discussions, and historical recollections to understand or re-understand the facts and causal/consequential dynamics of decisions and life-pursuits/ reactions which fashioned our particular course throughout the labyrinths of chosen and non-chosen life passages.

This learning certainly has practical significance as a "blueprint" for future purposeful action, but more frequently seems to function as "icing on the cake" of previous living which many of us need to explain, to help verify its worth, justify the pain/suffering/confusion we experienced, and to place ourselves in positions of esteemed social status as "sages" or philosophic "mentors" to gain the approval and veneration of others, to regain lost status produced by work and other social role relinquishment, and also to feel a sense of dignity and value as veteran participants in a "cosmic drama" to which we have, and continue to invest tremendous spirit, energy, and hope for reward and meaning and substantive value.

This type of learning activity sometimes involves the learning of principles or dynamics of living, but other times takes on the character of "learning how to learn" so that we not only understand more about human nature as thinking beings, but also build basic frameworks as "remedial corrections" for previous deficient approaches to educating ourselves, or as future platforms to use for a variety of different pragmatic or esoteric purposes which move us to areas of content beyond this form of "meta-education."

LO #4 (Attaining Personal Content Goals)

Sometimes we decide to pursue learning activities with the specific intention of gaining circumscribed and somewhat limited knowledge of particular subject areas which are not necessarily "convertible" into parallel "social" achievements (more money, new job, hobby acquisition), but are frequently topics which interest us for the sheer sake of "curiosity"; or constitute an array of intertwined or coordinated "curricula" which, when viewed collectively, produce an outcome which has special personal meaning as an achievement or conquest of a particular life aspiration, or even obstacle (e.g., completing college just to "say" we did and to "know" we are "educated").

Learning of this sort usually has a definitive beginning and end point, and often does not produce the desired personal "payoff" until it has been completed, and usually documented with some proof of participation or competence at the end. We enjoy these activities because we feel productive and can "parlay" personal satisfactions into the future by using various aspects of the acquired knowledge within the context of social interactions, or can expand upon unitary facts by applying additional "bits and pieces" of information to form "weblike" matrices of education to enhance self-esteem, areas of common interest with others, or "adaptive" capacity by improving ability to be "tuned-in" to a wider range of community or world issues concerning which we possess factual information.

There is frequently an internal sensation, of acute and chronic duration, of success which can date back to childhood parental expectations, or represent lifetime dreams which we have decided are necessary to complete unfinished puzzles or tapestries that signify a full and worthwhile life for ourselves. These "success" feelings can also herald a "moral" victory over the dark and lazy/resistive sides of our personalities, but generate rewards which seem more a part of social and cultural "hierarchies of adequacies," rather than primarily having a more "firmamental" or "eternal" global meaning. People typically complete a course of study, a college degree program, finish a revered book, or even satisfactorily conclude a series of topical discussions with family members--all of which appear to supplement some aspect of "emotional deficiency" by interjecting a section of learned content or material which has a retroactive intent of "remediation," more often than an exploratory or proactive visionary escapade into an unknown future.

LO #5 (Improving Social Capability and Contribution)

There are times, in growing older, when we feel personally secure and generally adequate, but notice that we are more distant from social interactions and community networks than we would like to be, and suffer, to various extents, from the isolation which comes from knowing we have something to contribute--but feeling stifled in the absence of a vehicle for external and interactive self-expression; or feeling that part of our "psyche" needs more nourishment from the extra-personal contacts and stimulation afforded within the mainstream of community life.

In our quest to contribute more to the betterment of society, which may reflect our generativity (discussed earlier in this book), or to enjoy the social interactive warmth of more frequent, but "productive" partnerships, we often discover that we lack knowledge, not only of the "places" and "processes" of entry into more active social life, but we may also lack particular social skills of communication and current knowledge which facilitate acceptance and retention in small group roles revolving around the planning, organization, implementation, and evaluation of various humane and recreational public events which may attract our interests.

Changes in former marital, residential, health, family, financial or other situations may also place us in situations where we must seek new friends or categories of acquaintances/resources to replace previous or lost associations--yet lack awareness of strategies, techniques, cultural nuances, needs, expectations, or common activities of other groups with which we are not educationally or experientially familiar. In trying to meet new people, therefore, we may decide to attend learning exercises in confidence building, public speaking, social skill development, personal needs assessment, etc.; or may directly seek knowledge of specific community activities and task requirements so we have the training, orientation, and socialization foundation knowledge to assume contributory roles as volunteers, activists, political campaign assistants, consultants, or just participants where we offer a relatively "full" personality with some social "retooling" as a more functional member of various types of social teams.

The rewards usually revolve around group task accomplishment (e.g., neighborhood improvement) where we share the "glory," yet we also feel more socially "responsible," personally useful, and even spiritually righteous in giving to others who do not directly ask for assistance, as one form of "charitable" contribution to joint efforts, which also "serve up" delicious portions of interpersonal warmth and camaraderie among the team participants.

LO #6 (Learn Survival Skills)

Arrival at stages of "older" age not only sadly places us in "mismatched" or "deviant" social and work roles which are marked by ostracism, rejection, termination (forced, coerced or voluntary), curtailment, or increased demands to "keep up the pace," but are often accompanied by personal awarenesses or beliefs that we have allowed ourselves to "lose touch" with the styles, attitudes, knowledge, language, technology, and basic survival and adaptational skills of our current "century," and therefore must get "retooled" or "updated" in various educational efforts to "get with it."

Although these evaluative decisions may be stimulated and pressured by societal norms and values, their ultimate cause and consequence is an individual judgment that may or may not be accurate or necessary in view of our own personal lifestyles and value/activity preferences. Also, many of us may initially pursue some form of "adjustment" or "update" training and realize, in the course of progressively assessing our potentials and interests versus social expectations and opportunities, that we were previously more satisfied than we thought, and decide to reconfirm our "adequacy" status, to "fight back" when external "assessors" impose judgments relative to our "success needs," or even withdraw from pressurized situations which lack flexibility to accept and functionally utilize "who" and "what" we are. In cases, however, where we do ratify the necessity or relevance of upgrading or improving practical knowledge or capabilities, some typical areas of formal or informal education pursuit are these:

-- home or job computer technology to avoid obsolescence and to become stylishly "literate" and informed;

-- management/supervisory skills to obtain promotions or raises in employment situations;

-- technical skills to operate modern automated and "robotic" equipment to maintain job security or to transfer to more desirable/less strenuous work roles in current or new organizations;

-- orientations and experiential practice and mental/physical conditioning to utilize new forms or upgraded prosthetic/health-aid devices or practices (e.g., tools for arthritis sufferers);

-- allied health and psychosocial education to understand and adapt to changes related to the "aging" process of maturational development and to handle stresses of loss or change (e.g., self-help books, non-crisis therapy sessions);

-- new vocational knowledge or skills for second or third separate career path for men, first or second formal employment for women usually;

-- skills and knowledge in "fix-it" or "savings" areas to conserve money or utilize free time, like home repair, auto mechanics, redecorating, bargain-shopping, sewing, clothes-making, energy-conservation, financial planning, etc.;

-- hobbies to fill leisure-time or "actualize" creative talents which have been dormant, yet "pressing" for improvement and concrete outcome expression;

-- nutrition, exercise--physiology, bio-feedback techniques, meditation to relax, improve health, take a better overall "care" of ourselves when we realize we have "neglected" basic life-satisfaction needs, improve motivation;

-- cultural "resocialization" to learn new languages and thought/value patterns of younger generations, understand world or community affairs, learn to appreciate modern art or music, develop increased comfort in participating in community affairs (computer banking, home video machines, "ticketron" sales, modern makeup or clothing style selection, utilizing modern transportation, underground high-speed trains, monorails soon to appear in some cities, international rapid jet travel, etc.).

LO #7   (Relationship Building)

A considerable amount of research on goals and "processes" of adult education confirms that a substantial number of participants become involved in continuing learning activities on formal or informal bases, to partly or totally meet needs for interpersonal contact, stimulation, warmth, encouragement, support and overall relationship building with moderate to serious "commitment" outcomes in mind.   This does not mitigate the quality of learning which evolves, or diminish the level of sincerity with which we pursue and "work at" the subjects or skills we are studying, but highlights the fact that these are given secondary "motivational" and goal-directed priority in preference for paramount concerns with emotional, intellectual, or psychic-spiritual connections with instructors or other learners.

In some cases, the development of strong relationship ties within a learning situation may mean that there is a sudden or gradual diminution of continued participation in similar future learning tasks or opportunities, yet in other situations, many of us may become emotionally close to "kindred spirits" and jointly pursue or increase learning endeavors with the added support and sharing emanating from new relationships.

In any case, those of us who learn for these reasons can typically (not always) expect to realize minimal specific beneficial "societal" outcomes or advantages from completion of educational activities, either because we have not systematically designed our learning with content-related end-products in mind, we change learning environments frequently when emotional needs are not satisfied, or we do receive "graduation" benefits but place little psychic or emotional value on these outcomes, and pay little attention to the options or advantages which accrue.

The increased free time we have as older men and women provides a substantial opportunity to meet new people through continued educational pursuits, although there are some disadvantages or obstacles we should keep in mind:

^ physical limitations increasingly may prohibit the breadth or intensity of involvement we desire because the "learning" parts of the experience place demands on our various thinking and working capacities;

^ we may be interested in relationships, but lack the prerequisite "credentials" to enroll in certain educational programs or opportunities and may, therefore, need to concentrate temporarily on strict learning objectives to "set up" future options for collateral relationship enhancement via more formal educational endeavors;

^ inability to develop satisfactory liaisons may cause us to drop out of educational pursuits eventually, particularly if we choose not to invest some degree of energy in being satisfied by the learning for its own values and benefits.

LO #8   (Filling Time)

Probably the least fulfilling and desirable utilization of continued adult learning is to simply prevent boredom, fill empty leisure-time "space," to avoid thinking about or handling other important but difficult life issues, or to pass the time and "wait to die" (as some people actually report). In these destructive, or at least minimally constructive orientations, there is little benefit from deep-seated emotional growth or self-fulfillment. We typically become socially irresponsible in refusing or neglecting to share what we learn for the benefit of others, the "demands" of the learning tasks sometimes cause even further declines in morale, and essentially "stop growing" intellectually and spiritually one step short of total "vegetabalism" and dormant withdrawal from the energy "centers" and "forces" of life. Of course, learning is a better way to pass time than non-learning, but we may be inclined to retain less and to reduce the application of learning to other life areas when we lack a "future-hopeful" orientation relative to change in our existential or "being" status as a direct or indirect symbolic result of "what" or "how" we learn.

If any of you find yourselves fitting into this category, I would strongly suggest stepping back momentarily to determine if other motivations or aspirations can be uncovered in your conscious or unconscious minds to serve as a more substantive and energetic "drive shaft" for future-generated education and personal development.

Personal Accomplishment and Leisure-Time

One of the horrible tragedies of "aging" is the attitude maintained or accepted by many "seniors," that the period of "prime" productivity and individual goal achievement has "faded into the sunset," and that the most meaningful accomplishments of life are associated with the physical, financial, health, and mental "fitness" periods of early and middle adulthood. With this "retro-tinted" perspective, older people and their families often seek emotional achievement "highs" or vortices of esteem building energy from memories and reconstructed historical accounts, without giving equal "billing" to current or future goals or achievements.

Although energy "erosions and recessions," along with various degrees of depleted financial resources, social role opportunities, influential control of fiscal resources and personnel, and fluctuating mental capacities certainly made many achievement tasks much tougher, and of longer duration to arrive at satisfying "end points," the latter years of "life" (as we know it) can be ideal times for certain types of personal accomplishments for the following reasons:

1.   A mature and more integrated self-awareness helps us to select truly significant target goals, and to maintain a "centrality" of focus and energy concentration for efficient and effective achievement outcomes.

2.   Qualitative thought and behavioral skills increases the likelihood of satisfactorily proficient "methods" to produce pride-worthy outcomes.

3.   Leisure time offers opportunity for comprehensive goals, or alternately specific and detailed intricate tasks, with limited interruptions or delays in maintaining consistency and concentration on the "finer points" of our work.

4.   Lifelong emotional development and spiritual enlightment enables us to invest symbolic and "transcendental" "ultra-physical" meaning to the accomplishments we manifest, with possibly more exciting emotional "payoffs" than we were able to enjoy with similar projects at younger ages because there were fewer "evaluative domains" for the appreciation of all life tasks.

5.   The length of "previous time lived" provides an enriched "experiential pathway," filled with a wider range of previous achievements that can provide continuity and connective arterial significance, as

we associate present or future-anticipated accomplishments with previous "milestones of our growth" to produce a stronger and clearer "system" or linear framework for an expansive scenario of our complete and holistic lives.

In getting ready, now, to briefly discuss various types of accomplishments we might pursue in our retirement years, it is important to keep in mind the dangers of equating personal achievement with traditional socially-sanctioned definitions of "youthful" productivity as seen within Westernized, industrial profit-oriented economic philosophies. Achievements usually require hard work, dedication, discipline, some isolation from interruptive distractions in our social systems, and moderate degrees of healthy anxiety and frustration relative to personal "mediocrity" but do not necessarily imply physical rather than mental activity, observable versus inner psycho-emotional successes, pragmatism instead of idiosyncratic "eccentricity" as criteria for outcomes, widespread versus personal or limited application of end-results, or monetary rather than esthetic "values" attached to any results we produce.

The main point is that many of us may derive considerable emotional satisfaction from some continuation of productive accomplishment in our lives, and may do ourselves and those around us a great disservice by deciding that this form of self-actualization is too hard, socially inappropriately silly, "uneventful," or of little long-term value--simply because we have a "retrospective depreciatory" rather than "prospective appreciatory" view of our lives. Time, of course, may appear to have concrete and limited incremental measurement standards, but our phenomenal minds always have the option of rearranging, recreating, or eliminating traditional time, space, value, distance, beginning, or end criteria to, instead, concentrate on other aspects or domains to define qualitative living, producing or functioning.

Some Areas of Later-Life Accomplishments

1.   Completion of college degrees, technical training programs, hobby workshops, creative-talent courses, therapy relationships, life-planning seminars, or programs to teach home repair/financial management/health maintenance, etc.

2. Fulfilling travel dreams, relocating to a more desirable geographic residence, visiting more with family or friends who live at a distance, exploring unknown activities in your town or community, searching through family historical records/albums/documents/storage chests to discover or rediscover exciting revelations or memories of the past (it's fun to share these with friends or family as well).

3. Enhancing physical fitness, developing new "motor" skills, developing nutritional and health management expertise, learning a new sport or active leisure activity, improving mental and physical "reactivity" and endurance, control eating/drinking, and stop smoking.

4. Changing some aspects of personal appearance, altering wardrobe styles, improving listening or communicating skills, developing new "mannerisms" that improve appearance and self-regard, becoming more flexible in stereotyped behavior patterns (be careful of skydiving, skateboards, and alligator wrestling!).

5. Improving ability to relax, developing stress reduction techniques, slowing down on unproductive or dissatisfying activities, "smelling life's multitude of 'roses,'" defining and meeting your own needs, getting rid of irrational fears and worries.

6. Developing or improving creative talents, "marketing" new or existing artistic projects, expanding or fine-tuning philosophical or analytic thinking capabilities, becoming a more active/knowledgeable/enthusiastic consumer of culture/art/music/literature, enhancing awareness and "relationships" with the aesthetic and symbolic "messages" of nature and the world around us.

7. Exacerbating the quality of intercultural interests, trying and cooking foreign foods, building friendships with people who are "different" from ourselves, reading about and becoming informed about other cultures, changing narrow views or limiting behavior patterns of our own culture as expressed in our individual lifestyles.

8. Becoming a community humanitarian, volunteering at social service agencies, contributing money to charities, becoming a foster grandparent, visiting the sick, involving oneself in community

improvement/beautification projects, writing letters/articles to "confront" human rights or community "deficit" issues in the public eye.

9. Creating a comprehensive plan or strategy to "define" your leisure time, plan fulfilling activities, learn to evaluate progress in enjoying older age, take greater charge of all aspects of your life, learn better ways to "fit in" with the interests and activities of your adult children or the grandkids, create plans to improve relationships with friends, conceptualize the "reasons" for living the rest of your life and implement activities that fulfill this "commitment to quality."

10. Rearrange your living space for greater comfort, redecorate to express more clearly and excitedly "who" you are, plan long range strategies to replace worn out furniture or improve the appearance/functionality of your space, become involved in "innovative" forms of environmental self-expression (e.g., paint your own pictures no matter what quality they have).

11. Start a new career, try to find work (full or part-time) in an interesting organization or activity, read all you can about a particular job or profession, sign yourself up as an apprentice or volunteer to learn new skills, start your own company in the basement (include selected friends in whatever you are interested in and disregard outcome "success" indicators--the "process" is probably more fun than the outcome), become a volunteer or paid consultant to help evaluate the input/ process/outcomes of someone else's business, volunteer for research programs at universities to contribute to worldwide knowledge building.

12. Start and manage some form of social group/club/learning center/ collective activity, build communicational linkages with other groups that are active (e.g., reading groups in libraries, international cultural exchange groups, church organizations in other cities), work on "out-reach" activities to interest others in your pursuits, improve cohesion with group bylaws, uniforms, shared ceremonies, etc.

13. Become a communicator and information processor, write letters and make phone calls to other interested people, become a "ham" radio operator, develop expertise in using newspapers and community resources to be aware of "what's going on" and to participate, answer or write "personal ads" in newspapers, become a knowledgeable

participant--listener in regular radio programs, write letters to T.V. stations to make suggestions, seek out "pen pals" in other countries.

Spiritual Excitement and Cosmic Veneration

The gradual "decline" and change of many areas of socially-extolled physical capability and appearance, the emptiness and "eco-dysfunctionalism" of community role loss and traditional productivity "obsolescence," the emotional pain and loneliness of "apparent" absence of loved ones through death or serious physical "invalidism," and the psychic struggle to find purpose and meaning of our existence as we experience the "shortness" of time and the "subjectivity" of each individual life journey--all cause most of us, at one point or another during our mature years, to give some degree of serious thought to our spiritual identities.

In some cases, we may have been "religious" in traditional ways from childhood, or may similarly have "deep" and "mystical" belief or intuitive value frameworks without regular church attendance or denominational affiliation; so that "aging spirituality" represents a continuation and confirmation of the "basics," and probably a growth maturation of some higher levels of awareness of God or other inspirational "forces," or development of greater perfection in the daily manifestation of our "faith" through good deeds, qualitative interactions, and "required" (formally or informally) allegiance to the principles and doctrines of each individual belief system.

With other individuals, spirituality or religion in the "twilight" years may accompany "crisis" conditions of our minds, hearts, or souls which represent pressured explorations of "security blankets" or core principles and explanations of the "life phenomena," which we feel or fear have been absent in our lives previously, and which we often anticipate in heightened exasperation or lowered depression, may represent necessary "core" beliefs to comfort the approaching fearful transition out of known physical existence, or essential foundation values to insure at least minimal rewards (or to avoid maximum punishments) as we face "potential" supreme "evaluators" in any "next lives" which are to "materialize."

The problem for most of us, I fear, whether we are in the spiritual "business as usual" category, or represent the "drowning searchers for life preservers," is that we may not only utilize the potentials and energies we have for spiritual growth and fulfillment in diminished, inferior, maladaptive, defensive, or insufficient ways; but ultimately rob ourselves and other's around us of the enormous and profound levels of "other-worldly," mystical, heavenly, transcendental, hyper-energetic/peaceful sensations, awareness or revelations which many spiritual believers and practitioners report on relatively regular bases, and which many of us "ordinary folks" experience very occasionally as "peak experiences" of visionary grandeur, "abundance," plurality, centrality, specificity, clarity, radiance, symmetry, depth, richness, triumph, relevance, sovereignty, etc.

As we experience "declines" in the more mundane arenas of life, we may also come face to face with ultimate questions of our most basic and fundamental purpose in living, which we all usually balance somewhat between enhancement of the self, social productivity and adjustment, interpersonal caring and positive deeds and achievement or awareness of some type of essence or "being" whose evaluative criteria seems far beyond and decidedly superior to the typical standards we experience in daily living. These spiritual domains are sometimes translatable into manifest "worldly" acts, but for others, represent conditions of emotion, absence of stress, presence of pacified tranquility, or almost unexplainable awareness of ultimate worth and value as part of cosmic or heavenly domains, which have no correlational anchors or connecting points within the mental, verbal, behavioral or cultural ideas and structures which organize and provide continuity to daily experience.

Current psychic and neuro-psychologic research has certainly alerted us to the extremely significant presence of "extra-human" potentials and capa- bilities in almost all of us to perceive, think, communicate and utilize psychic and kinetic energies in phenomenal ways. This not only tells us there are other worlds of probable vast proportions within each human mind, but that these separate minds are able to transfer associational and synergistic energies to one another and to extraneous repositories or "junctures" of interactive "space," which catapults collective "consciences" into third (neither he/she, nor I, but us) and fourth (not us but something beyond-and-including us) or fifth (beyond and not including us) dimensions of reality.

As we grow older and develop a lifetime of expertise in using thought and emotions, and as we move beyond many of the social and fiscal obligations/burdens/entrapments/constraints of daily struggle to conform to social standards, we may become eventually free enough of superficial and elementary psychic stress and mental routinization to use the cognitive principles of discipline, concentration, relaxation, abstraction, association, expansion, etc. to begin to truly explore and approach the highest levels of spiritual and emotional "being" and "awareness" which may ratify the value of all previous, present and future "living" for us in ways which are unimaginably far beyond our wildest imaginative dreams.

For many of us, then, the time of life for the most ultimate progress in qualitative living may only be the more advanced adult years--and many of us may sadly miss a potential chance to live as we have never lived before in our minds, our hearts, and our souls.

In this regard, some of the specific goals of spiritual enlightenment and veneration of the holistic self are noted in the following numbered paragraphs:

Goal Number One > To gain as many "visionary exposures" to life as possible which represent "aggregate montages" of the "totality" of our own former, present, or future thoughts, feelings or actions which are all integrated into some form of meaningful "whole" whereby everything is viewed as exquisitely positive and pure, with similarities and differences between intents and outcomes viewed as "functional" parts of a purposeful "machine" which has worth and value because of its existence and operation based on its own integrity, and the brilliance of its operational capabilities to sustain itself.

Goal Number Two > To appreciate fully the "central role" each of us plays as a "single responsive unit of life" which fulfills and completes the "mission" of an overriding and preeminent/grandiose generative "force," while sharing energy and interactive responsibilities with all other animals/minerals/vegetables; yet simultaneously experience our existence as prime "procreators" of new life and absolute/consummate tabernacles to define and retain concepts and ideas which existentially symbolize "all there is"; and to conclude diametrically, that both ends of this spectrum fit together perfectly without contradiction.

Goal Number Three > To achieve periods or moments of concentrated awareness of the influential potency and explosive/implosive, "convulsive" intensity of our human emotions and basic existence, which provides unequivocal exhilarating validation of all previous feelings of "all beings," and plunges our hearts and minds into funneled manifestation of "cavernous" appreciation and additional expression/awareness of the glory of neuro-psychic-spiritual capacity for "sensation," and confirms the beauty and value of "noncognitive" communication of "sensitivities" within ourselves, and between other "beings."

Goal Number Four > To experience a comprehensive matrix of specific as well as abstract "evaluative judgments" of the all-conclusive and "benedicta-torial" correctness of all previous actions, as examples of honorable integrity and principled conformity to righteous values, or as internally hopeful and courageous heroic efforts to attain goodness, despite detours through the painful, but cleansing "aquarian" experiences of equally laudable human fear/defense/escape/retaliation/inaction, etc.

Goal Number Five > To view our troubled/active/tired/energized/burdened/ defensive/vigilant "psyches" at the tranquil center of discordant and diamet-rically oppositional/contradictory life forces of good and bad, which has represented a growth--achievement--transcendence hierarchical, maze-like challenge which we have negotiated to perceive the causes and learned benefits of "logical inverse correlates," plus their equally logical irrelevance relative to global and abstract "truths" of life, while presently "resting" within a perfectly peaceful and non-antagonistic, "nullificational" domain from which we receive permanent solace in freedom from life's systems and philosophical distracting "controversies."

Goal Number Six > To command seemingly "eternal" clarity of vision con-cerning choices and obstacles, which will intuitively synthesize thoughts and behaviors into an interwoven symphony of complex movements which will ultimately produce positive outcomes and growth-producing processes, in a planned strategic journey to some ultimate "state" of success/learning/ appreciation/ reward which has been obscured from continuous vision pre-viously, but will represent automatic, "radar-controlled" "terminal culmination" for our predestined personal fulfillment.

Goal Number Seven > To discipline our thoughts and analytic capabilities throughout life to the point that we ultimately transport our minds into an "emotionally rich chamber" where some form of enhancing, expanding, puri-fying, clarifying or accepting "energy" blends with conceptual rigorous intensity and concentrated "associational" expertise to enable anxiety and pressure to relax and abate to the point of attaining intellectual understanding of previously unattainable specific or abstract perspectives which is accompanied by sensations of cosmic wisdom and humble understanding of simplicity plus complexity as they represent central facts of human existence, but inferior processes of "negotiating" life challenges until they are mastered--then relinquished--then reattained with accompanying dosages of spiritual motivation to "see the light" and emotional fervor in becoming fully human by moving our minds into communion with the greatest minds and thoughts of all time--which is ultimately a regression back to more simplistic childlike awareness and explanation.

Goal Number Eight > To attain feelings of genuine "love" which appears to be unification with a superior symbolic representation of comprehensive and intensively accepting appreciation of all human processes as natural and beautiful manifestations of composite "pasteurized" intentioned thought, mood and physical behavior; along with global admiration of human struggles to conquer "inferiority" through valiant expressions of energized effort and hope, and almost supernatural enjoyment of the personal "dignity" of survival instincts which push the human spirit to monumental efforts to "please," win, succeed, attain, grow, etc., coupled with saintly empathy for the disappointments experienced along the way which are never fully allowed to destroy the germinal and primordial spirit of "aliveness."

Goal Number Nine > To be enveloped periodically or even permanently in a mystical shroud of secure protection, loving "advocacy," and eternal nurturance which is accompanied by feelings of ultra-paramount and intimate "friendships" and unequivocal approval of our basic humanity, but positively infused with confrontational and stimulative encouragement to improve and attain the greatest heights of every form of qualitative existence; plus feelings of intimately known and shared aspirations with deep-seated "awarenesses" of acceptance of failure and total commitment of emotional and spiritual attentiveness to our needs and hopes forever.

Goal Number Ten > To forecast permanent continuity of the "self" and our ideals through the allegiance of subordinate and parallel "learners" who appreciate the cumulative quality of our sequential existence as it was transferred sanctimoniously in gradual or traumatic psychic "encounters" as part of supernatural and ultra-human destinies to expand through and for one another, along with sensations of extrapolated expansion of the continuously transported self into increasingly superior dimensions of worth and functionality which is only possible through the laborious process of chronologic expression of future selves who are dependent to some degree, on the value of our antecedent existence and generous sharing of wisdom at critical points of personal and historical/cultural development.

Goal Number Eleven > To become so intimately involved in loving relationships (with friends, spouse, relatives, children, animals, Supreme Beings, or even innate objects we have cared for which have also "served" us) that the degree of intimate sharing produces a "fused oneness" where the depth of unity powerfully excludes fearful external influences or intrusions; the forcefulness of combined psycho-spiritual energies elevates the intensely "accepting" participants to extreme levels of blissful completion and extension of the whole self; and the approval of each alternate partner for the other represents unmitigated advocacy, along with total "benediction" of the most basic and natural aspects of personal dignity, and specific human attributes which testify to the value of absolute uniqueness and freedom.

Goal Number Twelve > To microscopically, "magniscopically," and "intensiscopically" view through, and deep into our physical appearance to the point of surpassing superficial cultural criteria of "attractiveness," and fully relishing the brilliance of human construction/contour/countenance/coloration as pinnacles of the unimaginable quintessence of the concept of beauty itself, while also appreciating the miraculous capability of the observer to observe and attack "moving" and "enjoying" criteria to the "juncture" of the "physical" and mental; and to additionally triumphantly overcome and render insignificant any specific indicators of "pleasurable" demeanor, while simultaneously viewing each minute molecular or epidermic "aspect" of the self as a symbolic "amplification" of the mystery of creation and metabolism, and the magnificence of any life "substance."

Goal Number Thirteen > To develop highly acute and ultra-sensitively perceptive awareness of ourselves as communicational "mechanisms," senders/receivers, "conduit," etc., whereby we, as "learners and growers" are totally and "understandably" tuned-in to the multitude of simultaneous and alternating "messages" (sights, sounds, feelings, smells, intuitions, touches, etc.) emanating from our total ecological, psychophysiological, cosmic, and spiritual environments to the extent that our "centrability" and "incoming/interpreting" activities "electrify" our self-concepts of purpose and value. While, at the same time, we may also perceive heightened beliefs or evidence of our human power and influence on people or events through our reciprocal capability to send impactful signals and to contribute stimulating motivational messages to produce change, unify variant aspects of life/nature, validate being, or celebrate our own existence (I "am-ness").

Goal Number Fourteen > To arrive at a state of awareness of the self where personal pain, suffering, agitation, disconcertion, impatience, hopeful-anticipation, etc. are not only accepted as valuable experiences of the "balanced self" through which growth emerges, but also become examples of existential and universal "burdens" of responsibility to forever carry some "weights" of human kind in order to free others from this potentially devas-tating "sentence" for them, but to spiritually motivate us and others to envision, and work to achieve, superior "states" of existence as a direct function of perceiving the opposite, yet feeling that the depth of this pain enables us to surprisingly arrive at heightened awarenesses of the glory of feeling and being because of the intensity engendered by the negative emotions in life.

It is important for each of us to understand that spiritual "enlightment" is a very personal as well as possibly "generic" phenomena, which certainly varies in many ways from my subjective and limited "descriptions" of selected "awarenesses," and that, in some respects, our spiritual natures may not be able to be understood by any other humans wherein attempts to describe them in traditional language and thought may not only fall short of capturing the magnitude of their relevance, but may even seriously distort their true essence and meaning.

Although spirituality is a "tough subject" to tackle, on the other hand, we may all enhance the quality and meaning of our various collective and idiosyncratic lives by reaching for these illusive "stars" or inner "jewels," and pushing our minds and spirits into the "advanced realms" of humanness or ultra-humanness which each of us has probably experienced during at least one special moment in life, and may be able to capture permanently if we spend the time and effort "freeing" ourselves from more mundane thoughts and behaviors and struggling to discover the inner or outer core of true "personhood" which many describe as the prime reason, motivation, begin-ning, end, and ultimate relevance of our existence in concert with all other "things" that also exist, interact and move through various developmental paths.

Death and "Finality"

Although there has been some attempt by noted scholars and clinicians (e.g., Kubler-Ross) to describe and theorize the "dying" process, there is still a wealth of discovery and understanding yet to evolve about a phenomena which takes on a range of differing connotations, including ultimate loss, painful suffering, beginning of new life spiritual and physical victory, domain of "nothingness," peaceful rest, tumultuous struggle for life, final reward, final punishment, predestined outcome, unity with God, continuation of life in an alternate space/dimension, supernatural journey/awareness, unification symbol of all ecology, etc.

In this variegated light, therefore, we know little about specific developmental "stages" of this transitional process; have developed few, if any, consistent and valid taxonomies of psychic thought or feelings, or spiritual "action" which occurs; and have little definitive data on predictable "causes" of various "outcomes," as each of us learns or discovers various ways of interpreting and dealing with this seemingly inevitable "life" occurrence.

There is considerable information, of course, on various cultural separation and grief "rituals," but again, relatively incomprehensive and unsophisticated discovery of the "meanings" of life-relative-to-death process in loved ones we lose, and untested clinical experiments to manipulate or change typical approaches to death by those who are, and those who are not dying themselves to determine differentially valued adaptations/ compensations, and particularly to prepare any of us to predict or better utilize remaining periods of time in this "known" life, and in whatever existential or other domain ensues when traditional physical existence has ended. The most pronounced interactions with the dying person remain, in my opinion, within the circumscribed realm of medical and technological "comfort" and life "sustenance" areas of capability, with generally insufficient successful efforts to develop composite and "systemic" master plans of dying which include the full range of our physical, emotional, intellectual, social, religious, spiritual "selves" and interactions, which relate to the corresponding professional fields of health and allied health care, psychology, sociology, religion, spiritualism, metaphysics, anthropology, law, education, physics, and others.

The death phase of life has also been fearfully, reluctantly and igno- rantly not applied as a "focal point" of all other arenas of childhood and adult development, so we continue to avoid its discussion as a central component of historical and ahistorical life, and generally "refuse" to understand its nature and implications as a sociocultural plus psycho-spiritual phenomenon. This occurs since we do not trace its symbolic existence as a life concept, back through the antecedent life cycle to understand how and why we have, in fact, understood or not understood it in various alternate ways within and between different world animal, mineral, vegetable, and human cultures and environments.

With these problems of enriched understanding in mind, therefore, I would like to pose, what I feel, are some of the most significant questions about death that each of us should try to answer for ourselves--particularly since the inquiry and analytic procedure, itself, can help us grow toward greater self-understanding; and also because the answers we come up with may very significantly determine the case with which we approach and deal with this component of life, and the overall quality and value of this event or series of sequential or parallel eco-cosmic and psycho-spiritual events in our journey of individual and cultural existence.

Significant Questions About Our Death

1. Is "dying" really any form of "loss" to the dying person, or do we grieve ourselves in anticipation because we have learned to "experience" personal deficits or "withdrawals" as others have left us previously?

2. Is there any relationship between death and birth processes, and would understanding of the similarities or differences provide additional options for changing the feelings we have about either "beginnings," or "ends?"

3. When we control "premature death" through personal prevention of mortal "accidents," and medical technology's increasing influence on pathological illness and physiologic deterioration, does natural death "appear" to us in a different "light" relative to a "natural life" continuum?

4. Does the application of high level "sustenance" or "comforting" "technology" at the conclusion of life alter more positive or negative viewpoints we could develop about this "terminal state of being?"

5. To what extent does our psychological "wish for ending," "acceptance of finality," or "struggle for survival" influence the manner in which we ultimately experience the anticipatory prelude and actual event of dying?

6. To what extent does our former history of wins/losses, successes/failures predict and control the attitude we have about this final "contest?"

7. What options do we have of altering our "compartmental" delineations of the death phenomenon, and what influence does the art of "segmenting" or isolating any stage of the life process have on our interpretation of this or other aspects of existence?

8. Would rehearsal and exposure to the symbolic meanings of death at earlier ages help us to handle the real event in different ways?

9. Do we integrate the dying experience when we do earlier "mental work" to schedule it as an "intended" part of our learning and growing agenda?

10. Does family discussion of the "benefits" of our previous existence for everyone's future growth cause any reduction of the "loss" interpretation of dying?

11. Does the cultural perspective of human "superiority" isolate us in death processes from "unifying" natural associations with other forms of life, and represent "failure" rather than cooperative extension of "ecological energy?"

12. In what ways does our cultural orientation toward "youthful productivity" distance us emotionally from the more "passive" attributes of life, which are also present or maybe symbolized by "end of life decline?"

13. Does a strong positive self-concept and independent identity connect or isolate us from the "continuities" of the life journey, especially relative to concepts of "control," mastery, "survival," "aloneness," etc.?

14. To what extent does a cohesive religious or spiritual belief system assist us in feeling more positive or less anxious/sad about dying?

15. Do lingering childhood fears of the "unknown," along with cultural and cognitive learning and valuation of the "permanence" of phenomena, cause us to be "conditioned" to view death as a negative occurrence?

16. Do people who are capable of more abstract thinking handle death better than those of us who are more pragmatic or "concrete?"

17. Is there ever any possibility of improving mental and spiritual capacity to validly "see" what exists beyond natural life as we know it?

18. Is the experience of dying a self-fulfilling prophecy which we have decided upon earlier in life, or is it possible to be truly "open" to experience the unique "essence" of death as this actually unfolds in our lives?

19. Does the act of suicide actually change the experience of death as a result of person control, decision-making, alterations of morale/mood, time selection of death, cause of mortality, or other factors which hinge on the issue of voluntary vs. involuntary dying?

20. In what ways does "acceptance" of death alter the perception of the occurring experience, and how do we select various options for either acceptance or rejection of any life event or process?

21. Is death predominantly a mental or physical occurrence, does one life energy cause or result from changes in the other, and what possibilities or selective options exist for these two "domains" to fit and work together for a "positive" "terminal" experience?

As each of us may decide in his or her own way to grapple with any or all of the aforementioned issues, and hopefully reach some conclusions about our own approach, integration, and resolution of this aspect of "living," there are also some general guidelines which many clinicians feel are helpful in preparing for the coming of the "end" or "beginning." These are noted as follows:

General Guidelines to Prepare for Our Dying Experience

1. Try to decide what represents the major purpose and value of your life, and plan ways to symbolize and vividly represent "your essence" as you prepare for, actually experience, and conclude the final "ceremony" of your life.

2. Conclude all "unfinished business" and conflict with important people in your life, and move significant relationships to the "ultimate" in any qualitative "realms," which represent the primary meaning of each association to you and the other person.

3. Decide what aspects of your life, knowledge, awareness, and emotions are still "deficient" or absent from your life, and work on attaining some or all parts of these goals as you work through and undergo the dying phase of your growth. Also plan for yourself what you need to learn or "do" in any subsequent lives you may have, and enjoy the anticipation of this post-natural development.

4. Discuss all fears and apprehensions about death or "loss" as soon as possible, to help develop your awareness of any regressive childhood irrationalities or "fixations" which embody these thoughts, and to "purge" yourself of "disquieting" neurotic expectations, which will ruin any peaceful "expiration" which you are capable of achieving.

5. Decide upon, and practice, the "final" thought, word, feeling or "vision" you wish for yourself (or to receive from a loved one, priest, minister, etc.), and try to analyze and understand how this "ultimate sensation" cannot only inject greater meaning into your life before death, but also how it may represent a spiritual or heightened emotional "peak" to fulfill an ultimate goal or otherwise propel you from or toward a new domain of your "being."

6. Broaden your knowledge and comprehensive understanding of the principles and canons of any specific denominational religion, or spiritual philosophy which you use to guide your life, or by which you are "bound" through birth, cultural heritage, baptism, confirmation, other ceremonial rituals, philosophic predestination, lifelong allegiance, or default (if you let the chips fall in some arena of belief dictated by family choice, identity of presiding minister, etc.). Insure that you are

"squared" with your belief system, according to its principles or your interpretation of these principles, and also appreciate the positive "gains" you will receive through this "canonical" system of beliefs or "truths."

7. Clearly state, write, or energetically think about the generative contributions you wish to make developmentally in the lives of significant other people, your town, the community/world, or to yourself in subsequent lives, and give a testimonial and "benediction" of these "influences" by directly sharing them with those involved (or suitable representatives who may pass on your intentions), or at least directing concentrated psycho-spiritual-emotional energy into the transcendental passing and infusion of these good intents into the "energy receptors" of systems with which you cannot directly dialogue.

8. Ask directly for unmet emotional "gifts" you need from others, and plan as much time as possible to not only enjoy them, but to incorporate their added "energies" into your overall transitional scheme and spiritual procedure for qualitatively achieving the deepest levels of developmental and blossoming adequacy as you "crescendo" toward your final earthbound "destiny."

9. Spend considerable time alone and with others who care about you, reviewing the significant events, accomplishments, learnings, joys, and emotional "highs" of your life, to prepare a positive mental framework to comfortably accompany your final moments in this life, and also to give you an opportunity to reconcile with your historical "negatives" and convert their "traumatic" or "deleterious" natures into conceptions of their value for learning, growing, suffering purposefully or "balancing" the natural pros and cons of life.

10. Work very hard at initiating your "grieving process" concerning "loves" you will leave behind and miss, not only to fully invest or immerse yourself in the qualitative center and mass of their nurturance for you, but to also ultimately conclude your anger at yourself for failing, your disappointment at realizing your inadequacy, the fears you have of independence and unknown dangers in separation, the futility of giving in a productively oriented world with visions of the absence of further reciprocal receptions or paybacks--and ultimately to arrive at a peaceful state of awareness of the possible insignificance of "feeling" states when

this life has concluded, the miniscule relevance of human relationships with the "astronomical spiritual realms" of life, the unity and oneness of our "singular being" which was never possibly "connected" to other beings, the conclusive nature of wonderful interactions at each moment in chronologic time, the futility of conceptualizing "gains" which "will never" exist in the future, and the magnitude of our "connections" to all aspects of life which will or may never end with the circumscribed cessation of biologic "life" in one organism of the macro-expansive ecology of all that is, was, or ever will be.

11. Put your human mind at rest, and free it from all worries about life consequences in this world (especially with surviving loved ones) when you are no longer physically present, partly because there is absolutely nothing you can do to directly influence further outcomes from a post-mortem perspective, partly because you can take some actions presently to help others prepare which will be hindered by excessive worry, and partly because others may choose to permanently retain your essence and influence in their minds and hearts, and therefore, will always have the benefit of consultative contributions you can make, given their need to run their own lives independently.

12. Seek special assistance and support from God, the saints, other super-natural entities, spiritual leaders, or any mystical/emotional "centers of actualization" in helping you make a successful transition from what is to what will be, or was, and specifically use prayers, meditations, consultations, concentrated analyses, emotional sensitivities, etc. to differentiate the human and supernatural domains in your life, to help reduce your resistance to the "healing powers" of your chosen Life Guide, and to put into action any contributory human strengths to assist your "passage" and "transition" to come.

13. Work to place your thoughts, feelings, behaviors, and all other "dynamics" and "conditions" of your present existence into the expected berths, domains, spaces, roles, "essences," conditions or places of awareness in the next life, to not only assist in the movement as it approaches, but to avoid the crisis trauma which may develop as you unexpectedly and possibly rapidly transfer from one state to another. This does not suggest that you "die" while qualitative life continues, but that you practice and be familiar with the condition of death you see as "positive" before it actually happens, so that when the cessation of

your life begins (especially if it is slow and you can be aware of it) you can precede its moment to moment progress with progressive "arrivals" in your mental and spiritual life.

14. Realize that every human being always does the best and fulfills the most of which they are capable at every moment of existence, as dictated by their culture, learning, socialization, perspective and philosophy; and that we were probably never capable of being more than we were, while we were probably the "most" that anything can ever be--at the end, remember that we "were," and that was perfect, and there is nothing more that could have been done in the past. All there is, is tomorrow, and we will be our best there also. The beauty of life is that it is perfectly everything and nothing at the same time, and we have possibly never had any control over our existence, which was probably well and good because life is so incredibly beautiful in its perfection and imperfection together.